STUDIES IN CRITICAL PHILOSOPHY

Herbert Marcuse

Studies in Critical Philosophy

TRANSLATED BY JORIS DE BRES

BEACON PRESS   BOSTON

© NLB, 1972

'The Foundation of Historical Materialism' first published in *Die Gesell-schaft*, 1932, © Herbert Marcuse, 1932, this translation first published in 1972, © NLB, 1972; 'A Study on Authority' first published by Librairie Félix Alcan, 1936, © Herbert Marcuse, 1936, this translation first published in 1972, © NLB, 1972; 'Sartre's Existentialism' first published in *Philosophy and Phenomenological Research*, 1948, © *Philosophy and Phenomenological Research*, 1948; 'Karl Popper and the Problem of Historical Laws' first published in *Partisan Review*, 1959, © *Partisan Review*, 1959; 'Freedom and the Historical Imperative' first published in Éditions de la Baconnière, 1970, © Editions de la Baconnière, 1970, this version first published in 1972, © Herbert Marcuse, 1972.

Studies in Critical Philosophy was first published by New Left Books in 1972 and by Beacon Press in 1973.

Beacon Press books are published under the auspices of the Unitarian Universalist Association.

Simultaneous publication in Canada by Saunders of Toronto, Ltd.

All rights reserved.

Printed in the United States of America

9 8 7 6 5 4 3 2 1

Library of Congress Cataloging in Publication Data

Marcuse, Herbert, 1898–
    Studies in critical philosophy.
    CONTENTS: The foundation of historical materialism. — A study on authority. — Sartre's existentialism. [etc.]
    Includes bibliographical references.
    1. Dialectical materialism.   2. Authority.
3. Sartre, Jean Paul, 1905–   4. Popper, Sir Karl Raimund, 1902–
I. Title
B945.M2983S86   1973   146'.3   72–6235
ISBN 0–8070–1528–8
ISBN 0–8070–1529–6 (pbk.)

By Herbert Marcuse

Eros and Civilization: A Philosophical Inquiry into Freud

Reason and Revolution: Hegel and the Rise of Social Theory

One-Dimensional Man: Studies in the Ideology of Advanced Industrial Society

Negations: Essays in Critical Theory

An Essay on Liberation

Five Lectures: Psychoanalysis, Politics, and Utopia

Counterrevolution and Revolt

and, with Robert Paul Wolff and Barrington Moore, Jr.,

A Critique of Pure Tolerance

Translator's note : My thanks are due to Ben Fowkes for his careful checking of the translation and for his invaluable assistance in finding the English-language sources for the quotations in 'A Study on Authority'.

STUDIES IN CRITICAL PHILOSOPHY

The Foundation of
Historical Materialism

[1932]

Translator's note: This essay first appeared as 'Neue Quellen zur Grund-legung des Historischen Materialismus' in *Die Gesellschaft* (Berlin) in 1932, as a review of Marx's newly published *Economic and Philosophical Manu-scripts of 1844*. Marcuse quotes a great deal from the *Manuscripts*, and in order to make the source of these quotations available to the English-speaking reader I have given page references to the translation by Martin Milligan (Karl Marx, *Economic and Philosophical Manuscripts of 1844*, Lawrence and Wishart, London, 1970). The choice of this edition does not reflect any preference for Milligan's translation as opposed to others, except that it is currently the fullest, cheapest and most readily available. A few changes have been made in the translation.

The use of a particular translation of the *Manuscripts* means adjusting to the style of that translation for the sake of consistency. To a large extent the difficulties encountered are therefore difficulties not in translating Marcuse but in translating Marx. For the particular terminology used here (e.g. 'transcendence' and 'supersession', 'alienation' and 'estrangement', 'essence' and 'being') the reader should therefore refer to the 'Translator's and Editor's Note on Terminology' (pp. 57–60) as well as the footnotes in the Lawrence and Wishart edition. A fuller understanding of the problems involved in translating the concepts used in the *Manuscripts* can be gained by a comparison with relevant passages in other translations, notably T. B. Bottomore's *Karl Marx, Early Writings* (London, 1963) and David McLellan's *Karl Marx, Early Texts* (Oxford, 1971). Varying interpretations and translations of difficult concepts are discussed by Bottomore in his introduction and notes as well as in the introduction and notes to István Mészáros, *Marx's Theory of Alienation* (London, 1970).

The publication of the *Economic and Philosophical Manuscripts* written by Marx in 1844[1] must become a crucial event in the history of Marxist studies. These manuscripts could put the discussion about the origins and original meaning of historical materialism, and the entire theory of 'scientific socialism', on a new footing. They also make it possible to pose the question of the actual connections between Marx and Hegel in a more fruitful and promising way.

Not only does the fragmentary nature of the *Manuscripts* (substantial sections seem to have been lost and the analysis often breaks off at the crucial points; there are no final drafts ready for publication) necessitate a detailed interpretation constantly relating individual passages to the overall context, but the text also demands an exceptionally high level of technical knowledge on the part of the reader. For, if I may anticipate, we are dealing with a philosophical critique of political economy and its philosophical foundation as a theory of revolution.

It is necessary to place such strong emphasis on the difficulties involved right at the outset, in order to avert the danger that these manuscripts will once again be *taken too lightly* and hastily put into the usual compartments and schemata of Marx scholarship. This danger is all the greater because all the familiar categories of the subsequent critique of political economy are already found together in this work. But in the *Economic and Philosophical Manuscripts* the original meaning of the basic categories is clearer than ever before, and it could become necessary to revise the current interpretation of the later and more elaborate critique in the light of its origins. Perhaps this provisional review of the *Manuscripts* will suffice to show the inadequacy of the familiar thesis that Marx developed from providing a philosophical to providing an economic basis for his theory.

1. Volume 3 of the first section of the Marx-Engels-Gesamtausgabe (MEGA). They appeared almost simultaneously under the title *Nationalökonomie und Philosophie* in Kröner's Pocket Editions, Volume 91 (K. Marx, *Der Historische Materialismus. Die Frühschriften I*) pp. 283ff. This edition does not include the piece printed as the *First Manuscript* in MEGA, which is essential for an understanding of the whole. The reading of the text is at variance with MEGA in numerous instances.

We are dealing with a *philosophical* critique of political economy, for the basic categories of Marx's theory here arise out of his emphatic confrontation with the philosophy of Hegel (e.g. labour, objectification, alienation, supersession, property). This does not mean that Hegel's 'method' is transformed and taken over, put into a new context and brought to life. Rather, Marx goes back to the problems at the root of Hegel's philosophy (which originally determined his method), independently appropriates their real content and thinks it through to a further stage. The great importance of the new manuscripts further lies in the fact that they contain the first documentary evidence that Marx concerned himself explicitly with Hegel's *Phenomenology of Mind*, 'the true point of origin and the secret of the Hegelian philosophy' (p. 173).

If Marx's discussion of the basic problems of Hegel's philosophy informed the foundation of his theory it can no longer be said that this foundation simply underwent a transformation from a philosophical to an economic basis and that in its subsequent (economic) form philosophy had been overcome and 'finished' once and for all. Perhaps the foundation includes the philosophical basis in *all* its stages. This is not invalidated by the fact that its sense and purpose are not at all philosophical but practical and revolutionary: the overthrow of the capitalist system through the economic and political struggle of the proletariat. What must be seen and understood is that economics and politics have become the economic-political *basis* of the theory of revolution through a quite particular, philosophical interpretation of human existence and its historical realization. The very complicated relationship between philosophical and economic theory and between this theory and revolutionary praxis, which can only be clarified by an analysis of the whole situation in which historical materialism developed, may become clear after a full interpretation of the *Economic and Philosophical Manuscripts*. I only want to introduce this process in my paper. A rough formula which could be used as a starting point would be that the revolutionary critique of political economy itself has a philosophical foundation, just as, conversely, the philosophy underlying it already contains revolutionary praxis. The theory is in itself a practical one; praxis does not only come at the end but is already present in the beginning of the theory. To engage in praxis is not to tread on alien ground, external to the theory.

With these introductory remarks we can proceed to describe the overall content of the *Manuscripts*. Marx himself describes their purpose as the *critique of political economy* – a 'positive' critique, and thus one which, by revealing the mistakes of political economy and its inadequacy for the subject, also provides it with a basis to make it adequate for its task. The positive critique of political economy is thus a critical *foundation* of political economy. Within this critique the idea of political economy is completely transformed: it becomes the science of the necessary conditions for the communist revolution. This revolution itself signifies – quite apart from economic upheavals – a revolution in the whole history of man and the definition of his being: 'This communism . . . is the *genuine* resolution of the conflict between man and nature and between man and man – the true resolution of the strife between existence and essence, between objectification and self-confirmation, between freedom and necessity, between the individual and the species. Communism is the riddle of history solved, and it knows itself to be this solution' (p. 135).

If political economy can gain such central importance it is clear that, from a critical point of view, it must be treated from the outset as more than just another science or specialized scientific field. Instead it must be seen as the scientific expression of a problematic which involves the whole being of man. Thus we must begin by considering more closely *what sort of* political economy is here subject to criticism.

Political economy is criticized as the scientific justification or concealment of the total 'estrangement' and 'devaluation' of human reality represented in capitalist society – as a science which treats man as 'something unessential' (p. 130) whose whole existence is determined by the 'separation of labour, capital and land', and by an inhuman division of labour, by competition, by private property, etc. (p. 106). This kind of political economy scientifically sanctions the perversion of the historical-social world of man into an alien world of money and commodities; a world which confronts him as a hostile power and in which the greater part of humanity ceases to be anything more than 'abstract' workers (torn away from the reality of human existence), separated from the object of their work and forced to sell themselves as a commodity.

As a result of this 'alienation' of the worker and of labour, the realization of all man's 'essential powers' becomes the loss of their reality; the objective world is no longer 'truly human property' appropriated in 'free activity' as the sphere of the free operation and self-confirmation of the whole of human nature. It is instead a world of objects in private possession which can be owned, used or exchanged and whose seemingly unalterable laws even man must obey – in short, the universal 'domination of dead matter over mankind' (p. 102).

This whole situation has often been described under the headings of 'alienation', 'estrangement' and 'reification' and is a widely known element of Marxist theory. The important point is, however, to see how and from what angle Marx interprets it here at the starting-point of his theory.

At the beginning of his positive critique of political economy, at the point where he takes up the matter of alienation and estrangement, Marx states: 'We proceed from an economic fact *of the present*' (p. 107). But are alienation and estrangement 'economic facts' like, for example, ground rent or the price of commodities in its dependence on supply and demand or any other 'law' of the process of production, consumption and circulation?

Bourgeois political economy, as criticized here, does not regard alienation and estrangement as such as a fact (the circumstances to which these words refer are covered in the bourgeois theory under quite different headings); for socialist political economy this fact will only 'exist' if and in so far as the theory is placed on the foundation which Marx worked out in the context of the studies we are discussing. We must therefore ask what sort of fact this is (since it is essentially different from all other facts in political economy), and on what basis it becomes visible and can be described as such.

The description of the circumstance of alienation and estrangement seems initially to proceed completely on the ground of traditional political economy and its theorems. Marx significantly starts by dividing his investigation into the three traditional concepts of political economy: 'The Wages of Labour', 'The Profit of Capital' and 'The Rent of Land'. But more important, and a sign pointing in a completely new direction, is the fact that this division into three is soon exploded and abandoned: 'From page xxii to the end of the manuscript Marx wrote across the three columns, disregarding the headings. The text of these six pages (xxii–xxvii) is given in the present book under the title, "Estranged Labour"' (publisher's note, p. 6).

The development of the concept of labour thus breaks through the traditional framework for dealing with problems; the discussion continues with this concept and discovers the new 'fact' which then becomes the basis for the science of the communist revolution. Our interpretation must therefore set out from Marx's concept of labour.

When Marx depicts the manner of labour and the form of existence of the worker in capitalist society – complete separation from the means of production and from the product of his labour which has become a commodity, the balancing of wages around the minimum for mere physical survival, the severance of the worker's labour (performed as 'forced labour' in the capitalist's service) from his 'human reality' – all these features can in themselves still denote simple economic facts. This impression seems to be confirmed by the fact that Marx, 'by analysis from the concept of alienated labour', reaches the concept of 'private property' (p. 117) and thus the basic concept of traditional political economy.

But if we look more closely at the description of alienated labour we make a remarkable discovery: what is here described is not merely an economic matter. It is the alienation of man, the devaluation of life, the perversion and loss of human reality. In the relevant passage Marx identifies it as follows: 'the concept of alienated labour, i.e. of alienated man, of estranged labour, of estranged life, of estranged man' (p. 117).

It is thus a matter of man as man (and not just as worker, economic subject and the like), and of a process not only in economic history but in the history of man and his reality. In the same sense he writes about private property: 'Just as *private property* is only the sensuous expression of the fact that man becomes *objective* for himself and at the same time becomes to himself a strange and inhuman object, . . . so the positive abolition of private property [is] the sensuous appropriation for and by man of the human essence and of human life' (pp. 138ff.).

It is not because Marx is limited by a particular kind of philosophical terminology that he so often speaks here of 'human essential powers' and 'man's essential being', or, for example, that he calls 'the established objective existence of industry . . . the open book of man's essential powers' or wants to grasp its 'connection with man's essential being' (p. 142) and, in the places quoted above, uses a *philosophical* framework to describe labour and private property. His interpretation rather attempts to make it clear that the whole critique and foundation of political economy grew explicitly on a philosophical basis and out of a philosophical dispute, and that the philosophical concepts used cannot be regarded as remnants which were later discarded or as a disguise which we can strip off. As the result of an idea about the essence of man and its realization, evolved by Marx in his dispute with Hegel, a simple economic fact appears as the perversion of the human essence and the loss of human reality. *It is only on this foundation* that an economic fact is capable of becoming the real basis of a revolution which will genuinely transform the essence of man and his world.

What we are trying to show is this: from the outset the basic concepts of the critique – alienated labour and private property – are not simply taken up and criticized as economic concepts, but as concepts for a crucial process in human history; consequently the 'positive abolition' of private property by the true appropriation of human reality will revolutionize the entire history of mankind. Bourgeois political economy has to be basically transformed in the critique for this very reason: it never gets to see man who is its real subject. It disregards the essence of man and his history and is thus in the profoundest sense not a 'science of people' but of non-people and of an inhuman world of objects and commodities. 'Crude and thoughtless communism' (p. 133) is just as sharply criticized for the same reason: it too does not centre on the reality of the human essence but operates in the world of things and objects and thus itself remains in a state of 'estrangement'. This type of communism only replaces individual private property by 'universal private property' (p. 132); 'it wants to destroy everything which is not capable of being possessed by all as private property. It wants to do away by force with talent, etc. For it, the sole purpose of life and existence is direct, physical possession. The task of the labourer is not done away with, but extended to all men' (pp. 133ff.).

The objections to the absolute economism of Marxist theory, which have been thoughtlessly raised time and again right up to the present day, were already raised here by Marx himself against the crude communism which he opposed: for him the latter is merely the simple 'negation' of capitalism and as such exists on the same level as capitalism – but it is precisely that level which Marx wants to abolish.

Before starting our interpretation we need to avert another possible misunderstanding. If Marx's critique of political economy and his foundation of revolutionary theory are here dealt with as *philosophy* this does not mean that thereby 'only theoretical' philosophical matters will be included, which minimize the concrete historical situation (of the proletariat in capitalism) and its praxis. The starting point, the basis and the goal of this investigation is precisely the particular historical situation and the praxis which is revolutionizing it. Regarding the situation and praxis from the aspect of the history of man's essence makes the acutely practical nature of the critique even more trenchant and sharp: the fact that capitalist society calls into question not only economic facts and objects but the entire 'existence' of man and 'human reality' is for Marx the decisive justification for the proletarian revolution as a *total and radical* revolution, unconditionally excluding any partial upheaval or 'evolution'. The justification does not lie outside or behind the concepts of alienation and estrangement – it is precisely this alienation and estrangement itself. All attempts to dismiss the philosophical content of Marx's theory or to gloss over it in embarrassment reveal a complete failure to recognize the historical origin of the theory: they set out from an essential separation of philosophy, economics and revolutionary praxis, which is a product of the reification against which Marx fought and which he had already overcome at the beginning of his critique.

I

In capitalist society labour not only produces commodities (i.e. goods which can be freely sold on the market), but also produces 'itself and the worker as a commodity', the worker becoming 'an ever cheaper commodity the more commodities he creates' (pp. 107ff.). The worker not only loses the product of his own labour and creates alien objects for alien people; he is not only 'depressed spiritually and physically to the condition of a machine' through the increasing division and mechanization of labour, so that 'from being a man [he] becomes an abstract activity and a belly' (p. 68) – but he even has to 'sell himself and his human identity' (p. 70), i.e. he must himself become a commodity in order to exist as a physical subject. So instead of being an expression of the whole man, labour is his alienation; instead of being the full and free realization of man it has become a 'loss of realization'. 'So much does labour's realization appear as loss of realization that the worker loses realization to the point of starving to death' (p. 108).

It should be noted that even in this depiction of the 'economic fact' of alienated labour the simple economic description is constantly broken through: the economic 'condition' of labour is cast back onto the 'existence' of the working man (p. 67); beyond the sphere of economic relations the alienation and estrangement of labour concern the essence and reality of man as 'man' and only for this reason can the loss of the object of labour acquire such central significance. Marx makes this quite clear when he states that the 'fact' he has just described is the 'expression' of a more general state of affairs: 'This fact expresses merely that the object which labour produces – labour's product – confronts it as something alien, as a power independent of the producer. The product of labour is labour which has been embodied in an object, which has become material: it is the objectification of labour' (p. 108), and when he says: 'All these consequences' (of the capitalist economic system) 'result from the fact that the worker is related to the product of his labour as to an alien object' (ibid.). The economic fact of estrangement and reification[2] is thus grounded in a particular attitude by man (as a worker) towards the object (of his labour). 'Alienated labour' must now be understood in the sense of this kind of relation of man to the object, and no longer as a purely economic condition. 'The alienation of the worker in his product means not only that his labour becomes an object, an external existence, but that it exists outside him, independently, as something alien to him, and that it becomes a power on its own confronting him. It means that the life which he has conferred on the object confronts him as something hostile and alien' (pp. 108ff.). And it will further be shown that the economic fact of 'private property' too is *grounded* in the situation of alienated labour, understood as the activity of man: 'Private property is thus the product, the result, the necessary consequence, of

2. 'Reification' denotes the general condition of 'human reality' resulting from the loss of the object of labour and the alienation of the worker which has found its 'classical' expression in the capitalist world of money and commodities. There is thus a sharp distinction between reification and objectification (the latter will be discussed more fully below). Reification is a specific ('estranged', 'untrue') *mode* of objectification.

alienated labour, of the external relation of the worker to nature and to himself' (p. 117).

An amazing, idealistic distortion of the actual facts seems to have taken place here: an economic fact is supposed to have its roots in a general concept and in the relation of man to the object. 'Private property thus results by analysis from the concept of alienated labour' ibid.) – this is Marx, not Hegel, writing! The apparent distortion expresses one of the crucial discoveries of Marx's theory: the breakthrough from economic fact to human factors, from fact (*Tat'sache'*) to act (*Tat'handlung'*), and the comprehension of fixed 'situations' and their laws (which in their reified form are out of man's power) *in motion, in the course of their historical development* (out of which they have fallen and become fixed). (Cf. the programmatic introduction of the new approach to the problem on pp. 118–19). We cannot go into the revolutionary significance of this method here; we shall continue to pursue the line of approach outlined at the beginning.

If the concept of alienated labour includes the relation of man to the object (and, as we shall see, himself) then the concept of labour as such must also cover a human activity (and not an economic condition). And if the alienation of labour signifies the total loss of realization and the estrangement of the human essence then labour itself must be grasped as the real expression and realization of the human essence. But that means once again that it is used as a *philosophical* category. Despite the above development of the subject we would be loth to use the often misused term ontology in connection with Marx's theory, if Marx himself had not expressly used it here: thus he says that only 'through the medium of private property does the *ontological* essence of human passion come into being, in its totality as in its humanity',[3] and he suggests that 'man's feelings, passions, etc., are not merely anthropological phenomena . . . but truly ontological affirmations of being (of nature)' (ibid.).[4]

3. p. 165 (my italics).
4. Cf. the passage in Feuerbach which clearly underlies the sentence quoted: 'Human feelings thus do not have an empirical, anthropological significance in the

Marx's positive definitions of labour are almost all given as counter-concepts to the definition of *alienated* labour, and yet the ontological nature of this concept is clearly expressed in them. We shall extract three of the most important formulations: 'Labour is man's coming-to-be for himself within alienation, or as alienated man' (p. 177), it is 'man's act of self-creation or self-objectification' (p. 188), 'life-activity, productive life itself' (p. 113). All three of these formulations, even if they did not occur within the context of Marx's explicit examination of Hegel, would still point to Hegel's ontological concept of labour.[5] The basic concept of Marx's critique, the concept of alienated labour, does in fact arise from his examination of Hegel's category of objectification, a category developed for the first time in the *Phenomenology of Mind* around the concept of labour.[6] The *Economic and Philosophical Manuscripts* are direct evidence of the fact that Marx's theory has its roots in the centre of Hegel's philosophical problematic.

We can deduce the following from these definitions of labour: labour is 'man's act of self-creation', i.e. the activity through and in which man really first becomes what he is by his nature as man. He does this in such a way that this becoming and being are there *for himself*, so that he can know and 'regard' himself as what he is (man's 'becoming-for-himself'). Labour is a knowing and conscious activity: in his labour man relates to himself and to the object of his labour; he is not directly one with his labour but can, as it were, confront it and oppose it (through which, as we shall see, human labour fundamentally distinguishes itself as 'universal'

sense of the old transcendental philosophy; they have an ontological, metaphysical significance' (*Grundsätze der Philosophie der Zukunft*, § 33; *Sämtliche Werke II*, 1846, p. 324).

5. Cf. for example: Being-for-itself 'comes into its own through labour'. In labour the consciousness of the worker 'is externalized and passes into the condition of permanence', 'in working, consciousness, as the form of the thing formed, becomes an object for itself' (*Phenomenology of Mind*, trans. J. B. Baillie, London, 1966, pp. 238–40).

6. For these connections I must refer the reader to the extensive interpretation of Hegel's concept of labour in my book, *Hegels Ontologie und die Grundlegung einer Theorie der Geschichtlichkeit*. Cf. Hegel's definition of labour in the new edition of the *Jenenser Realphilosophie II* (Leipzig, 1931, especially pp. 213ff.).

and 'free' production from the 'unmediated' production of, for example, the nest-building animal). The fact that man in his labour is there 'for himself' in objective form is closely related to the second point: man is an 'objective' or, more exactly, an 'objectifying' being. Man can only realize his essence if he realizes it as something *objective*, by using his 'essential powers' to produce an 'external', 'material', objective world. It is in his work in this world (in the broadest sense) that he is real and effective. 'In creating a world of objects by his practical activity, in his work upon inorganic nature, man proves himself a conscious species being . . .' (p. 113). In this activity man shows himself as the human being he is according to his 'species' as distinct from animal, vegetable and inorganic being (we will examine the central concept of objectification at a later stage below). Labour, understood in this way, is the specifically human 'affirmation of being' in which human existence is realized and confirmed.

Thus even the most provisional and general characterization of Marx's concept of labour has led far beyond the economic sphere into a dimension in which the subject of the investigation is human existence in its totality. The interpretation cannot progress any further before this dimension has been described. We must first answer the question of how and from what starting-point Marx defines man's existence and essence. The answer to this question is a prerequisite for understanding what is really meant by the concept of estranged labour and for understanding the whole foundation of revolutionary theory.

II

There are two passages in the *Economic and Philosophical Manuscripts* in which Marx gives an explicit definition of man, encompassing the totality of human existence: on pages 112–14 and 179–83. Even if they are only a sketchy outline, these passages give a clear enough indication of the real basis of Marx's critique. On several occasions (pp. 135, 137, 181) Marx describes 'positive communism', which will achieve the abolition of estrangement and reification, as 'humanism' – a terminological hint that for him the basis is a particular kind of realization of the human essence. The development of this humanism, as far as it is a positive definition of the human essence, is here primarily influenced by Feuerbach: as early as in the preface we read: 'positive criticism as a whole – and therefore also German positive criticism of political economy – owes its true foundation to the discoveries of Feuerbach' (p. 236, note 3), and 'it is only with Feuerbach that positive, humanistic and naturalistic criticism begins' (p. 64). Later the 'establishment of true materialism and of real science' is described as Feuerbach's 'great achievement' (p. 172). In our interpretation, however, we shall not follow the road of philosophical history and trace the development of 'humanism' from Hegel through Feuerbach to Marx, but attempt to unfold the problem from Marx's text itself.

'Man is a species being, not only because in practice and in theory he adopts the species as his object (his own as well as those of other things), but – and this is only another way of expressing it – also because he treats himself as the actual, living, species; because he treats himself as a *universal* and therefore a free being' (p. 112). The definition of man as a 'species being' has done a lot of damage in Marx-scholarship; our passage is so valuable because it exposes the real origins of Marx's concept of 'species'. Man is a 'species being', i.e. a being which has the 'species' (his own and that of the rest of existence) as its object. The species of a being is that which this being is according to its 'stock' and 'origin'; it is the 'principle' of its being that is common to all the particular features of what it is: the general essence of this being. If man can make the species of every being into his object, the general essence of every being can become objective for him: he can possess every being as that which it is in its essence. It is for this reason (and this is expressed in the second half of the sentence quoted) that he can *relate* freely to every being: he is not limited to the particular actual state of the being and his immediate relationship to it, but he can take the being as it is in its essence

beyond its immediate, particular, actual state; he can recognize
and grasp the *possibilities* contained in every being; he can exploit,
alter, mould, treat and take further ('pro-duce') any being according to its 'inherent standard' (p. 114). Labour, as the specifically
human 'life activity', has its roots in man's nature as a 'species
being'; it presupposes man's ability to relate to the 'general'
aspect of objects and to the possibilities contained in it. Specifically human *freedom* has its roots in man's ability to relate to
his *own* species: the self-realization and 'self-creation' of man. The
relationship of man as a species being to his objects is then more
closely defined by means of the concept of free labour (free
productions).

Man as a species being is a 'universal' being: *every* being can
for him become objective in its 'species character'; his existence
is a universal relationship to objectivity. He has to include these
'theoretically' objective things in his praxis; he must make them
the object of his 'life activity' and work on them. The whole of
'nature' is the medium of his human life; it is man's means of life;
it is his prerequisite, which he must take up and reintroduce into
his praxis. Man cannot simply accept the objective world or
merely come to terms with it; he must appropriate it; he has to
transform the objects of this world into organs of his life, which
becomes effective in and through them. 'The universality of man
appears in practice precisely in the universality which makes all
nature his inorganic body – both inasmuch as nature is (1) his
direct means of life and (2) the material, the object, and the
instrument of his life activity. Nature is man's inorganic body –
nature, that is, in so far as it is not itself the human body' (p. 112).

The thesis of nature as a means for man implies more than
merely that man is dependent simply for his physical survival on
objective, organic and inorganic nature as a means of life, or that
under the direct pressure of his 'needs' he 'produces' (appropriates, treats, prepares, etc.) the objective world as objects for food,
clothing, accommodation, etc. Marx here explicitly speaks of
'spiritual, inorganic nature', 'spiritual nourishment' and 'man's
physical and spiritual life' (p. 112). This is why the universality

of man – as distinct from the essentially limited nature of animals – is *freedom*, for an animal 'produces only under the dominion of immediate physical need' while man 'only truly produces in freedom therefrom' (p. 113). An animal thus only produces itself and 'what it immediately needs for itself or its young. It produces one-sidedly, whilst man produces universally' (ibid.). Man does not have objects merely as the environment of his immediate life activity and does not treat them merely as objects of his immediate needs. He can 'confront' any object and exhaust and realize its inner possibilities in his labour. He can produce 'in accordance with the laws of beauty' and not merely in accordance with the standard of his own needs (p. 114). In this freedom man reproduces 'the whole of nature', and through transformation and appropriation furthers it, along with his own life, even when this production does not satisfy an immediate need. Thus the history of human life is at the same time essentially the history of man's objective world and of 'the whole of nature' ('nature' in the wider sense given to this concept by Marx, as also by Hegel).[7] Man is not *in* nature; nature is not the *external* world into which he first has to come out of his own inwardness. Man *is* nature. Nature is his 'expression', 'his work and his reality' (p. 114). Wherever we come across nature in human history it is '*human* nature' while man for his part is always 'human *nature*' too. We can thus see provisionally to what extent consistent 'humanism' is immediately 'naturalism' (pp. 135, 181).

On the basis of the unity thus achieved between man and nature Marx moves towards the crucial definition of *objectification*, through which the specifically human relationship to objectivity, the human way of producing, is more concretely determined as universality and freedom. Objectification – the definition of man as an 'objective being' – is not simply a further point appended to the definition of the unity of man and nature, but is the closer and deeper foundation of this unity. (Objectification as such belongs – like his participation in nature – to the essence of

7. Cf. *Phenomenology of Mind*, p. 220, the concept of 'inorganic nature', and pp. 234ff. of my book *Hegels Ontologie, etc.*

man, and can thus not be 'superseded'; according to revolutionary theory only a particular form of objectification – reification, 'estrangement' – can and must be superseded.)

As a natural being man is an 'objective being', which for Marx is a 'being equipped and endowed with objective (i.e. material) essential powers' (p. 180), a being who relates to real objects, 'acts objectively', and 'can only *express* his life in real, sensuous objects' (pp. 181ff.). Because the power of his being thus consists in living out (i.e. through and in external objects) everything he is, his 'self-realization' at the same time means 'the establishment of a real, objective world, which is overpowering because it has a form external to him and is thus not part of his being' (p. 180). The objective world, as the necessary objectivity of man, through the appropriation and supersession of which his human essence is first 'produced' and 'confirmed', is part of man himself. It *is* real objectivity only for self-realizing man, it is the 'self-objectification' of man, or human objectification. But this same objective world, since it is real objectivity, can appear as a precondition of his being which does *not* belong to his being, is beyond his control, and is 'overpowering'. This conflict in the human essence – that it is in itself objective – is the root of the fact that objectification can become reification and that externalization can become alienation. It makes it possible for man completely to 'lose' the object as part of his essence and let it become independent and overpowering. This possibility becomes a reality in estranged labour and private property.

Marx then attempts to implant objectification and the conflict appearing within it even more deeply into the definition of man. 'An objective being ... would not act objectively if the quality of objectivity did not reside in the very nature of his being. He creates, posits objects alone, *because* he is posited by objects – because at bottom he is nature' (p. 180). The quality of being posited by objects is, however, the fundamental determinant of 'sensuousness' (to have senses, which are affected by objects) and thus Marx can identify objective being with sensuous being, and the quality of having objects outside oneself with the quality of being sensuous: 'To be sensuous, i.e. real, is to be an object of the senses, a sensuous object, and therefore to have objects out-side oneself which are subject to the operations of one's senses', and this passage: '*To be* objective, natural and sensuous, and at the same time to have object, nature and sense outside oneself, or oneself to be object, nature and sense for a third party, is one and the same thing' (p. 181). (The second identification also included here will be discussed below.) Thereby 'sensuousness' for Marx moves into the centre of his philosophical foundation: 'Sensuous-ness (see Feuerbach) must be the basis of all science' (p. 143).

It is already clear from the above deduction that 'sensuousness' is here an ontological concept within the definition of man's essence and that it comes before any materialism or sensualism. The concept of sensuousness here taken up by Marx (via Feuer-bach and Hegel) goes back to Kant's *Critique of Pure Reason*. There it is said that sensuousness is the human perception through which alone objects are *given* to us. Objects can only be given to man in so far as they 'affect' to him. Human sen-suousness is affectibility.[8] Human perception as sensuousness is receptive and passive. It receives what it is given, and it is dependent on and needs this quality of being given. To the extent to which man is characterized by sensuousness he is 'posited' by objects, and he accepts these prerequisites through cognition. As a sensuous being he is an affixed, passive and suffering being.

In Feuerbach, to whom Marx explicitly refers in the passage quoted, the concept of sensuousness originally tends in the same direction as in Kant. In fact when Feuerbach, in opposition to Hegel, wants to put the receptivity of the senses back at the starting-point of philosophy, he initially almost appears as the preserver and defender of Kantian criticism against 'absolute idealism'. 'Existence is something in which not only I, but also the others, and especially the *object*, participate.'[9] 'Only through the *senses* does an object in the true sense become given – not

8. Second impression, B. 33.
9. Feuerbach, *Sämtliche Werke II*, p. 309.

through thinking for itself'; 'an object is given not to my Ego but to my non-Ego, for only where I am passive does the conception of an activity existing outside me, i.e. objectivity, come into being' (ibid., pp. 321ff.). This accepting, passive being with needs, dependent on given things, which finds its expression in man's sensuousness, is developed by Feuerbach into the 'passive principle' (ibid., pp. 257ff.) and placed at the apex of his philosophy – although he goes in a direction quite different from that of Kant. The definition of man as purely a passive being 'with needs' is the original basis for Feuerbach's attack on Hegel and his idea of man as a purely free, creative consciousness: 'only a passive being is a necessary being. Existence without needs is superfluous existence . . . A being without distress is a being without ground . . . A non-passive being is a being without being. A being without suffering is nothing other than a being without sensuousness and matter' (ibid., pp. 256f.).

The same tendency to go back to sensuousness is now also discernible in Marx – a tendency to comprehend man's being defined by needs and his dependence on pre-established objectivity by means of the sensuousness in his own being. This tendency in turn is subject to the aim of achieving a real, concrete picture of man as an objective and natural being, united with the world, as opposed to Hegel's abstract 'being', freed from pre-established 'naturalness', which posits both itself and all objectivity. In line with Feuerbach, Marx says: 'as a natural, corporeal, sensuous, objective being [man] is a *passive*, conditioned and limited creature' (p. 181) and: 'To be sensuous is to *be passive*. Man as an objective, sensuous being is therefore a *passive* being – and because he feels what he suffers, a passionate being' (p. 182). Man's passion, his real activity and spontaneity is ascribed to his passivity and neediness, in so far as it is an aspiration to a pre-established object existing outside him: 'Passion is the essential force of man energetically bent on its object' (p. 182).[10] And: 'The rich man is simultaneously the man *in need of* a totality

10. The ontological concept of passion is found similarly in Feuerbach (*Werke II*, p. 323).

of human manifestations of life – the man in whom his own realization exists as an inner necessity, as *need*' (p. 144).

We can now understand why Marx emphasizes that 'man's feelings, passions, etc. . . . are truly ontological affirmations of being of [nature]' (p. 165). The distress and neediness which appear in man's sensuousness are no more purely matters of cognition than his distress and neediness, as expressed in estranged labour, are purely economic. Distress and neediness here do not describe individual modes of man's behaviour at all; they are features of his whole *existence*. They are ontological categories (we shall therefore return to them in connection with a large number of different themes in these *Manuscripts*).

It was necessary to give such an extensive interpretation of the concept of sensuousness in order to point once again to its real meaning in opposition to its many misinterpretations as the basis of materialism. In developing this concept Marx and Feuerbach were in fact coming to grips with one of the crucial problems of 'classical German philosophy'. But in Marx it is this concept of sensuousness (as objectification) which leads to the decisive turn from classical German philosophy to the theory of revolution, for he inserts the basic traits of *practical* and *social* existence into his definition of man's essential being. As objectivity, man's sensuousness is essentially practical objectification, and because it is practical it is essentially a social objectification.

III

We know from Marx's *Theses on Feuerbach* that it is precisely the concept of human *praxis* that draws the line of demarcation between himself and Feuerbach. On the other hand, it is through this (or more exactly, through the concept of labour) that he reaches back beyond Feuerbach to Hegel: 'The outstanding achievement of Hegel's *Phenomenology* and of its final outcome . . . is thus . . . that Hegel . . . grasps the essence of labour and comprehends objective man – true, because real man – as the outcome of man's own labour' (p. 177). Things are thus not as simple as we would expect; the road from Feuerbach to Marx is not characterized by a straight rejection of Hegel. Instead of this, Marx, at the origins of revolutionary theory, once again appropriates the decisive achievements of Hegel on a transformed basis.

We saw that man's sensuousness signified that he is posited by pre-established objects and therefore also that he *has* a given, objective world, to which he *relates* 'universally' and 'freely'. We must now describe more closely the way in which he possesses and relates to the world.

In Feuerbach man's possession of, and relation to, the world remains essentially theoretical, and this is expressed in the fact that the way of relating, which really permits 'possession' of reality, is 'perception'.[11] In Marx, to put it briefly, labour replaces this perception, although the central importance of the theoretical relation does not disappear: it is combined with labour in a relationship of dialectical interpenetration. We have already suggested above that Marx grasps labour, beyond all its economic significance, as *the* human 'life-activity' and the genuine realization of man. We must now present the concept of labour in its inner connection to the definition of man as a 'natural' and 'sensuous' (objective) being. We shall see how it is in labour that the distress and neediness, but also the universality and freedom of man, become real.

'Man is directly a natural being. As a natural being and as a living natural being he is on the one hand endowed with natural powers of life – he is an *active* natural being. These forces exist in him as tendencies and abilities – as instincts. On the other hand, as a natural, corporeal, sensuous, objective being he is a suffering, conditioned and limited creature. . . . That is to say, the objects of his instincts exist outside him, as *objects* independent of him; yet these objects are objects that he *needs* – essential objects,

11. e.g. *Werke II*, pp. 258, 337. The indications of a more profound definition, which doubtless exist in Feuerbach, are not followed through. Cf., for example, the concept of 'resistance' *II*, pp. 321ff.), etc.

indispensable to the manifestation and confirmation of his essential powers' (p. 181). Objects are thus not primarily objects of perception, but of needs, and as such objects of the powers, abilities and instincts of man. It has already been pointed out that 'need' is not to be understood only in the sense of physical neediness: man needs 'a totality of human manifestations of life' (p. 144). To be able to realize himself he needs to express himself through the pre-established objects with which he is confronted. His activity and his self-affirmation consist in the appropriation of the 'externality' which confronts him, and in the transference of himself into that externality. In his labour man supersedes the mere objectivity of objects and makes them into 'the means of life'. He impresses upon them the form of his being, and makes them into 'his work and his reality'. The objective piece of finished work *is* the reality of man; man *is* as he has realized himself in the object of his labour. For this reason Marx can say that in the object of his labour man sees himself in objective form, he becomes 'for himself', he perceives himself as an object. 'The object of labour is, therefore, the objectification of man's species life: for he duplicates himself not only, as in consciousness, intellectually, but also actively, in reality, and therefore he contemplates himself in a world that he has created' (p. 114).

Objectification of the 'species life': for it is not the isolated individual who is active in labour, and the objectivity of labour is not objectivity for the isolated individual or a mere plurality of individuals – rather it is precisely in labour that the specifically human *universality* is realized.

Thus we can already discern the second basic characteristic of objectification: it is essentially a 'social' activity, and objectifying man is basically 'social' man. The sphere of objects in which labour is performed is precisely the sphere of common life-activity: in and through the objects of labour, men are shown *one another* in their reality. The original forms of communication, the essential relationship of men to one another, were expressed in the common use, possession, desire, need and enjoyment, etc. of the objective world. All labour is labour with and for and against others, so that in it men first mutually reveal themselves for what they really are.[12] Thus every object on which a man works in his individuality is 'simultaneously his own existence for the other man, the existence of the other man, and that existence for him' (p. 136).

If the objective world is thus understood in its totality as a 'social' world, as the objective reality of human society and thus as human objectification, then through this it is also already defined as a *historical* reality. The objective world which is in any given situation pre-established for man is the reality of a past human life, which, although it belongs to the past, is still present in the form it has given to the objective world. A new form of the objective world can thus only come into being on the basis, and through the supersession of an earlier form already in existence. The real human and his world arise first in this movement, which inserts the relevant aspect of the past into the present: 'History is the true natural history of man', his 'act of origin' (p. 182), 'the creation of man through human labour' (p. 145). Not only man emerges in history, but also nature, in so far as it is not something external to and separated from the human essence but belongs to the transcended and appropriated objectivity of man: 'world history' is 'the emergence of nature for man' (ibid.).

It is only now, after the totality of the human essence as the unity of man and nature has been made concrete by the practical-social-historical process of objectification, that we can understand the definition of man as a 'universal' and 'free' species being. The history of man is at the same time the process of 'the whole of nature'; his history is the 'production and reproduction' of the whole of nature, furtherance of what exists objectively through once again transcending its current form. In his 'universal' relationship[13] to the whole of nature, therefore, nature is ulti-

12. Cf. the comprehensive formulation in *The Holy Family*: 'that the object as being for man or as the objective being of man is at the same time the existence of man for other men, his human relation to other men, the social relation of man to man' (*The Holy Family*, Moscow, 1956, p. 60).

13. Feuerbach: 'Man is not a particular being like the animal, but a *universal* being, thus not a limited and unfree but an unlimited and free being, for universality,

mately not a limitation on or something alien outside him to which he, as something other, is subjected. It is his expression, confirmation, activity: 'externality is ... the *self-externalizing world of sense* open to the light, open to the man endowed with senses' (p. 192).

We now want to summarize briefly the definitions brought together in the concept of man as a universal and free being. Man 'relates' to himself and whatever exists, he can transcend what is given and pre-established, appropriate it and thus give it his own reality and realize himself in everything. This freedom does not contradict the distress and neediness of man, of which we spoke at the beginning, but is based upon it in so far as it is freedom only as the transcendence of what is given and pre-established. Man's 'life-activity' is 'not a determination with which he directly merges' like an animal (p. 113), it is 'free activity', since man can 'distinguish' himself from the immediate determination of his existence, 'make it into an object' and transcend it. He can turn his existence into a 'means' (ibid.), can himself give himself reality and himself 'produce' himself and his 'objectivity'. It is in this deeper sense (and not only biologically) that we must understand the sentence that 'man produces man' (pp. 136, 137) and that human life is genuinely 'productive' and 'life-engendering life' (p. 113).

Thereby Marx's definition returns to its starting-point: the basic concept of 'labour'. It is now clear to what extent it was right to deal with labour as an ontological category. As far as man, through the creation, treatment and appropriation of the objective world, gives himself his own reality, and as far as his 'relationship to the object' is the 'manifestation of human reality' (p. 139), labour is the real expression of human freedom. Man becomes free in his labour. He freely realizes himself in the object of his labour: 'when, for man in society, the objective world everywhere becomes the world of man's essential powers – human reality, and

---

absence of limitations, and freedom are inseparable. And this freedom does not for example exist in a particular capacity ... but extends over his whole being' (*Werke*, *II*, p. 342).

for that reason the reality of his *own* essential powers – . . .
all objects become for him the objectification of himself, become
objects which confirm and realize his individuality, become *his*
objects: that is, *man himself* becomes the object' (p. 140).

IV

In the preceding sections we have attempted to present in its
context the definition of man underlying the *Economic and
Philosophical Manuscripts* and to reveal it as the basis of the
critique of political economy. It almost appears, despite all
protestations to the contrary, as if we are moving in the field of
philosophical investigations, forgetting that these *Manuscripts* are
concerned with the foundation of a theory of revolution and hence
ultimately with revolutionary *praxis*. But we only need to put the
result of our interpretation next to its starting point to find that
we have reached the point where the philosophical critique in
itself directly becomes a practical revolutionary critique.

The fact from which the critique and the interpretation set out
was the alienation and estrangement of the human essence as
expressed in the alienation and estrangement of labour, and hence
the situation of man in the historical facticity of capitalism. This
fact appears as the total *perversion* and *concealment* of what the
critique had defined as the essence of man and human labour.
Labour is not 'free activity' or the universal and free self-
realization of man, but his enslavement and loss of reality. The
worker is not man in the totality of his life-expression, but a non-
person, the purely physical subject of 'abstract' activity. The
objects of labour are not expressions and confirmations of the
human reality of the worker, but alien things, belonging to someone other than the worker – 'commodities'. Through all this the
existence of man does not become, in estranged labour, the
'means' for his self-realization. The reverse happens: man's self
becomes a means for his mere existence. The pure physical
existence of the worker is the goal which his entire life-activity

serves. 'As a result, therefore, man [the worker] only feels himself freely active in his animal functions – eating, drinking, pro-creating, or at most in his dwelling and in dressing-up, etc., and in his human functions he no longer feels himself to be anything but an animal. What is animal becomes human and what is human becomes animal' (p. 111).

We have seen that Marx describes this estrangement and loss of reality as the 'expression' of a total perversion of the behaviour of man as man: in his relationship to the product of his labour as an 'alien object exercising power over him' and simultaneously in the relationship of the worker to his own activity as 'an alien activity not belonging to him' (ibid.). This reification is by no means limited to the worker (even though it affects him in a unique way); it also affects the non-worker – the capitalist. The 'dominion of dead matter over man' reveals itself for the capitalist in the state of private property and the manner in which he has and possesses it. It is really a state of being possessed, of being had, slavery in the service of property. He possesses his property not as a field of free self-realization and activity but purely as capital: 'Private property has made us so stupid and one-sided that an object is only *ours* when we have it – when it exists for us as capital, or when it is directly possessed, eaten, drunk, worn, inhabited, etc., – in short, when it is *used* by us . . . the life which they [realizations of possession] serve as means is the life of private property, labour, and conversion into capital' (p. 139). (We shall return to the definition of 'true possession' underlying this description of 'false property' below.)

If historical facticity thus reveals the total perversion of all the conditions given in the definition of the human essence, does it not prove that this definition lacks content and sense, and that it is only an idealistic abstraction, which does violence to historical reality? We know the cruel derision with which, in his *German Ideology*, which appeared only a year after these *Manuscripts*, Marx destroyed the idle talk of the Hegelians, such people as Stirner and the 'true socialists', about *the* essence, *the* man, etc. Did Marx himself, in his definition of the human essence, give in to this idle chatter? Or does a radical change take place in Marx's fundamental views between our *Manuscripts* and the *German Ideology*?

There is indeed a change, even if it is not in his fundamental views. It must be emphasized again and again that in laying the foundations of revolutionary theory Marx is fighting *on various fronts*: on the one hand against the pseudo-idealism of the Hegelian school, on the other against reification in bourgeois political economy, and then again against Feuerbach and pseudo-materialism. The meaning and the purpose of his fight thus varies according to the direction of his attack and defence. Here, where he is principally fighting reification in political economy, which turns a particular kind of historical facticity into rigid 'eternal' laws and so-called 'essential relationships', Marx presents this facticity in contrast to the real essence of man. But in doing this he brings out its truth, because he grasps it within the context of the real history of man and reveals the necessity of its being overcome.

These changes, then, result from shifts in the terrain of the conflict. But the following point is still more decisive. To play off essence (the determinants of 'the' man) and facticity (his given concrete historical situation) against each other is to miss completely the new standpoint which Marx had already assumed at the outset of his investigations. For Marx essence and facticity, the situation of essential history and the situation of factual history, are no longer separate regions or levels independent of each other: the historical experience of man is *taken up into the definition of his essence*. We are no longer dealing with an abstract human essence, which remains equally valid at every stage of concrete history, but with an essence which can be defined in *history* and *only* in history. (It is therefore quite a different matter when Marx speaks of the 'essence of man', as opposed to Bruno Bauer, Stirner and Feuerbach!)[14] The fact that despite or precisely because of

14. The *German Ideology* says of the critique in the *Deutsch-Französische Jahrbücher*: 'Since at that time this was done in philosophical phraseology, the traditionally occurring philosophical expressions such as 'human essence', 'species' etc., gave the German theoreticians the desired excuse for . . . believing that here again it

this it is always man himself that matters in all man's historical praxis is so self-evident that it is not worth discussing for Marx, who grew up in a direct relationship with the most lively period of German philosophy (just as the opposite seems to have become self-evident for the epigones of Marxism). Even in Marx's extremely bitter struggle with German philosophy in the period of its decline, a philosophical impetus lives on which only complete naïveté could misconstrue as a desire to destroy philosophy altogether.

The discovery of the historical character of the human essence does not mean that the history of man's essence can be identified with his factual history. We have already heard that man is never directly 'one with his life-activity'; he is, rather, 'distinct' from it and 'relates' to it. Essence and existence *separate* in him: his existence is a 'means' to the realization of his essence, or – in estrangement – his essence is a means to his mere physical existence (p. 113). If essence and existence have thus become separated and if the real and free *task* of human praxis is the unification of both as factual realization, then the authentic task, when facticity has progressed so far as totally to *pervert* the human essence, is the *radical abolition* of this facticity. It is precisely the unerring contemplation of the essence of man that becomes the inexorable impulse for the initiation of radical revolution. The factual situation of capitalism is characterized not merely by economic or political crisis but by a catastrophe affecting the human essence; this insight condemns any mere economic or political *reform* to failure from the outset, and unconditionally requires the cataclysmic transcendence of the actual situation through *total revolution*. Only after the basis has been established in this way, so firmly that it cannot be shaken by any merely economic or political arguments, does the question of the *historical conditions and the bearers* of the revolution arise: the question of the theory of class struggle and the dictatorship of the proletariat. Any critique which only pays attention to this theory,

was a question merely of giving a new turn to their theoretical garments . . .' (*The German Ideology*, Moscow, 1968, p. 259).

without coming to grips with its real foundation, misses the point.

We shall now look at the *Manuscripts* to see what they contribute to the preparation of a positive theory of revolution and how they treat the real supersession of reification, the supersession of alienated labour and of private property. We shall once again limit ourselves to the basic state of affairs expressed in the economic and political facts. What also belongs to this positive theory of revolution is – as we shall show – an investigation of the *origin* of reification: an investigation of the historical conditions and emergence of private property. Two main questions must therefore be answered: 1. How does Marx describe the accomplished supersession of private property, i.e. the state of the human essence after the total revolution? 2. How does Marx handle the problem of the origin of private property or the emergence and development of reification? Marx himself explicitly asked both these questions: the answer is given mainly on pages 115–17 and 135–42.

The total estrangement of man and his loss of reality had been traced back to the alienation of labour. In the analysis, *private property* had been revealed as the manner in which alienated labour 'must express and present itself in real life' (p. 115) and as the 'realization of alienation' (p. 117) (we shall return to the close connection between alienated labour and private property below). The supersession of alienation, if it is to be a genuine supersession (and not merely 'abstract' or theoretical), must supersede the real form of alienation (its 'realization'); and so 'the entire revolutionary movement necessarily finds both its empirical and its theoretical basis in the movement of private property – more precisely, in that of the economy' (p. 136).

Through this connection with alienated labour private property is already *more* than a specific economic category: this extra element in the concept of private property is sharply emphasized by Marx: 'Material, immediately sensuous private property is the material, sensuous expression of *estranged human* life. Its movement – production and consumption – is the sensuous revelation of the movement of all production until now, i.e. the realization of the reality of man' (pp. 136ff.). Through the explanatory 'i.e. the realization . . . of man' which he adds Marx expressly emphasizes the fact that 'production', of which the movement of private property is the 'revelation', is not economic production but the self-producing process of the whole of human life (as interpreted above). The extent to which private property expresses the movement of estranged human life is more closely described in the following passage: 'Just as private property is only the sensuous expression of the fact that man becomes objective for himself and at the same time becomes to himself a strange and inhuman object: just as it expresses the fact that the assertion of his life is the alienation of his life, that his realization is his loss of reality . . . so the positive transcendence of private property . . .' is more than economic transcendence: namely the positive 'appropriation' of the whole of human reality (pp. 138ff.). Private property is the real expression of the way in which estranged man objectifies himself, 'produces' himself and his objective world and realizes himself in it. Private property therefore constitutes the realization of an entire form of human *behaviour* and not just a given physical '*state*' external to man,[15] or 'a *merely objective* being' (p. 128).

But if an estranged form of behaviour which has lost reality is thus realized in private property, then private property itself can only represent an estranged and unreal form of true and essential human behaviour. There must therefore be *two real 'forms'* of property: an estranged and a true form, a property which is merely private and a property which is 'truly human' (p. 119).[16]

15. This turn from a state outside men to a human relation again illustrates the new problematic of Marx's theory: his penetration through the veil of abstract reification towards the comprehension of the objective world as the field of historical-social praxis. Marx emphasizes that this way of posing the question had already entered traditional political economy when Adam Smith recognized labour as the 'principle' of economics, but its real sense was immediately completely concealed again since this kind of political economy 'merely formulated the laws of *estranged* labour' (p. 117; my italics).

16. Marx directs his heaviest attacks in the *German Ideology* precisely against the concept of 'truly human property' (particularly in his polemic against the 'true socialists', op. cit., pp. 516ff.); here, within Marx's foundation of the theory of revolution, this concept obviously has a significance quite different from that in Stirner and the 'true socialists'.

There must be a form of 'property' belonging to the essence of man, and positive communism, far from meaning the abolition of all property, will be precisely the *restoration* of this truly human form of property.

How can one 'define the general nature of private property, as it has arisen as a result of estranged labour, in its relation to *truly human* and *social property*' (p. 118)? The answer to this question must at the same time make clear the meaning and goal of the positive supersession of private property. 'The meaning of private property – apart from its estrangement – is the *existence of essential objects* for man, both as objects of gratification and as objects of activity' (p. 165).

This is the most general positive definition of true property: the availability and usability of all the objects which man needs for the free realization of his essence. This availability and usability is realized as *property* – which is by no means self-evident, but is based on the idea that man never simply and directly has what he needs, but only really possesses objects when he has appropriated them. Thus the purpose of labour is to give to man as his own possessions objects which have been treated and to make them into a world through which he can freely engage in activity and realize his potentialities. The essence of property consists in 'appropriation'; a particular manner of appropriation and realization through appropriation is the basis of the state of property, and not mere having and possessing. We must now more closely define this new concept of appropriation and property which underlies Marx's analysis.

We have seen how private property consists in an untrue mode of having and possessing objects. In conditions of private property an object is 'property' when it can be 'used'; and this use consists either in immediate consumption or in its capacity to be turned into capital. 'Life-activity' stands in the service of property instead of property standing in the service of free life-activity; it is not the 'reality' of man which is appropriated but objects as things (goods and commodities) and even this kind of appropriation is 'one-sided': it is limited to the physical behaviour of man and to objects which can immediately 'gratify' or be turned into capital. In contrast to this, 'true human property' is now described in its true appropriation: 'the sensuous appropriation for and by man of the human essence and of human life, of objective man, of human achievements – should not be conceived merely in the sense of *immediate*, one-sided *gratification* – merely in the sense of *possession*, of *having*. Man appropriates his total essence in a total manner, that is to say, as a whole man.' This total appropriation is then more closely described: 'Each of his human relations to the world – seeing, hearing, smelling, tasting, feeling, thinking, observing, experiencing, wanting, acting, loving – in short, all the organs of his individual being . . . are in their objective orientation or in their orientation to the object, the appropriation of that object' (pp. 138–9).

Beyond all economic and legal relations, appropriation as the basis of property thus becomes a category which comprehends the universal and free relationship of man to the objective world: the relationship to the object which is becoming one's own is 'total' – it 'emancipates' *all* the human senses. The *whole* man is at home in the *whole* objective world which is 'his work and his reality'. The *economic and legal* supersession of private property is not the *end*, but only the *beginning* of the communist revolution. This universal and free appropriation is *labour*, for as we saw, the specifically human relationship to the object is one of creating, positing, forming. But in this case labour would no longer be an alienated and reified activity, but all-round self-realization and self-expression.

The inhumanity represented by reification is thus abolished at the point where it was most deeply rooted and dangerous: in the concept of property. Man no longer 'loses' himself in the objective world, and his objectification is no longer reification, if objects are withdrawn from 'one-sided' ownership and possession and remain the work and reality of the one who 'produced' or realized them and himself in them. It is not, however, the isolated individual or an abstract plurality of individuals which has been realized in them, but *social* man, man *as* a social being. Man's return to his true property is a return into his social essence; it is the liberation of society.

V

'Man is not lost in his object only when the object becomes for him a *human* object or objective man. This is possible only when the object becomes for him a *social* object, he himself for himself a social being, just as society becomes a being for him in this object' (p. 140). There are thus two conditions for breaking through reification as outlined above: the objective relations must become human – i.e. social – relations and they must be recognized and consciously preserved as such. These two conditions are fundamentally interrelated, for the objective relations can only become human and social if man himself is conscious of them *as such*, i.e. in his *knowledge* of both himself and the object. Thus we again encounter the central role which a particular kind of insight (man's 'coming-to-be for himself') plays in the foundation of Marx's theory. To what extent can cognition, the recognition of objectification as something social, become the real impulse for the abolition of all reification?

We know that objectification is essentially a social activity and that it is precisely in his objects and in his labour on them that man recognizes himself as a social being. The insight into objectification, which breaks through reification, is the insight into society as the subject of objectification. For there is no such thing as 'society' as a subject outside the individual; Marx expressly warns against playing society as an independent entity off against the individual: 'Above all we must avoid postulating "Society" again as an abstraction *vis-à-vis* the individual. The individual *is the social being*. His life, even if it may not appear in the direct form of a communal life in association with others, *is* therefore an expression and confirmation of social life' (pp. 137–8).

Insight into objectification thus means insight into how and through what man and his objective world *as social relations* have become what they are. It means insight into the historical-social situation of man. This insight is no mere theoretical cognition or arbitrary, passive intuition, but *praxis*: the supersession of what exists, making it a 'means' for free self-realization.

This also means that the insight which defines this task is by no means available to everyone: it can only be known by those who are actually *entrusted with this task* by their historical-social situation (we cannot pursue the way in which the proletariat becomes the bearer of this insight in the situation analysed by Marx: its content is presented at the close of Marx's *Introduction to the Critique of Hegel's Philosophy of Right*). It is not a matter of *the* task for man *as such* but of a particular historical task in a particular historical situation. It is therefore necessary that 'the transcendence of the estrangement always proceeds from that form of the estrangement which is the dominant power' (p. 154). Because it is dependent on the conditions pre-established by history, the praxis of transcendence must, in order to be genuine transcendence, reveal these conditions and appropriate them. Insight into objectification as insight into the historical and social situation of man reveals the historical conditions of this situation and so achieves the *practical force and concrete form* through which it can become the lever of the revolution. We can now also understand how far questions concerning the *origin* of estrangement and insight into the *origin* of private property must be an integrating element in a positive theory of revolution.

Marx's handling of the question of the origins of private property shows the pioneering new 'method' of his theory. Marx is fundamentally convinced that when man is conscious of his history he cannot fall into a situation which he has not himself created, and that only he himself can liberate himself from any situation. This basic conviction already finds its expression in the concept of freedom in the *Manuscripts*. The phrase that the liberation of the working class can only be the work of the working class itself resonates clearly through all the economic explanations; it only enters into 'contradiction' with historical materialism if the latter is falsified into a vulgar materialism. If the relations of production have become a 'fetter' and an alien force determining man, then this is only because man has at some stage himself alienated himself from his power over the relations of production. This is also true if one sees the relations of production as being determined primarily by the given 'natural' forces of production (e.g. climatic or geographical conditions, the condition of the land, the distribution of raw materials) and ignores the fact that all these physical data have always existed in a form historically handed down and have formed a part of particular human and social 'forms of intercourse'. For the situation of man which exists through such pre-existing forces of production only becomes an historical and social situation through the fact that man 'reacts' to what he finds pre-existing, i.e. through the manner in which he appropriates it. In truth these relations of production which have been reified into alien, determining forces are always objectifications of particular social relations, and the abolition of the estrangement expressed in these relations of production can only be total and real if it can account for economic revolution in terms of these human relations. Thus the question of the origin of private property becomes a question of the activity through which man *alienated* property from himself: 'How, we now ask, does *man* come to *alienate*, to estrange, his *labour*? How is this estrangement rooted in the nature of human development?' And being aware of the crucial importance of this new way of formulating the question, Marx adds: 'We have already gone a long way to the solution of this problem by *transforming* the question of the *origin of private property* into the question of the relation of *alienated labour* to the course of humanity's development. For when one speaks of private property, one thinks of dealing with something external to man. When one speaks of labour, one is directly dealing with man himself. This new formulation of the question already contains its solution' (pp. 118–19).

The answer to this question is not contained in the *Economic and Philosophical Manuscripts*; it is worked out in his later critiques of political economy. The *Economic and Philosophical*

Manuscripts do, however, contain a proof within the definition of man's essence that objectification always carries within it a tendency towards reification and labour a tendency towards alienation, so that reification and alienation are not merely chance historical facts. In connection with this it is also shown how the worker even through his alienation 'engenders' the non-worker and thus the domination of private property (pp. 116–17), and how he therefore has his fate in his own hands at the origin of estrangement and not just after liberation.

Marx gives his definition of estrangement as self-estrangement in a reference to the real achievement of Hegel's *Phenomenology*: 'The real, active orientation of man to himself as a species being ... is only possible through the *utilization* of all the powers he has in himself and which he has as belonging to a species ..., treating these generic powers as objects and this, to begin with, is again *only possible in the form of estrangement*' (p. 177; my italics).

We fail to find an explanation here as to why this is, to begin with, only possible in the form of estrangement; and it is, strictly speaking, impossible to give one, for we are confronted with a state of affairs that has its roots in man – as an 'objective' being – and which can only be revealed as such. It is man's 'need' – as already interpreted above – for objects alien to him, 'overpowering' and 'not part of his being', to which he must relate *as if* they were external objects, although they only become real objects through and for him. Objects first confront him *directly* in an external and alien form and only become *human* objects, objectifications of man, through conscious historical and social appropriation. The expression of man thus first tends towards alienation and his objectification towards reification, so that he can only attain a universal and free reality through 'the negation of negation': through the *supersession* of his alienation and the *return* out of his estrangement.

After the possibility of alienated labour has been shown to have its roots in the essence of man the limits of philosophical description have been reached and the discovery of the real origin of alienation becomes a matter for economic and historical analysis. We know that for Marx the starting point for this analysis is the *division of labour* (cf., for example, p. 159); we cannot go further into this here and shall only look quickly at the way Marx shows that already with the alienation of labour the worker 'engenders' the domination of the capitalist and thereby of private property. At the head of this analysis there stands the sentence: 'Every self-estrangement of man, from himself and from nature, appears in the relation in which he places himself and nature to *men other than* and differentiated from himself' (p. 116; my italics). We are already acquainted with the context of this sentence: the relation of man to the object on which he works is directly his relation to other men with whom he shares this object and himself as something social. So that although the worker in the self-alienation of his labour 'possesses' the object as something alien, overpowering and not belonging to him, this object nowhere confronts him as an isolated thing, belonging to no one and, as it were, outside humanity. The situation is rather this: 'If the product of labour does not belong to the worker, if it confronts him as an alien power, then this can only be because it belongs to some *other man than the worker*' (p. 115). With the alienation of labour the worker immediately stands as 'servant' in the service of a 'master': 'Thus, if the product of his labour . . . is for him an alien . . . object . . . then his position towards it is such that someone else is master of this object, someone who is alien. . . . If he is related to his own activity as to an unfree activity, then he is related to it as an activity performed in the service, under the dominion, the coercion, and the yoke of another man' (pp. 116ff.).

It is not a case of a 'master' existing first, subordinating someone else to himself, alienating him from his labour, and making him into a mere worker and himself into a non-worker. But nor is it a case of the relationship between domination and servitude being the simple consequence of the alienation of labour. The alienation of labour, as estrangement from its own activity and from its object, already *is* in itself the relationship between worker and non-worker and between domination and servitude.

These distinctions seem to be of only secondary importance, and they do in fact disappear into the background again in the later, purely economic analysis. Nevertheless they must be expressly emphasized in the context of the *Manuscripts*, if only for the fact that they are relevant to Marx's crucial reaction to Hegel. Domination and servitude are here not concepts for particular (pre- or early capitalist) formations, relations of production, etc. They give a general description of the social condition of man in a situation of estranged labour. In this sense they point back to the ontological categories of 'domination and servitude' developed by Hegel in his *Phenomenology* (II, pp. 145ff.).[17] We cannot discuss here Marx's further description of the relation between domination and servitude, but we shall select one important point: 'everything which appears in the worker as an *activity* of alienation, of estrangement, appears in the non-worker as a *state* of alienation, of estrangement' (p. 119).

We know that the transcendence of estrangement (a state in which both master *and* servant find themselves, although not in the same way) can only be based on the destruction of reification, i.e. on the practical insight into the activity of objectification in its historical and social situation. Since it is only in *labour* and in the objects *of his labour* that man can really come to understand himself, others and the objective world in their historical and social situation, the master, as a *non*-worker, cannot come to this insight. Since what is actually a specific human activity appears to him as a material and objective state of affairs, the worker has an (as it were) irreducible advantage over him. He is the real factor of transformation; the destruction of reification can only be *his* work. The master can only come to this revolutionary insight if he becomes a worker, which, however, would mean transcending his own essence.

From every point of approach and in all directions this theory, arising out of the philosophical critique and foundation of

17. I have gone into this in my essay 'Zum Problem der Dialektik' (*Die Gesellschaft*, 12, 1931).

political economy, proves itself to be a *practical theory*, a theory whose immanent meaning (required by the nature of its object) is particular praxis; only particular praxis can solve the problems peculiar to this theory. 'We see how the resolution of the *theoretical* antitheses is *only* possible in a *practical* way, by virtue of the practical energy of man. Their resolution is therefore by no means merely a problem of understanding, but a *real* problem of life, which *philosophy* could not solve precisely because it conceived this problem as *merely* a theoretical one' (pp. 141–2). We could add to this sentence: which philosophy can solve, however, if it grasps it as a *practical* problem, i.e. if it transcends itself as 'only theoretical' philosophy, which in turn means, if it really 'realizes' itself as philosophy for the first time.

Marx calls the practical theory which solves this problem, in so far as it puts man as a historical and social being in the centre, 'real humanism' and identifies it with 'naturalism' to the extent to which, if it is carried through, it grasps the unity of man and nature: the 'naturalness of man' and the 'humanity of nature'. If the real humanism outlined here by Marx as the basis of his theory does not correspond to what is commonly understood as Marx's 'materialism', such a contradiction is entirely in accordance with Marx's intentions: 'here we see how consistent naturalism and humanism distinguishes itself both from idealism and materialism, constituting at the same time the unifying truth of both' (p. 181).

VI

Finally we need to examine briefly Marx's critique of Hegel, which was envisaged as the conclusion of the whole *Manuscripts*. We can make the discussion brief because we have already gone into Marx's elaboration of the positive foundations of a critique of Hegel (the definition of man as an 'objective', historical and social, practical being) in the context of our interpretation of the critique of political economy.

Marx begins by pointing out the necessity of discussing a question which has still not been adequately answered: 'How do we now stand as regards the Hegelian dialectic?' (p. 170). This question, coming at the conclusion of his positive critique of political economy and the foundation of revolutionary theory, shows how much Marx was aware of working in an area opened up by Hegel and how he experienced this fact – in contrast to almost all the Hegelians and almost all his later followers – as a scientific-philosophical obligation towards Hegel. After briefly dispatching Bruno Bauer, Strauss, etc., whose 'critical critique' makes the need to come to terms with Hegel anything but superfluous, Marx immediately gives his support to Feuerbach: 'the only one who has a serious, critical attitude to the Hegelian dialectic and who has made genuine discoveries in this field' (p. 172). Marx mentions three such discoveries: Feuerbach (1) recognized philosophy (i.e. the purely speculative philosophy of Hegel) as a 'form and manner of existence of the estrangement of the essence of man', (2) established 'true materialism' by making 'the social relationship "of man to man" the basic principle of his theory' and (3) precisely through this principle opposed Hegel's mere 'negation of negation', which does not go beyond negativity, with a 'self-supporting positive, positively based on itself' (pp. 172ff.). With this enumeration, Marx simultaneously articulated the three main directions of his own critique of Hegel, and it is to these that we now turn.

'One must begin with Hegel's *Phenomenology*, the true point of origin and the secret of the Hegelian philosophy' (p. 173). From the beginning Marx tackles Hegel's philosophy where its origin is still visible in an unconcealed form: in the *Phenomenology*. If at the beginning of the critique it may still have looked as if it was really only a critique of what one is accustomed to regard as Hegel's 'dialectic', we now see that what Marx criticizes as the dialectic is the foundation and actual 'content' of Hegel's philosophy – not its (supposed) 'method'. And while Marx criticizes, he simultaneously extracts the positive aspects, the great discoveries made by Hegel – i.e. only because for Marx there are genuinely positive discoveries in Hegel, on the basis of which he can and must do further work, can and must Hegel's philosophy become for him the subject of a critique. We shall begin with the negative part of his critique – Marx's collation of Hegel's 'mistakes' – so that we can then extract the positive aspects from these negative ones and show that the mistakes are really only mistaken interpretations of genuine and true states of affairs.

In the *Phenomenology* Hegel gives 'speculative expression' to the movement of the history of the 'human essence', but not of its real history, only its 'genetic history' (p. 173). That is, he gives the history of the human essence, in which man first becomes what he is and which has, as it were, always already taken place when the real history of man occurs. Even with this general characterization Marx has grasped the sense of the *Phenomenology* more profoundly and accurately than most interpreters of Hegel. He then proceeds to a critique of the core of Hegel's own problematic: Hegel's philosophical description of the history of the human essence fails at the start, because Hegel from the outset grasps it only as abstract 'self-consciousness' ('thought', 'mind') and thus overlooks its true concrete fullness: 'For Hegel the essence of man – man – equals self-consciousness' (p. 178); the history of the human essence runs its course purely as the history of self-consciousness or even as history within self-consciousness. What Marx had shown to be crucial for the definition of man's essence and what he had put at the centre of his conceptual structure – the 'objectivity' of man, his 'essential objectification' – is precisely what is ominously given a different meaning and perverted by Hegel. The object (i.e. objectivity as such) is in Hegel only an object *for consciousness* in the very strong sense that consciousness is the 'truth' of the object and that the latter is only the negative side of consciousness: having been 'posited' (created, engendered) by consciousness as its alienation and estrangement, it must also be 'transcended' by consciousness again, or 'taken back' into consciousness. The object is thus, by the nature of its existence, a purely negative thing, a 'nullity' (p. 182); it is merely an object of abstract thought, for Hegel reduces self-consciousness to abstract thought. 'The main point is that the object of consciousness is nothing else but self-consciousness, or that the object is only objectified self-consciousness – self-consciousness as an object. . . . The issue, therefore, is to surmount the object of consciousness. Objectivity as such is regarded as an estranged human relationship which does not correspond to the essence of man' (p. 178). For Marx, however, objectivity was precisely the human relationship in which man could alone come to self-realization and self-activity; it was 'real' objectivity, the 'work' of human labour and certainly not the object of abstract consciousness. From this standpoint Marx can say that Hegel fixes man as 'a non-objective, spiritual being' (p. 178). This being never exists with genuine objects but always only with the self-posited negativity of itself. It is actually always 'at home with itself' in its 'otherness as such' (p. 183). It is thus ultimately 'non-objective', and 'a non-objective being is a . . . *non-being*' (p. 182).

This also constitutes a critique of the *Phenomenology* in so far as it claims to present the movement of the history of man's essential being. If this being whose history is being presented is a '*non-being*', then this history must also be 'inessential' in the full sense of the word. Marx perceives Hegel's discovery of the movement of human history in the movement of 'objectification as loss of the object, as alienation' (p. 177) and in the 'transcendence' of this alienation as it recurs in many forms in the whole of the *Phenomenology*. But the objectification is only apparent, 'abstract and formal', since the object only has 'the semblance of an object' and the self-objectifying consciousness remains 'at home with itself' in this seeming alienation (pp. 183ff.). Like estrangement itself, its supersession is only a semblance: alienation remains. The forms of estranged human existence which Hegel cites are not forms of estranged real life but only of consciousness and knowledge: what Hegel deals with and supersedes are not 'real religion, the real state, or real nature, but religion as a subject of knowledge, i.e. Dogmatics; the same with Jurisprudence, Political Science and Natural Science' (pp. 186–7). Because alienation is thus only superseded in the mind and not in reality, i.e. because 'this supersession of thought leaves its object standing in reality', Marx can say the whole *Phenomenology*, and indeed the whole of Hegel's system in so far as it is based on the *Phenomenology*, remains within estrangement. This comes out in Hegel's system as a whole in the fact, for example, that 'nature' is not grasped as man's 'self-externalizing world of sense' in its existential unity with man or its 'humanity', but is taken as externality 'in the sense of alienation, of a mistake, a defect, which ought not to be', – a 'nothing' (p. 192).

We shall not go into the other features of the negative critique here: they are already familiar from the *Critique of Hegel's Philosophy of Right*; e.g. the conversion of mind into an absolute, the hypostatization of an absolute subject as the bearer of the historical process, the inversion of subject and predicate (p. 188), etc. What must be borne in mind is that Marx regards all these 'inadequacies' as within a real state of affairs. If Hegel posits the human essence as a 'non-being', then it is the non-being of a real being and thus a real non-being; if he has 'only found the abstract, logical, speculative expression for the movement of history' (p. 173), then this is still an expression for the movement of real history; if he has described objectification and estrangement in their abstract forms, then he has still seen objectification and estrangement as essential movements of human history. The emphasis of Marx's critique of Hegel is definitely on the *positive* part, to which we now proceed.

'The outstanding achievement of Hegel's *Phenomenology* and of its final outcome, the dialectic of negativity as the moving and generating principle, is thus first that Hegel conceives the self-creation of man as a process, conceives objectification as loss of the object, as alienation and as transcendence of this alienation; that he thus grasps the essence of *labour* and comprehends objective man . . . as the outcome of man's own labour' (p. 177). The full significance of the interpretation of the *Phenomenology* given here by Marx could only be grasped if we unfolded the central problematic of Hegel's work, which we obviously cannot do here; it would also only then become apparent with what unheard of sureness Marx sees through all the mystifying and misleading interpretations (which begin even within Hegel's work) and gets back to the bedrock of the problems which were raised, for the first time in modern philosophy, in the *Phenomenology*.

In the sentence quoted above Marx has brought together all the discoveries of Hegel which he recognizes as crucial: in what follows we want briefly to explain these, for Marx, 'positive moments of the Hegelian dialectic'.

The *Phenomenology* presents the 'self-creation of man', which means, after what has already been said, the process in which man (as an organic, living being) becomes what he is according to his essence – i.e. human essence. It thus gives the 'genetic history' (p. 173) of the human essence or man's essential history. Man's 'act of creation' is an 'act of self-genesis' (p. 188), i.e. man gives his essence to himself: he must first make himself what he is, 'posit' himself, and 'produce' himself (we have already gone into the meaning of this concept). This history which is given into man's own hands is grasped by Hegel as a 'process' characterized by alienation and its supersession. The process as a whole stands under the title of 'objectification'. The history of man thus occurs and fulfils itself as objectification: the reality of man consists of creating real objects out of all his 'species powers', or 'the establishing of a real, objective world' (p. 180). It is this establishing of an objective world which Hegel treats merely as the alienation of 'consciousness' or knowledge, or as the relation of abstract thought to 'thinghood', while Marx grasps it as the 'practical' realization of the whole of man in historical and social labour (ibid.).

Hegel defines the relation of knowledge to the objective world in such a way that this objectification is simultaneously the loss of the object, i.e. the loss of reality or estrangement, so that, 'to begin with, [it] is again only possible in the form of estrangement' (p. 177). That is to say: knowledge, in the process of becoming objective, initially *loses* itself in its objects: they confront it as something alien and other, in the form of an external world of things and matters which have lost their inner connection with the consciousness which has expressed itself in them and now continue as a power independent of consciousness. In the *Phenomenology*, for example, morality and right, the power of the state and wealth appear as estranged objective worlds and it is here that Marx accuses Hegel of dealing with these worlds only as 'worlds of thought' and not as real worlds (pp. 174ff.), since for Hegel they are externalizations of 'Mind' only and not of real, total human existence.

Although objectification consists initially in the loss of the object or estrangement, it is precisely this estrangement which in Hegel becomes the recovery of true being. 'Hegel conceives man's self-estrangement, the alienation of man's essence, man's loss of objectivity and his loss of realness as self-discovery, change of his nature, objectification and realization' (pp. 187–8). The human essence – always conceived in Hegel as exclusively knowledge – is such that it must not only express but alienate itself, not only objectify itself but lose its object, to be able to discover itself. Only if it has really lost itself can it come to itself, only in its 'otherness' can it become what it is 'for itself'. This is the 'positive meaning' of negation, 'the dialectic of negativity as the moving and generating principle' (p. 177). We should have to go into the foundations of Hegel's ontology to justify and clarify this assertion: here we need only show how Marx interprets this discovery by Hegel.

Through the positive concept of negation just referred to, Hegel conceives 'labour as man's act of self-genesis' (p. 188); 'he grasps labour as the essence of man – as man's essence in the act of proving itself' (p. 177). With reference to this Marx goes so far as to say: 'Hegel's standpoint is that of modern political economy' (ibid.) – a seemingly paradoxical statement in which, however, Marx summarizes the colossal, almost revolutionary concreteness of Hegel's *Phenomenology*. If labour is here defined as man's essence in the act of proving itself this obviously refers to labour not purely as an economic, but as an 'ontological' category, as Marx defines it in this very passage: 'Labour is man's coming-to-be for himself within alienation, or as alienated man' (p. 177). How does it come about that Marx should take precisely the category of labour to interpret Hegel's concept of objectification as self-discovery in estrangement and of realization in alienation?

It is not only because Hegel uses labour to reveal the objectification of the human essence and its estrangement, or because he depicts the relation of the labouring 'servant' to his world as the first 'supersession' of estranged objectivity (II, pp. 146 ff.). It is not only because of this; although the fact that this is viewed as the real beginning of human history in the *Phenomenology* is neither a coincidence nor the result of a purely arbitrary decision, but expresses the innermost direction of the entire work. Marx has thereby – albeit in an exaggerated form – discovered the original meaning of the history of the human essence as it is elaborated in the *Phenomenology* in the form of the history of self-consciousness. It is praxis, free self-realization, always taking up, superseding and revolutionizing pre-established 'immediate' facticity. It has already been pointed out that Marx holds Hegel's real mistake to be the substitution of 'Mind' for the subject of this praxis. Hence for Marx, 'the only labour which Hegel knows and recognizes is abstract mental labour' (p. 177). But this does not alter the fact that Hegel grasped labour as man's essence in the act of proving itself – a fact which retains its vital importance: despite the 'spiritualization' of history in the *Phenomenology*, the actual leading concept through which the history of man is explicated is transforming 'activity' (II, pp. 141, 196, 346, 426, etc.).

If the inner meaning of objectification and its supersession is thus praxis, then the various forms of estrangement and their supersession can also be more than mere 'examples' taken out of real history and put alongside each other with no necessary connection. They must have have their roots in human praxis and be an integral part of man's history. Marx expresses this insight in the sentence that Hegel has found 'speculative expression for the movement of history' (p. 173) – a sentence which (as already stated) must be understood positively just as much as negatively and critically. And if the forms of estrangement are rooted as historical forms in human praxis itself, they cannot be regarded simply as abstract theoretical forms of the objectivity of consciousness; under this logical-speculative 'disguise' they must have ineluctable practical consequences, they must of necessity be effectively superseded and 'revolutionized'. A critique must lie hidden already in the *Phenomenology*: critique in the revolutionary sense which Marx gave to this concept. 'The *Phenomenology* is, therefore, an occult critique – still to itself obscure and mystifying: but inasmuch as it keeps steadily in view man's estrangement . . . there lie concealed in it all the elements of the critique already *prepared and elaborated* in a manner often rising far above the Hegelian standpoint'. In its separate sections it contains 'the critical elements of whole spheres such as religion, the state, civil life, etc. – but still in an estranged form' (p. 176).

Thereby Marx has expressed in all clarity the inner connection between revolutionary theory and Hegel's philosophy. What seems amazing, as measured by this critique – which is the result of a *philosophical* discussion – is the decline of later interpretations of Marx (even – *sit venia verbo* – those of Engels!) by people who believed they could reduce Marx's relationship to Hegel to the familiar transformation of Hegel's 'dialectic', which they also completely emptied of content.

These suggestions will have to suffice; above all we cannot go into the question if and how the 'mistakes' with which Marx charges Hegel can really be attributed to him. It has perhaps become clear through this paper that the discussion really starts at the centre of Hegel's problematic. Marx's critique of Hegel is not an appendage of the preceding critique and foundation of political economy, for his examination of political economy is itself a continuous confrontation with Hegel.

A Study on Authority

[1936]

Publisher's note : First published as *Studie über Autorität und Familie* in *Studien über Autorität und Familie*, Librairie Félix Alcan, Paris, 1936.

The authority relationship, as understood in these analyses, assumes two essential elements in the mental attitude of he who is subject to authority: a certain measure of freedom (voluntariness: recognition and affirmation of the bearer of authority, which is not based purely on coercion) and conversely, submission, the tying of will (indeed of thought and reason) to the authoritative will of an Other. Thus in the authority relationship freedom and unfreedom, autonomy and heteronomy, are yoked in the same concept and united in the single person of he who is subject. The recognition of authority as a basic force of social praxis attacks the very roots of human freedom: it means (in a different sense in each case) the surrender of autonomy (of thought, will, action), the tying of the subject's reason and will to pre-establish contents, in such a way that these contents do not form the 'material' to be changed by the will of the individual but are taken over as they stand as the obligatory norms for his reason and will. Yet bourgeois philosophy put the autonomy of the person right at the centre of its theory: Kant's teachings on freedom are only the clearest and highest expression of a tendency which has been in operation since Luther's essay on the freedom of the Christian man.

The concept of authority thus leads back to the concept of freedom: it is the practical freedom of the individual, his social freedom and its absence, which is at stake. The union of internal autonomy and external heteronomy, the disintegration of freedom in the direction of its opposite is the decisive characteristic of the concept of freedom which has dominated bourgeois theory since the Reformation. Bourgeois theory has taken very great pains to justify these contradictions and antagonisms.

The individual cannot be simultaneously free and unfree, autonomous and heteronomous, unless the being of the person is conceived as divisible and belonging to various spheres. This is quite possible once one ceases to hypostatize the I as the 'substance'. But the decisive factor is the mode of this division. If it is undertaken dualistically, the world is split in half: two relatively self-enclosed spheres are set up and freedom and unfreedom as totalities divided between them in such a way that one sphere is wholly a realm of freedom and the other wholly a realm of unfreedom. Secondly, what is internal to the person is claimed as the realm of freedom: the person as member of the realm of Reason or of God (as 'Christian', as 'thing in itself', as intelligible being) is free. Meanwhile, the whole 'external world', the person as member of a natural realm or, as the case may be, of a world of concupiscence which has fallen away from God (as 'man', as 'appearance'), becomes a place of unfreedom. The Christian conception of man as 'created being' 'between' *natura naturata* and *natura naturans*, with the unalterable inheritance of the Fall, still remains the unshaken basis of the bourgeois concept of freedom in German Idealism.

But the realm of freedom and the realm of unfreedom are not simply contiguous with or superimposed on each other. They are founded together in a specific relation. For freedom – and we must hold fast to this astonishing phrase despite its paradoxical nature – is the condition of unfreedom. Only because and in so far as man is free can he be unfree; precisely because he is 'actually' (as a Christian, as a rational person) completely free must he 'unactually' (as a member of the 'external' world) be unfree. For the full freedom of man in the 'external' world as well would indeed simultaneously denote his complete liberation from God, his enslavement to the Devil. This thought reappears in a secularized form in Kant: man's freedom as a rational being can only be 'saved' if as a sensual being he is entirely abandoned to natural necessity. The Christian doctrine of freedom pushes the liberation of man back until it pre-dates his actual history, which then, as the history of his unfreedom, becomes an 'eternal' consequence of this liberation. In fact, strictly speaking there is no liberation of man in history according to this doctrine or, to put it more precisely, Christian doctrine has good reasons for viewing such a liberation as primarily something negative and evil, namely the partial liberation from God, the achievement of freedom to sin (as symbolized in the Fall).

As an 'internally' free being man is born into a social order which, while it may have been posited or permitted by God, by no means represents the realm in which the existence or non-existence of man is decided upon. Whatever the nature of this order may be, the inner freedom of man (his pure belief and his pure will, provided they remain pure) cannot be broken in it. 'The power of the temporal authority, whether it does right or wrong, cannot harm the soul.'[1]

This absolute inwardness of the person, the transcendent nature of Christian freedom *vis-à-vis* all worldly authority, must at the same time mean an 'internal' weakening and breaking of the authority relationship, however completely the individual may submit externally to the earthly power. For the free Christian knows that he is 'actually' raised above worldly law, that his essence and his being cannot be assailed by it and that his subordination to the worldly authorities is a 'free' act, which he does not 'owe' them. 'Here we see that all works and all things are free to a Christian through his faith. And yet because the others do not yet believe, the Christian bears and holds with them, *although he is not obliged to do these things*. He does this freely. . .'[2] This simultaneous recognition and transcendence of the whole system of earthly authorities announces a very important element in the Christian-bourgeois doctrine of freedom – its *anti-authoritarian tendency*. The social meaning of this doctrine of freedom is not simply that the individual should submit *in toto* to any earthly authority and thus affirm *in toto* the given system of authorities at any time. The Protestantism of Luther and Calvin which gave the Christian doctrine of freedom its decisive form for bourgeois society, is bound up with the emergence of a new, 'young' society which had first to conquer its right to exist in a bitter struggle against existing authorities. Faced with the universal bonds of traditionalist feudalism it absolutely required the liberation of the individual within the earthly order as well

1. Luther, *Treatise on Good Works* (1520), in *Selected Writings of Martin Luther*, vol. I, Philadelphia, 1967, p. 174.
2. Op. cit., p. 118 (my italics).

(the individual free subject of the economic sphere later essentially became the model of its concept of the individual) – it required the liberation of the territorial sovereign from the authority of an internationally centralized Church and a central imperial power. It further required the liberation of the 'conscience' from numerous religious and ethical norms in order to clear the way for the rise of the bourgeoisie. In all these directions an *antiauthoritarian attitude* was necessary: and this will find its expression in the writers we shall discuss.

However, this anti-authoritarian tendency is only the complement of an order which is directly tied to the functioning of as yet opaque relationships of authority. From the very outset the bourgeois concept of freedom left the way open for the recognition of certain metaphysical authorities and this recognition permits external unfreedom to be perpetuated within the human soul.

This point announced a fresh duality in the Protestant-bourgeois concept of freedom: an opposition between Reason and Faith, rational and irrational (in fact anti-rational) factors. As opposed to the rational, 'calculating' character of the Protestant-capitalist 'spirit' which is often all too strongly emphasized, its irrational features must be particularly pointed out. There lies an ultimate lack of order at the very root of this whole way of life, rationalized and calculated down to the last detail as an 'ideal type', this whole 'business' of private life, family and firm: the accounts do not, after all, add up – neither in the particular, nor in the general 'business'. The everyday self-torture of 'inner-worldly asceticism' for the sake of success and profit still ultimately has to experience these things, if they really occur, as unforeseeable good fortune. The individual is confronted again and again with the fear of loss: the reproduction of the whole society is only possible at the price of continual crises. The fact that the production and reproduction of life cannot be rationally mastered by this society constantly breaks through in the theological and philosophical reflections on its existence. The terrible hidden God of Calvinism is only one of the most severe forms of such a breakthrough: Luther's strong defence of the 'unfree will' is a similar case, as is the yawning gulf between the pure form of the universal law and the material for its fulfilment in Kant's ethic. The bourgeoisie fought its greatest battles under the banner of 'Reason' but it is precisely bourgeois society which totally deprives reason of its realization. The sector of nature controlled by man through rational methods is infinitely larger than in the Middle Ages; society's material process of production has in many instances been rationalized down to the last detail – but as a *whole* it remains 'irrational'. These antagonisms appear in the most varied forms in the ambivalence of bourgeois relationships of authority: they are rational, yet fortuitous, objective, yet anarchic, necessary, yet bad.

Luther's pamphlet *The Freedom of a Christian* brought together for the first time the elements which constitute the specifically bourgeois concept of freedom and which became the ideological basis for the specifically bourgeois articulation of authority: freedom was assigned to the 'inner' sphere of the person, to the 'inner' man, and at the same time the 'outer' person was subjected to the system of worldly powers; this system of earthly authorities was transcended through private autonomy and reason; person and work were separated (person and office) with the resultant 'double morality'; actual unfreedom and inequality were justified as a consequence of 'inner' freedom and equality. Right at the start of the work[1] are those two theses which, following on from St Paul, express the internally contradictory nature of the Christian concept of freedom with a conscious emphasis on this paradoxical antinomy: 'A Christian is free and independent in every respect, a bondservant to none. A Christian is a dutiful servant in every respect, owing a duty to everyone' (p. 357). And the dissolution of the contradiction: the first sentence deals with 'the spiritual man, his freedom and his supreme righteousness', the second sentence refers to 'the outer man': 'In as far as he is free, he requires to do nothing. In as far as he is a servant he must do everything' (p. 369). That expresses clearly and sharply the dualistic doctrine of the two realms, with freedom entirely assigned to the one, and unfreedom entirely assigned to the other.

The more specific determinations of internal freedom are all given in a counter-attack on external freedom, as negations of a merely external state of freedom: 'No outer thing . . .' can make

1. Luther, *The Freedom of a Christian* (1520), in *Reformation Writings of Martin Luther*, vol. I, London, 1952, pp. 357ff.

the free Christian 'free or religious', for his freedom and his 'servitude' are 'neither bodily nor outward'; none of the external things 'touches the soul, either to make it free or captive' (pp. 357–8). Nothing which is in the world and stems from the world can attack the 'soul' and its freedom; this terrible utterance, which already makes it possible entirely to deprecate 'outer' misery and to justify it 'transcendentally', persists as the basis of the Kantian doctrine of freedom; through it, actual unfreedom is subsumed into the concept of freedom. As a result, a peculiar (positive and negative) ambiguity enters into this concept of freedom: the man who is enclosed in his inner freedom has so much freedom over all outer things that he becomes free *from* them – he doesn't even *have* them any more, he has no control over them (p. 367). Man no longer *needs* things and 'works' – not because he already has them, or has control over them, but because in his self-sufficient inner freedom he doesn't need them at all. 'If such works are no longer a prerequisite, then assuredly all commandments and laws are like broken chains; and if his chains are broken, he is assuredly free' (p. 362). Internal freedom here really seems to be transformed into external freedom. But the realm of external freedom which opens up is, from the standpoint of 'spiritual' salvation as a whole, a realm of 'things indifferent': what man is free to do here, what can be done or not done, is in itself irrelevant to the salvation of his soul. 'But "free" is that in which I have choice, and may use or not, yet in such a way that it profit my brother and not me.'[2] The 'free' things in this realm can also be called the 'unnecessary' things: 'Things which are not necessary, but are left to our free choice by God, and which we keep or not.'[3] Freedom is a total release and independence, but a release and independence which can never be freely fulfilled or realized through a deed or work. For this freedom so far precedes every deed and every work that it is always already realized when man begins to act. His freedom can never be the result of an action;

2. Luther, *The First Lent Sermon at Wittenberg* (9 March 1522), in *Selected Writings*, vol. II, p. 238.
3. Luther, *The Third Lent Sermon at Wittenberg* (11 March 1522), in op. ci vol. II, p. 243.

the action can neither add to nor diminish his freedom. Earthly 'works' are not done to fulfil the person who requires this; the fulfilment must have occurred 'through faith before all works' ... 'works follow, once the commandments have been met' (p. 364).

But what sense is left in the earthly work of man if it always lags behind fulfilment? For the 'internal' man there is in fact no sense at all. Luther is quite clear on this point: 'Works are lifeless things, they can neither honour nor praise God . . .' (loc. cit). A sentence pregnant with consequences: it stands at the beginning of a development which ends with the total 'reification' and 'alienation' of the capitalist world. Luther here hit on the nodal points of the new bourgeois *Weltanschauung* with great accuracy: it is one of the origins of the modern concept of the subject as person. Straight after he has proclaimed that works are 'lifeless things' he continues: 'But here we seek him who is not done, as works are, but is an initiator and a master of work' (loc. cit). What is sought is the person (or that aspect of the person) who (or which) is not done (by another) but who is and stays the real subject of activity, the real master over his works: the autonomously acting person. And at the same time – this is the decisive point – this person is sought in contradistinction to his ('lifeless') works: as the negation and negativity of the works. Doer and deed person and work are torn asunder: the person as such essentially never enters into the work, can never be fulfilled in the work, eternally precedes any and every work. The true human subject is never the subject of *praxis*. Thereby the person is relieved to a previously unknown degree from the responsibility for his praxis, while at the same time he has become free for all types of praxis: the person secure in his inner freedom and fullness can only now really throw himself into outer praxis, for he knows that in so doing nothing can basically happen to him. And the separation of deed and doer, person and praxis, already posits the 'double morality' which, in the form of the separation of 'office' and 'person' forms one of the foundation stones of Luther's ethics:[4]

4. Luther, *Sermon on the Ban* (1520), in *Luther's Works*, vol. 39, ed. H. Lehmann,

later we shall have to return to the significance of this divorce. But we have not yet answered the question. What meaning can the praxis of a person thus separated from his works still possess? His praxis is at first completely 'in vain': it is obvious that man as a person 'is free from all commandments, and quite voluntarily does all that he does without recompense, and apart from seeking his own advantage or salvation. He already has sufficient, and he is already saved through his faith and God's grace. What he does is done just to please God' (p. 372). The person does not need the works, but they must nevertheless be done, so that 'man may not go idle and may discipline and care for his body' (p. 371). The praxis which has been separated from the being of the person serves the sinful body, which is struggling against inner freedom, as a discipline, an incentive and a divine service. Here we cannot elaborate any further on this conception of inner-worldly ascetism, or its suitability for rationalizing life and its various modifications in Lutheranism and Calvinism; we need only point out that it is implanted in the Protestant concept of freedom, to which we now return.

Man is embedded in a system of earthly order which by no means corresponds to the fundamental teachings of Christianity. This contradiction provides a function for the 'double morality' as combined with the sharp distinction between the 'Christian' and the worldly human existence, between 'Christian' morality and 'external morality, which is the motive force in offices and works'. The former refers only to the 'inner' man: his 'inner' freedom and equality,[5] his 'inner' poverty, love and happiness (at its clearest in Luther's interpretation of the Sermon on the Mount, 1530).[6] The 'external' order, on the other hand, is measured completely by the rules to which praxis and works are subjected when taken in isolation from the person. It is very

Philadelphia, 1970, p. 8; and *Whether Soldiers, Too, Can Be Saved* (1526), in *Selected Writings*, vol. III, p. 434.

5. Luther, *Temporal Authority: To What Extent It Should be Obeyed* (1523), *Selected Writings*, vol. II, p. 307: emphasizing the exclusively 'inner' equality of men.

6. Translated into English in *Luther's Works*, vol. 21, ed. J. Pelikan, Philadelphia, 1956, pp. 3ff.

characteristic that here – in accordance with the idea of praxis as the discipline and service performed by an utterly sinful existence – the earthly order appears essentially as a system of 'authorities' and 'offices', as an order of universal subordination, and that these authorities and offices in turn essentially appear under the sign of the 'sword'. (In one of his fiercest passages about worldly authority, still in anti-authoritarian idiom, Luther calls the Princes of God 'jailers', 'hangmen' and 'bailiffs'.)[7] This whole system of subordination to authorities and offices can admittedly be justified as a whole by referring to the ordinances of God: it has been set up to punish the bad, to protect the faithful and to preserve the peace – but this justification is by no means sufficient to sanction the system of subordination that exists at any one time, the particular office or the particular authority and the way it uses the 'sword'. Can an unchristian authority be ordained by God and lay claim to unconditional subordination? Here the separation of office and person opens up a path which has far reaching consequences: it holds fast to the unconditional authority of the office, while it surrenders the officiating person to the fate of possible rejection. 'Firstly a distinction must be made: office and person, work and doer, are different things. For an office or a deed may well be good and right in itself which is yet evil and wrong if the person or doer is not good or right or does not do his work properly.'[8] There was already a separation of this kind before Luther, in Catholicism, but in the context of the doctrine of the inner freedom of the Christian man and of the rejection of any justification by 'works' it paves the way for the theoretical justification of the coming, specifically bourgeois, structure of authority.

The dignity of the office and the worthiness of the officiating person no longer coincide in principle. The office retains its unconditional authority, even if the officiating person does not deserve this authority. From the other side, as seen by those

7. *Selected Writings*, vol. II, p. 303.
8. *Selected Writings*, vol. III, p. 434, and cf. *Werke*, ed. Buchwald, Berlin 1905, vol. III, pt 2, p. 393.

subject to authority, in principle every 'under-person' is equal as a person to every 'over-person': with regard to 'inner' worthiness he can be vastly superior to the authority. Despite this he must give it his complete obedience. There is a positive and a negative justification for this. Negatively: because after all the power of the wordly authority only extends over 'life and property, and external affairs on earth',[9] and thus can never affect the being of the person, which is all that matters. Positively; because without the unconditional recognition of the ruling authorities the whole system of earthly order would fall apart, otherwise 'everyone would become a judge against the other, no power or authority, no law or order would remain in the world; there would be nothing but murder and bloodshed'.[10] For in this order there is no way in which one person can measure the worthiness of another or measure right and wrong at all. The system of authority proclaimed here is only tenable if earthly justice is taken out of the power of the people or if the existing injustice is included in the concept of earthly justice. God alone is judge over earthly injustice, and 'what is the justice of the world other than that everyone does what he owes in his estate, which is the law of his own estate: the law of man or woman, child, servant or maid in the house, the law of the citizen or of the city in the land . . .'.[11] There is no tribunal that could pass judgement on the existing earthly order – except its own existing tribunal: 'the fact that the authority is wicked and unjust does not excuse tumult and rebellion. For it is not everyone who is competent to punish wickedness, but only the worldly authority which wields the sword . . .'.[12] And just as the system of worldly authorities is its own judge in matters of justice, so also in matters of mercy: the man who appeals to God's mercy in the face of the blood and terror of this system is turned away. 'Mercy is neither here nor there; we are now speaking of the word of God, whose will is that

9. *Temporal Authority* (1523), in *Selected Writings*, vol. II, p. 295.
10. *Admonition to Peace: A Reply to the Twelve Articles of the Peasants in Swabia* (1525), in *Selected Writings*, vol. III, p. 327.
11. *Werke*, ed. Buchwald, Berlin, 1905, vol. III, pt 2, p. 300.
12. *Admonition to Peace*, in *Selected Writings*, vol. III, p. 325.

62

the King be honoured and rebels ruined, and who is yet surely as merciful as we are.' 'If you desire mercy, do not become mixed up with rebels, but fear authority and do good.'[13]

We are looking here only at those consequences which arise from this conception for the new social structure of authority. A rational justification of the existing system of worldly authorities becomes impossible, given the absolutely transcendental character of 'actual' justice in relation to the worldly order on the one hand, and the separation of office and person and the essential immanence of injustice in earthly justice on the other. In the Middle Ages authority was tied to the particular bearer of authority at the time; it is the 'characteristic of him who communicates the cognition of a judgement'[14] and as a 'characteristic' it is inseparable from him; he always 'has' it for particular reasons (which again can be rational or irrational). Now the two are torn apart: the particular authority of a particular worldly bearer of authority can now only be justified if we have recourse to authority in general. Authority must exist, for otherwise the worldly order would collapse. The separation of office and person is only an expression for the autonomization (*Verselbständigung*) and reification of authority freed from its bearer. The authority-system of the existing order assumes the form of a set of relationships freed from the actual social relationships of which it is a function; it becomes eternal, ordained by God, a second 'nature' against which there is no appeal. 'When we are born God dresses and adorns us as another person, he makes you a child, me a father, the one a lord, the other a servant, this one a prince, that one a citizen and so on.'[15] And Luther accuses the peasants who protested against serfdom of turning Christian freedom into 'something completely of the flesh': 'Did not Abraham and other patriarchs and prophets also have slaves?'[16]

13. *An Open Letter on the Harsh Book against the Peasants* (1525), in *Selected Writings*, vol. III, p. 371.
14. Grimmich, *Lehrbuch der theoretischen Philosophie auf thomistischer Grundlage*, Freiburg, 1893, p. 177.
15. *Werke*, ed. Buchwald, Berlin, 1905, vol. II, pt 2, p. 296.
16. *Admonition to Peace*, in *Selected Writings*, vol. III, p. 339.

It is no coincidence that it is the essence of 'Christian freedom' which is held up to the rebellious peasants, and that this does not make them free but actually confirms their slavery. The recognition of actual unfreedom (particularly the unfreedom caused by property relations) is in fact part of the sense of this concept of freedom. For if 'outer' unfreedom can attack the actual being of the person, then the freedom or unfreedom of man is decided on earth itself, in social praxis, and man is, in the most dangerous sense of the word, free from God and can freely become himself. The 'inner', *a priori* freedom makes man completely helpless, while seeming to elevate him to the highest honour: it logically precedes all his action and thought, but he can never catch his freedom up and take possession of it.

In the young Marx's formulation, this unfreedom conditioned by the internalization of freedom, this dialectic between the release from old authorities and the establishment of new ones is a decisive characteristic of Protestantism: 'Luther, without question, defeated servitude through devotion, but only by substituting servitude through conviction. He shattered the faith in authority, by restoring the authority of faith. . . . He freed man from external religiosity by making religiosity the innermost essence of man.'[17]

One of the most characteristic passages for the unconditional acceptance of actual unfreedom is Luther's admonition to the

17. Marx, *Introduction to a Contribution to the Critique of Hegel's Philosophy of Right*, in *Karl Marx : Early Writings*, trans. T. B. Bottomore, London, 1963, p. 53.
The contradiction between anti-authoritarian and authoritarian tendencies which pervades the whole of Luther's work has been clearly elaborated by R. Pascal, *The Social Basis of the German Reformation*, London, 1933. Pascal shows that this contradiction is determined by the social and economic situation of the urban petty bourgeoisie, to whose interests Luther's Reformation corresponds. Pascal further strongly emphasizes the basically authoritarian character of Lutheranism, into which the anti-authoritarian streams are ultimately also fitted, so that after the achievement of the socially necessary economic and psychological liberations they work completely in the interests of the stabilization and strengthening of the existing world order. Even on the rare occasions when Luther breaks his doctrine of unconditional obedience to the worldly authority (as in 1531 with regard to the question of armed resistance to the Emperor by the Princes, after Luther had finally had to abandon his hope of winning the Emperor for the Protestant cause), the position he takes is by no means revolutionary but conservative: the Emperor appears as the wanton destroyer of an order which must be preserved under all circumstances.

Christian slaves who had fallen into the hands of the Turks, telling them not to run away from their new lords or to harm them in any other way: 'You must bear in mind that you have lost your freedom and become someone's property, and that without the will and knowledge of your master you cannot get out of this without sin and disobedience.' And then the interesting justification: 'For thus you would rob and steal your body from your master, which he has bought or otherwise acquired, after which it is not your property but his, like a beast or other goods in his possession.'[18] Here, therefore, certain worldly property and power relationships are made the justification of a state of unfreedom in which even the total abandonment of the Christian to the unbeliever is of subordinate importance to the preservation of these property relationships.[19]

With the emergence of the independence of worldly authority, and its reifications, the breach of this authority, rebellion and disobedience, becomes the social sin pure and simple, a 'greater sin than murder, unchastity, theft, dishonesty and all that goes with them.'[20] 'No evil deed on earth' is equal to rebellion; it is a 'flood of all wickedness'.[21] The justification which Luther gives for such a hysterical condemnation of rebellion reveals one of the central features of the social mechanism. While all other evil deeds only attack individual 'pieces' of the whole, rebellion attacks 'the head itself'. The robber and murderer leave the head that can punish them intact and thus give punishment its chance; but rebellion

18. *On War Against the Turk* (1529), in *Selected Writings*, vol. IV, p. 42.

19. Thomas Münzer's attack on Luther deals precisely with this connection between Luther's concept of authority and a particular property order: 'The poor flatterer wants to cover himself with Christ in apparent goodness. . . . But he says in his book on trading that one can with certainty count the princes among the thieves and robbers. But at the same time he conceals the real origin of all robbery. . . . For see, our lords and princes are the basis of all profiteering, theft and robbery; they make all creatures their property. The fish in the water, the birds of the air, the plants on the earth must all be theirs (Isaiah 5). Concerning this they spread God's commandment among the poor and say that God has commanded that you shall not steal, but it does them no good. So they turn the poor peasant, the artisan and all living things into exploiters and evil-doers' (*Hoch verursachte Schutzrede* (1525), in *Flugschriften aus der Reformationszeit*, vol. X, Halle, 1893, p. 25).

20. *Treatise on Good Works*, in *Selected Writings*, vol. I, p. 163.

21. *An Open Letter*, in *Selected Writings*, vol. III, p. 381.

'attacks punishment itself' and thereby not just disparate portions
of the existing order, but this order itself (op. cit., pp. 380–81),
which basically rests on the credibility of its power of punishment
and on the recognition of its authority. 'The donkey needs to feel
the whip and the people need to be ruled with force; God knew
that well. Hence he put a sword in the hands of the authorities
and not a featherduster' (op. cit., p. 376). The condition of
absolute isolation and atomization into which the individual is
thrown after the dissolution of the medieval universe appears here,
at the inception of the new bourgeois order, in the terribly truth-
ful image of the isolation of the prisoner in his cell: 'For God has
fully ordained that the under-person shall be alone unto himself
and has taken the sword from him and put him into prison. If he
rebels against this and combines with others and breaks out and
takes the sword, then before God he deserves condemnation and
death.'[22]

Every metaphysical interpretation of the earthly order embodies
a very significant tendency: a tendency towards *formalization*.
When the existing order, in the particular manner of its materiality, the material production and reproduction of life, becomes
ultimately valueless with regard to its 'actual' fulfilment, then it
is no more than the form of a social organization as such, which is
central to the organization of this life. This form of a social order
ordained by God for the sinful world was for Luther basically a
system of 'over-persons' and 'under-persons'. Its formalization
expressed itself in the separation of dignity and worthiness, of
office and person, without this contradiction giving any rightful
basis for criticism or even for the reform of this order. It was thus
that the encompassing system of worldly authorities was safeguarded: it required unconditional obedience (or, if it intruded on
'Christian freedom', it was to be countered with spiritual weapons
or evaded).

But danger threatened from another quarter. Initially, the
unconditional freedom of the 'person', proclaimed by Luther,
encouraged an anti-authoritarian tendency, and, indeed, precisely

22. *Selected Writings*, vol. III, p. 466.

on account of the reification of authority. The dignity of the office was independent of the worthiness of its incumbent; the bourgeois individual was 'privately' independent of authority. The assertion of Christian freedom and the allied conception of a 'natural realm' of love, equality and justice was even more destructive. Although it was separated from the existing social order by an abyss of meaning, it must still have threatened the completely formalized social order simply by its claims and its full materiality. The ideas of love, equality and justice, which were still effective enough even in their suppressed Lutheran form, were a recurrent source of anxiety to the rising bourgeois society owing to their revolutionary application in peasant revolts, Anabaptism and other religious sects. The smoothing-out of the contradictions appearing here, and the incorporation of these destructive tendencies into the bourgeois order, was one of the major achievements of Calvin. It is significant that this synthesis was only possible because the contradictions were simultaneously breaking out anew in a different dimension – although now in a sphere no longer transcending the bourgeois order as a whole but immanent in it. The most important marks of this tendency are Calvin's 'legalism' and his doctrine of the 'right to resist'.

It has often been pointed out in the relevant literature that in Calvin the Lutheran 'natural law' disappears. The dualism of the two 'realms' is removed:[23] admittedly Calvin too had sharply to emphasize that (precisely because of his increased interest in the bourgeois order) 'the spiritual kingdom of Christ and civil government are things very widely separated'[24] but the Christian realm of freedom is no longer effective as the material antithesis of the earthly order. In the face of the completely sinful and evil world there is ultimately only the person of God who, through the sole mediation of Christ, has chosen individuals for redemption

---

23. Beyerhaus, *Studien zur Staatsanschauung Calvins*, Berlin, 1910, points out that although 'theoretically' a distinction is made between the two spheres, 'practically' they become a unity precisely in the realization of Calvin's idea of the state (p. 50).

24. Calvin, *Institutes of the Christian Religion*, trans. F. L. Battles, London, 1961, Book IV, ch. XX, para. 1.

by a completely irrational system of predestination. Luther had been greatly disturbed by the tensions between his teaching and the teachings of the 'Sermon on the Mount', where the transcendence of the existing order is most clearly expressed and a devastating critique of this order made, which no degree of 'internalization' could ever completely suppress: in Calvin these tensions no longer exist. The more inexorably Calvin elaborates the doctrine of eternal damnation, the more the positive biblical promises lose their radical impulse.[25] The way is made clear for a view of the wordly order which does not recognize its dubious antithesis. This does not mean that the world is somehow 'sanctified' in the Christian sense: it is and remains an order of evil men for evil men, an order of concupiscence. But in it, as the absolutely prescribed and sole field for their probation, Christians must live their life to the honour and glory of the divine majesty, and in it the success of their praxis is the *ratio cognoscendi* (reason of knowing) of their selection. The *ratio essendi* (reason of existence) of this selection belongs to God and is eternally hidden from men. Not love and justice but the terrible majesty of God was at work in the creation of this world, and the desires and drives, the hopes and laments of men are correspondingly directed not towards love and justice but towards unconditional obedience and humble adoration. Very characteristically, Calvin conceived original sin, i.e. the act which once and for all determined the being and essence of historical man, as disobedience, *inoboedientia*,[26] or as the crime of lese-majesty (while in St Augustine's interpretation of original sin as *superbia* [overwhelming pride] – which Calvin aimed to follow here – there is still an element of the defiant freedom of the self-affirming man). And obedience is also the mechanism which holds the wordly order together: a system, emanating from the family, of *subjectio* and *superioritas*, to which God has given his name for protection: 'The titles of Father, God and Lord, all meet in him alone, and hence, whenever any one of

25. H. Engelland, *Gott und Mensch bei Calvin*, Munich, 1934, pp. 113ff.
26. Cf. Barnikel, *Die Lehre Calvins vom unfreien Willen* . . . , Bonn dissertation, 1927, pp. 104ff; Beyerhaus, op. cit., p. 79.

them is mentioned our mind should be impressed with the same feeling of reverence' (*Institutes*, Book II, ch. VIII, para. 35).

By freeing the worldly order from the counter-image of a Christian realm of love, equality and justice and making it as a whole a means for the glorification of God, the formalization operative in Luther is withdrawn; the sanction granted it now also affects its materiality: '. . . in all our cares, toils, annoyances, and other burdens, it will be no small alleviation to know that all these are under the superintendence of God. The magistrate will more willingly perform his office, and the father of the family confine himself to his proper sphere. Every one in his particular mode of life will, without refining, suffer its inconveniences, cares, uneasiness, and anxiety, persuaded that God has laid on the burden' (op. cit., Book III, ch. X, para. 6). The new direction manifests itself in the often described activism and realism of Calvin's disciples: in the concept of an occupation as a vocation, in Calvin's 'state rationalism', in his extensive and intensive practico-social organization. With the abolition of Luther's formalization, the separation of office and person and the 'double morality' linked with it also disappear in Calvin (although it will be shown that this does not remove the reification of authority, i.e. the understanding of it as an element of a natural or divine feature of an institution or a person instead of as a function of social relationships): the religious moral law – and essentially in the form represented in the decalogue, which it is claimed is also a 'natural' law – is regarded as the obligatory norm for the practical social organization of the Christian 'community'. This was a step of great significance. It is true that the decalogue complied to a much greater degree with the demands of the existing social order than with the radical transcendental Christianity of the New Testament, and that it provided a considerably greater amount of latitude. Nevertheless, the new form of the law stabilized a norm, against which the officiating authorities could be 'critically' measured. 'But now the whole doctrine is pervaded by a spirit which desires to see society shaped and moulded for a definite purpose, and a spirit which can criticize law and authority according to the eternal standards of divine and natural law.'[27] Luther's irrationalist doctrine of authority as 'power for power's sake', as Troeltsch characterized it in a much disputed phrase, has been abandoned. In so far as obedience to the officiating authority leads to a transgression of the law, this authority loses its right to obedience.[28] It is a straight line from here to the struggle of the *Monarchomachi* against absolutism. From a source very close to Calvin, from his pupil, Théodore de Beza, comes the famous work *De jure magistratum in subditos* which presents the opinion that 'even armed revolution is permissible, if no other means remain . . .'.[29]

Yet these tendencies already belong to the later development of the bourgeoisie; in Calvin the right to resist in the face of worldly authorities is in principle limited from the start. Immediately after his warning to unworthy princes ('May the princes hear, and be afraid') Calvin continues: 'But let us at the same time guard most carefully against spurning or violating the venerable and majestic authority of rulers, an authority which God has sanctioned by the surest edicts, although those invested with it should be most unworthy of it, and, as far as in them lies, pollute it with their iniquity. Although the lord takes vengeance on unbridled domination, let us not therefore suppose that that vengeance is committed to us, to whom no command has been given but to obey and suffer. I speak only of private men' (*Institutes*, Book IV, ch. XX, para. 31). Worldly authority retains its independence and its reification. And in a characteristic modification of the Lutheran concept of the *homo privatus* as a free person, this *homo privatus* is now primarily unfree: he is the man who obeys and suffers. In no case is the *homo privatus* entitled to change the system of officiating authorities:[30] 'The subject as a private person has no independent political rights, rather he has the ethical-religious

27. Troeltsch, *The Social Teaching of the Christian Churches*, trans. O. Wyon, vol. II, London, 1931, p. 616.
28. Ibid., p. 618.
29. Ibid., p. 629.
30. Troeltsch, op. cit., p. 616; Lobstein, *Die Ethik Calvins*, Strasburg, 1877, p. 116.

duty to bear patiently even the extremities of oppression and persecution.'[31] Even in the case of the most blatant transgression of the Law, when obedience to the worldly authority must lead to disobedience to God, Calvin allows only a 'right of passive resistance'. Where the Christian organization of society is actually already under attack the right of veto is allowed only to the lower magistrates themselves, never to the 'people' or to any postulated representatives of the people. And so in Calvin too we encounter the Lutheran idea of the immanence of the law within the existing system of worldly authorities: decisions regarding their rightness or wrongness are made exclusively within their own order, among themselves.

The direct ordination of the system of worldly authorities by God, when combined with the Calvinist concept of God as the absolute 'sovereign', means both a strengthening and a weakening of worldly authorities – one of the many contradictions which arose when the Christian idea of transcendence ceased to be effective. Direct divine sanction increases the power of the earthly authorities: 'The lord has not only declared that he approves of and is pleased with the function of magistrates, but also strongly recommended it to us by the very honourable titles which he has conferred upon it',[32] – although at the same time it should not thereby under any circumstances be allowed to lead to a diminution or a division of the sovereignty of God. All worldly power can only be a 'derivative right': authority is a 'jurisdiction as it were delegated by God'. But for the people this delegacy is irremovable and irrevocable.[33] The relationship of God to the world appears essentially as the relationship of an unlimited sovereign to his subjects. Beyerhans has pointed out, with due caution, although clearly enough, that Calvin's concept of God 'betrays the influence of worldly conceptions of law and power'.[34]

A good index for the status of Protestant-bourgeois man in relation to the system of worldly order is the contemporary version

31. Beyerhaus, op. cit., p. 97.
32. *Institutes*, Book IV, ch. XX, para. 4.
33. Beyerhaus, op. cit., p. 87.
34. Beyerhaus, op. cit., p. 79.

of the concept of freedom. On the road from Luther to Calvin the concept of *libertas christiana* becomes a 'negative' concept. 'Christian freedom . . . is not understood positively as mastery over the world but in a purely negative manner as the freedom from the damning effect of the law.'[35] Calvin's interpretation of *libertas christiana* was essentially based on the polemic interpretation of Christian freedom. Luther's concept of freedom had not been positive in Lobstein's sense either. But in the establishment of an unconditional 'inner' freedom of the person there was none the less an element which pointed forward towards the real autonomy of the individual. In Calvin this moment is forced into the background. The threefold definition of *libertas christiana* in the *Institutes* (Book III, ch. XIX, paras 2, 4, 7) is primarily negative in all its three elements: (*a*) freedom of the conscience from the necessity of the law – not indeed as a higher authority to be relied on against the validity of the law, but (*b*) as 'voluntary' subordination to the law as to the will of God: 'they voluntarily obey the will of God, being free from the yoke of the law itself',[36] and (in the sense already indicated in Luther) (*c*) freedom from external things 'which in themselves are but matters indifferent', and which 'we are now at full liberty either to use or omit'.[37] We should stress, precisely in view of this last definition that, combined with Calvin's idea of vocation and of probation in the vocation, the adiaphorous character of the external things has become a strong ideological support for Protestant economic praxis under capitalism. The negativity of this concept of freedom is revealed here by its inner connection with a social order which despite all external rationalization is basically anti-rational and anarchic, and which, in view of its final goal, is itself negative.

What remains as a positive definition of freedom is freedom in the sense of freedom to obey. For Calvin it is no longer a problem that 'spiritual freedom can very well coexist with political servitude' (*Institutes*, Book IV, ch. XIX, para 1). But the difficulty of

35. Lobstein, op. cit., p. 148.
36. Op. cit., Book III, ch. XIX, para. 4. Cf. in I Peter, ch. 2, verse 16: 'The purpose of our liberty is this, that we should obey more readily and more easily' (Lobstein, op. cit., p. 37).   37. Op. cit., Book III, ch. XIX, para. 7.

uniting freedom and unfreedom reappears in the derivative form of the union of freedom and the unfree will. Calvin agrees with Luther that Christian freedom not only does not require free will, but that it excludes it. Both Luther and Calvin base the unfree will on a power which man simply cannot eradicate: on the depravity of human nature which arose from the Fall and the absolute omnipotence of the divine will. The unfree will is an expression of the eternal earthly servitude of men:[38] it cannot and may not be removed without exploding the whole Christian-Protestant conception of man and the world. For Calvin, not only man's sensuality but also his reason is ultimately corrupt. This provides the theological justification for an anti-rationalism which strongly contrasts with Catholic teaching. In the Catholic doctrine there was still an awareness that reason and freedom are correlative concepts, that man's rationality will be destroyed if it is separated from the free possibility of rational acting and thinking. For Thomas Aquinas, man, as a rational animal, is necessarily also free and equipped with free will: 'And forasmuch as man is rational is it necessary that man have a free will.'[39] In Luther reason itself attests to the fact 'that there is no free will either in man or in any other creature'.[40] Reason is here characteristically appraised as the index of human unfreedom and heteronomy: thus we read in Luther's *Treatise on Good Works*, after the interpretation of the first four commandments: 'These four preceding commandments do their work in the mind, that is, they take man prisoner, rule him and bring him into subjection so that he does not rule himself, does not think himself good, but rather acknowledges his humility and lets himself be led, so that his pride is restrained.'[41] To this should be added the loud warnings which Luther gives against an overestimation of human reason and its realm ('We must not start something by trusting in

38. 'For where there is servitude, there is also necessity.' Cf. Barnikel, op. cit., p. 113.

39. *Summa Theol.* I, quaestio 83, art. 1.

40. *Martin Luther on the Bondage of the Will*, translation of *De Servo Arbitrio*, (1525) by J. I. Packer and O. R. Johnston, London, 1957, p. 317; cf. Barnikel, op. cit., p. 46.   41. *Treatise on Good Works*, in *Selected Writings*, vol. I, p. 182.

the great power of human reason . . . for God cannot and will not
suffer that a good work begin by relying upon one's own power
and reason'),[42] and the rejection of a rational reform of the social
order in Calvin. This is all a necessary support for the demand for
unconditional subordination to independent and reified wordly
authorities, for which any rational justification is rejected.

But this doctrine of the 'unfree will' contains a new contradiction which must be resolved. How can man conceivably still be
responsible for himself if the human will is fully determined?
Man's responsibility must be salvaged: the Christian doctrine of
sin and guilt, the punishment and redemption of man requires it,
but the existing system of worldly order requires it too, for – as
we have indicated – this system for both Luther and Calvin is
essentially tied to the mechanism of guilt and punishment. Here
the concept of 'psychological freedom' offers a way out: Calvin
expounds the concept of a necessity (*necessitas*) which is not
coercion (*coactio*) but a 'spontaneous necessity'. The human will
is necessarily corrupt and necessarily chooses evil. This does not
mean, however, that man is forced, 'against his will' to choose
evil; his enslavement in sin is a 'voluntary enslavement' (*servitus
voluntaria*). 'For we did not consider it necessary to sin, other than
through weakness of the will; whence it follows that this was
voluntary.'[43] Thus despite the *necessitas* of the will, responsibility
can be ascribed for human deeds. The concept of enslavement or
voluntary necessity signifies one of the most important steps
forward in the effort to perpetuate unfreedom in the essence of
human freedom: it remains operative right up until German
Idealism. Necessity loses its character both as affliction and as the
removal of affliction; it is taken from the field of man's social
praxis and transferred back into his 'nature'. In fact necessity is
restored to nature in general and thus all possibility of overcoming
it is removed. Man is directed not towards increasingly overcoming necessity but towards voluntarily accepting it.

42. *To the Christian Nobility of the German Nation Concerning the Reform of the
Christian Estate* (1520), in *Selected Writings*, vol. I, p. 261.
43. Calvin, *Opera*, vol. VI, p. 280.

As is well known, a programmatic reorganization of the family and a notable strengthening of the authority of the *pater familias* took place in the context of the bourgeois-Protestant teachings of the Reformation. It was firstly a necessary consequence of the toppling of the Catholic hierarchy; with the collapse of the (personal and instrumental) mediations it had set up between the individual and God, the responsibility for the salvation of the souls of those not yet responsible for themselves, and for their preparation for the Christian life, fell back on the family and on its head, who was given an almost priestly consecration. On the other hand, since the authority of the temporal rulers was tied directly to the authority of the *pater familias* (all temporal rulers, all 'lords' become 'fathers'), their authority was consolidated in a very particular direction. The subordination of the individual to the temporal ruler appears just as 'natural', obvious, and 'eternal' as subordination to the authority of the father is meant to be, both deriving from the same divinely ordained source. Max Weber emphasizes the entry of 'calculation into traditional organizations brotherhood' as a decisive feature of the transformation of the family through the penetration of the 'capitalist spirit': the old relationships of piety decay as soon as things are no longer shared communally within the family but 'settled' along business lines.[44] But the obverse side of this development is that the primitive, 'naïve' authority of the *pater familias* becomes more and more a planned authority, which is artificially generated and maintained.

The key passages for the doctrine of the authority of the *pater familias* and of the 'derivation' of worldly authorities from it are Luther's exegeses of the Fourth Commandment in the *Sermon on Good Works* and in the *Large Catechism*, and Calvin's interpretation in the *Institutes*, Book II, ch. VIII. Luther directly includes within the Fourth Commandment 'obedience to over-persons, who have to give orders and rule', although there is no explicit mention of these. His justification, thus, characteristically, runs

44. Max Weber, *General Economic History*, trans. F. H. Knight, Glencoe, 1930, p. 356.

as follows: 'For all authority has its root and source in parental
authority. For where a father is unable to bring up his child
alone, he takes a teacher to teach him; if he is too weak, he takes
his friend or neighbour to help him; when he departs this life, he
gives authority to others who are chosen for the purpose. So he
must also have servants, men and maids, under him for the house-
hold, so that all who are called master stand in the place of parents,
and must obtain from them authority and power to command.
Wherefore in the bible they are all called fathers.'[45] Luther saw
clearly that the system of temporal authorities constantly depends
on the effectiveness of authority within the family. Where
obedience to father and mother are not in force 'there are no good
ways and no good governance. For where obedience is not maintained in houses, one will never achieve good governance, in a
whole city, province, principality or kingdom'.[46] Luther saw that
the system of society which he envisaged depended for its survival
as such on the continued functioning of parental authority;
'where the rule of the parents is absent, this would mean the end
of the whole world, for without governance it cannot survive'.[47]
For the maintenance of this world 'there is no greater dominion
on earth than the dominion of the parents',[48] for there is 'nothing
more essential than that we should raise people who will come
after us and govern'.[49] The wordly order always remains in view
as a system of rulers and ruled to be maintained unquestioningly.

On the other hand, however, parental authority (which is
always paternal authority in Luther) is also dependent on worldly
authority: the *pater familias* is not in a position to carry out the
upbringing and education of the child on his own. Alongside the
parents, there is the school, and the task of educating the future
rulers in all spheres of social life is impressed on it too. Luther

45. *The Large Catechism* (1529), in *Luther's Primary Works*, trans. H. Wace and
C. A. Buchheim, London, 1896, p. 58.
46. Quoted from *Luther als Pädagog*, ed. E. Wagner (Klassiker der Pädagogik,
Vol. II), Langensalza, 1892, p. 70.
47. Ibid., p. 73.
48. Ibid., p. 64.
49. Ibid., p. 119.

sees the reason for divinely sanctioned parental authority in the breaking and humiliation of the child's will: 'The commandment gives parents a position of honour so that the self-will of the children can be broken, and they are made humble and meek':[50] 'for everyone must be ruled, and subject to other men'.[51] Once again it is the image of the wordly order as universal subordination and servitude which is envisaged by Luther, a servitude whose simple 'must' is no longer even questioned. The freedom of the Christian is darkened by the shadow of the coming bourgeois society; the dependence and exploitation of the greatest part of humanity appears implanted in the 'natural' and divine soil of the family; the reality of class antagonisms is turned into the appearance of a natural-divine hierarchy, exploitation becomes the grateful return of gifts already received. For that is the second ground for unconditional obedience: 'God gives to us and preserves to us through them [the authorities] as through our parents, our food, our homes, protection and security';[52] 'we owe it to the world to be grateful for the kindness and benefits that we have received from our parents.'[53] And servants and maids ought even to 'give up wages' out of pure gratefulness and joy at being able to fulfil God's commandment in servitude.[54]

The personal characteristics which the coming social order wishes to produce require a change in all human values from earliest childhood. Honour (*Ehrung*) and fear (*Furcht*) or, taken together, reverence (*Ehrfurcht*) take the place of love as the determining factor in the relationship between the child and its parents.[55] 'For it is a far higher thing to honour than to love, since honouring does not simply comprise love [but] obedience, humility and reverence, as though towards some sovereign hidden there.'[56] The terrible majesty of Calvin's God comes to the surface

50. *Selected Writings*, vol. I, p. 168.
51. Op. cit., p. 164.
52. *Luther's Primary Works*, p. 60.
53. Op. cit., p. 56.
54. Op. cit., p. 59.
55. For a contrary passage, cf. *Luther als Pädagog*, p. 64.
56. *Luther's Primary Works*, p. 52.

in the authority of the *pater familias*. It is precisely discipline and fear which raises honouring one's parents above love: 'honour is higher than mere love, for it includes within it a kind of fear which, combined with love, has such an effect on a man that he is more afraid of injuring them than of the ensuing punishment'.[57] Just as disobedience is the greatest sin, obedience is the highest 'work' after those commanded in Moses's first tablet; 'so that to give alms and all other work for one's neighbour is not equal to this'.[58]

There are also passages in Luther in which parental and governmental authority are explicitly contrasted. Thus in the *Table Talks*: 'Parents look after their children much more and are more diligent in their care of them than the government is with its subjects. . . . The power of the father and mother is a natural and voluntary power and a dominion over children which has grown of itself. But the rule of the government is forced, an artificial rule.'[59] There is also some wavering on the question of the extension of the 'double morality' of office and person to parental authority. In the *Sermon on Good Works* (1520) Luther says: 'Where the parents are foolish and raise their children in a wordly manner, the children should in no way be obedient to them. For according to the first three Commandments God is to be held in higher esteem than parents.'[60] Nine years later, in the *Large Catechism*, he writes: 'Their [the parents'] condition or defect does not deprive them of their due honour. We must not regard their persons as they are, but the will of God, who ordered and arranged things thus.'[61]

In the passages quoted above one can see the tendency towards a separation of natural and social authority. Luther did not advance any further along the road from the 'natural' unity of the family to the 'artificial' and 'forced' unity of society; he was satisfied with establishing that the family is the 'first rule, in which

57. *Selected Writings*, vol. I, p. 163.
58. *Luther's Primary Works*, p. 56.
59. *Luther als Pädagog*, p. 53.
60. *Selected Writings*, vol. I, p. 166.
61. *Luther's Primary Works*, p. 52.

all other types of rule and domination have their origins'.[62] Calvin went a little further in this direction; he presents an exceptionally interesting psychological interpretation: 'But as this command to submit is very repugnant to the perversity of the human mind (which, puffed up with ambitious longings, will scarcely allow itself to be subjected) that superiority which is most attractive and least invidious is set forth as an example calculated to soften and bend our minds to the habits of submission. From that subjection which is most tolerable, the lord gradually accustoms us to every kind of legitimate subjection, the same principle regulating all.'[63]

Calvin agrees with Luther on the close association between subjection to authority in general and parental authority;[64] we saw how for him too the titles *Dominus* and *Pater* are interchangeable. But Calvin ascribes to the authority relationship of the family a quite definite function within the mechanism of subjection to social authorities. This function is psychological. Since subjection is actually repugnant to human nature, man should, through a type of subordination which by its nature is pleasant and will arouse the minimum of ill will, be gradually prepared for types of subordination which are harder to bear. This preparation occurs in the manner of a softening, bowing and bending; it is a continual habituation, through which man becomes accustomed to subjection. Nothing need be added to these words: the social function of the family in the bourgeois authority-system has rarely been more clearly expressed.

62. *Luther als Pädagog*, p. 70. Cf. Levin Schücking, *Die Familie im Puritanismus*, Leipzig, 1929, p. 89.
63. *Institutes*, Book II, ch. VIII, para. 35.
64. Troeltsch, op. cit., p. 603.

There are two ways of coming to an appreciation of the level reached by Kant in dealing with the problem of authority: the impact and the transformation of the 'Protestant ethic' could be traced in the Kantian doctrine of freedom, or the problem of authority and freedom could be developed immanently from the centre of Kant's ethics. The inner connections between Lutheran and Kantian ethics are plainly apparent. We shall point only to the parallels given by Delekat:[1] the conception of 'inner' freedom as the freedom of the autonomous person: the transfer of ethical 'value' from the legality of the 'works' to the morality of the person; the 'formalization' of ethics; the centring of morality on reverential obedience to duty as the secularization of 'Christian obedience'; the doctrine of the actual unconditional authority of worldly government. But with this method those levels of Kantian ethics which cannot be comprehended under the heading of the 'Protestant ethic' would be given too short a shrift and appear in a false light. The second way would indeed be a genuine approach, but would require an extensive elaboration of the whole conceptual apparatus of Kantian ethics, which we cannot provide within the framework of this investigation. We will necessarily have to choose a less adequate route: there are as it were two central points around which the problematic of authority and freedom in Kant's philosophy is concentrated: firstly, the philosophical foundation itself, under the heading of the autonomy of the free person under the law of duty, and secondly the sphere of the 'application' of ethics, under the heading of the 'right of resistance'. In this second section Kant deals with the problem in the context of a comprehensive philosophical interpretation of the

1. *Handbuch der Pädagogik*, ed. Nohl-Pallat, vol. I, Langensalza, 1928, pp. 221ff.

legal framework of bourgeois society.² The level of concreteness
of the present treatment admittedly cannot compensate for its
vast distance from the actual philosophical foundation, but it
offers a good starting point.

In the small treatise, *Reply to the Question: What is Enlightenment?* (1784), Kant explicitly poses the question of the relation
between social authority and freedom. To think and to act
according to an authority is for Kant characteristic of 'immaturity', a 'self-inflicted immaturity', for which the person is
himself to blame. This self-enslavement of man to authority has
in turn a particular social purpose, in that civil society 'requires a
certain mechanism, for some affairs which are in the interests of
the community, whereby some members of the community must
behave purely passively, so that they may, by means of an artificial consensus, be employed by the government for public ends
(or at least deterred from vitiating them)'.³ Bourgeois society has
an 'interest' in 'disciplining' men by handling them in an
authoritarian manner, for here its whole survival is at stake. In
the closing note of his *Anthropology*, Kant described religion as a
means of introducing such a discipline and as a 'requirement' of
the constituted bourgeois order 'so that what cannot be achieved
through external compulsion can be effected through the inner
compulsion of the conscience. Man's moral disposition is utilized
for political ends by the legislators. . . .'⁴

How can one square man's 'natural' freedom with society's
interest in discipline? For Kant firmly believes that the free
autonomy of man is the supreme law. It presupposes the exit of
man from the state of immaturity which is his own fault'; this
process is, precisely, 'enlightenment'. Nothing is needed for this

2. *Translator's note:* 'Bourgeois society' is here a translation of 'bürgerliche
Gesellschaft', more usually rendered as 'civil society'. While Kant and Hegel
certainly used the term in the sense of 'civil society', Marcuse used it in 1936 in the
sense of 'bourgeois society', since, as he states in relation to Kant's concept of 'civil
society', the 'actual features of bourgeois society are so much a part of it that this
formulation is justified' (*infra*, p. 82).

3. *Kant's Political Writings*, trans. H. B. Nisbet, ed. H. Reiss, Cambridge, 1970,
p. 56.

4. *Werke*, ed. Cassirer, Berlin, 1912, vol. VIII, p. 227.

except freedom, the freedom 'to make *public* use of one's reason in all matters'.[5] The freedom which confronts authority thus has a public character; it is only through this that it enters the concrete dimension of social existence; authority and freedom meet within *bourgeois society* and are posed as problems of bourgeois society. The contradiction is no longer between the 'inner' freedom of the Christian man and divinely ordained authority, but between the 'public' freedom of the citizen and bourgeois society's interest in discipline. Kant's solution remains dualistic; his problematic is in parallel with Luther's: 'the *public* use of man's reason must always be free, and this alone can bring about enlightenment among men; the *private* use of the same may often be very strictly limited, yet without thereby particularly hindering the progress of enlightenment'.[6] That seems to be the exact opposite of Luther's solution, which, while unconditionally preserving the 'inner' freedom of the private person, had also unconditionally subordinated public freedom to the worldly authority. But let us see what Kant means by the 'public' and 'private' use of freedom. 'But by the public use of one's own reason I mean that use which anyone may make of it *as a man of learning* addressing the entire *reading public*. What I term the private use of reason is that which a person may make of it in a particular *civil* post or office with which he is entrusted.'[7] What is 'private' is now the bourgeois 'office', and its bearer has to subordinate his freedom to society's interest in discipline. Freedom in its unrestricted, public nature, on the other hand, is shunted off into the dimension of pure scholarship and the 'world of readers'. Social organization is privatized (the civil 'office' becomes a private possession) and in its privatized form appears as a world of disciplined, controlled freedom, a world of authority. Meanwhile the 'intellectual world' is given the appearance of being actually public and free but is separated from public and free *action*, from real social praxis.

Kant places the problem of authority and freedom on the foundation of the actual social order, as a problem of 'bourgeois

5. *Kant's Political Writings*, p. 55.   6. Loc. cit.   7. Loc. cit.

society'. Even if this concept is by no means historically defined in Kant, but signifies the overall 'idea' of a social order (as a 'legal order'), the actual features of bourgeois society are so much a part of it that the above formulation is justified. We must examine Kant's explication of bourgeois society more closely in order to describe adequately his attitude to the problem of authority. It is to be found in the first part of the *Metaphysics of Morals*, in the *Metaphysical Elements of the Theory of Law.*

Bourgeois society is, for Kant, the society which 'safeguards Mine and Thine by means of public laws'.[8] Only in a bourgeois context can there be an external Mine and Thine, for only in this context do public laws 'accompanied by power' guarantee 'to everyone his own';[9] only in bourgeois society does all 'provisional' acquisition and possession become 'peremptory'.[10] Bourgeois society essentially achieves this legally secure position for the Mine and the Thine in its capacity as 'legal order', indeed, it is regarded as the 'ultimate purpose of all public right' to ensure the peremptory security of the Mine and Thine.

What then is 'right', this highest principle of the bourgeois order? Right is 'the sum total of those conditions under which the will of one person can be united with the will of another in accordance with a universal law of freedom'.[11] All formulations of Kant's concept of right signify a synthesis of opposites: the unity of arbitrary will and right, freedom and compulsion, the individual and the general community. This synthesis must not be thought of as a union which is the sum of individual 'parts'; instead, one should 'see the concept of right as consisting immediately of the possibility of combining universal reciprocal coercion with the freedom of everyone'.[12]

'Only the external aspect of an action'[13] is subject to right in Kant's view. The person as a 'moral' subject, as the locus of transcendental freedom, stands entirely outside the dimension of right. But the meaning of right here is the order of bourgeois

8. *Werke*, vol. VII, p. 44.   9. Op. cit., p. 59.
10. Op. cit., p. 68, and *Kant's Political Writings*, p. 163.
11. *Kant's Political Writings*, p. 133.
12. *Kant's Political Writings*, p. 134.   13. Loc. cit.

society. Transcendental freedom only enters into the legal order in a very indirect way, in so far as the universal law of rights is meant to counteract certain hindrances to the 'manifestations' of transcendental freedom.[14] With this relegation of law to the sphere of 'externality', both law and the society ordered by law are relieved of the responsibility for 'actual' freedom and opened up for the first time to unfreedom. In the synthesis of law we thus have the concerns of the 'externally' acting man before us; what do they look like?

We see a society of individuals, each one of whom appears with the natural claim to the 'free exercise of his will', and confronts everyone else with this claim (since the field of possible claims is limited); a society of individuals, for each one of whom it is a 'postulate of practical reason' to have as his own very external object of his will[15] and who all, with equal rights, confront each other with the natural striving after 'appropriation' and 'acquisition'.[16] Such a society is a society of universal insecurity, general disruption and all-round vulnerability. It can only exist under a similarly universal, general and all-round order of coercion and subordination, the essence of which consists in securing what is insecure, stabilizing what is tottering and preventing 'lesions'. It is highly significant that almost all the basic concepts of Kant's theory of right are defined by negative characteristics like securing, lesion, restriction, prevention and coercion. The subordination of individual freedom to the general authority of coercion is no longer 'irrationally' grounded in the concupiscence of the 'created being' and in the divinely ordained nature of government, but grows immanently out of the requirements of bourgeois society – as the condition of its existence.

But Kant still feels the contradiction between a society of universal coercion and the conception of the 'naturally' free individual. The synthesis of freedom and coercion must not occur in such a way that the original freedom of the individual is sacrificed to social heteronomy. Coercion must not be brought to the

14. Op. cit., p. 133. Cf. Haensel, *Kants Lehre vom Widerstandsrecht*, Berlin, 1926, pp. 10ff.   15. *Werke*, vol. VII, p. 48.   16. Op. cit., p. 70.

individual from without, the limitation of freedom must be a self-limitation, the unfreedom must be voluntary. The possibility of a synthesis is found in the idea of an original 'collective-general' will to which all individuals agree in a resolution of generally binding self-limitation under laws backed by power. That this 'original contract' is only an 'Idea'[17] needs no further discussion, but before we examine its content we must note the significance of its 'ideal' character for the development of the problem under discussion.

Firstly it transforms the historical facticity of bourgeois society into an *a priori* ideal. This transformation, which is demonstrable in Kant's theory of right at the very moment of its occurrence, does not simply mean the justification of a particular social order for all eternity; there is also at work in it that tendency towards the transcendence of the bourgeois authority-system which had already emerged in the Reformers of the sixteenth century. These destructive moments appear in the replacement of a (believed and accepted) fact by a (postulated) 'as if'. For Luther, divinely ordained authority was a given fact; in Kant the statement 'All authority is from God' only means we must conceive of authority '*as if*' it did not come from men, 'but none the less must have come from a supreme and infallible legislator'.[18] Correspondingly, the idea of a 'general will' only requires that every citizen be regarded 'as if he had consented within the general will'.[19] Certainly the 'transcendental As If' signifies a marked shift in the weight of authority towards its free recognition by the autonomous individual, and this means that the structure of authority has become rational – but the guarantees which are set up within the legal order itself against the destruction of the authority relationship are correspondingly stronger.

The 'original contract' is, so to speak, a treaty framework into which the most varied social contents are inserted. But this

17. *Translator's note:* 'Idea' is used here in the Kantian sense of a regulative principle of reason not found in experience but required to give experience an order and unity it would otherwise (according to Kant) lack.

18. *Kant's Political Writings*, p. 143 (Marcuse's emphasis).

19. Op. cit., p. 79.

multiplicity of elements is centred on one point; on the universal, mutual effort to make possible and secure 'peremptory' property, the 'external Mine and Thine', on the 'necessary unification of everyone's private property'.[20] In this way the mere 'fortuitousness' and arbitrariness of 'empirical' property is transformed into the legal validity and regularity of 'intelligible' property in accordance with the postulate of practical reason.[21] We must briefly follow this road through its most important stages, for it is at the same time the route towards the foundation of (social) authority.

Our starting-point is the peculiar (and defining) character of private property as something external, with which 'I am so connected that the use which another would like to make of it without my permission would injure me'.[22] The fact that someone else can use something possessed by me at all presupposes a very definite divorce between the possession and its possessor, presupposes that property does not merely consist in physical possession. The actual 'technical explanation' of the concept of 'private property' must therefore include this feature of 'property with physical possession': 'that which is externally mine is that which, if I am hindered in its use, would injure me, *even if I am not then in possession of it* (if the object is not in my hands)'.[23] What type of property is this property 'even without possession', which is the real subject dealt with by the legal order?

The separation of empirical and intelligible property lies at the basis of one of Kant's most profound insights into the actual structure of bourgeois society: the insight that all empirical property is essentially 'fortuitous' and is based on acquisition by 'unilateral will' ('appropriation') and thus can never present a universally binding legal title; 'for the unilateral will cannot impose on everyone an obligation which is in itself fortuitous. . .'.[24] This empirical property is not therefore sufficient to justify its all-round and lasting security at the centre of the

---

20. *Werke*, vol. VI, p. 130.
22. Ibid., p. 47.
24. Ibid., pp. 66ff.
21. Ibid., vol. VII, paras 6, 7 and 11.
23. Ibid., p. 51.

bourgeois legal order; instead of this, the possibility of an external Mine and Thine as a 'legal relationship' is 'completely based on the axiom that a purely rational form of property without possession is possible'.[25]

The way in which Kant constructs this axiom and in which he effects the return from empirical property to a 'purely rational form of property' in many ways corresponds to bourgeois sociology's handling of the problem. Kant says: 'In order to be able to extend the concept of property beyond the empirical and to be able to say that every external entity subjected to my will can be counted as mine by right if it is . . . in my power without being in possession of it, all conditions of the attitude which justifies empirical property must be eliminated [ignored] . . .';[26] the 'removal of all empirical conditions in space and time', abstraction from the 'sensuous conditions of property'[27] leads to the concept of 'intellectual appropriation'. By this route Kant arrives at the idea of an original joint ownership of the land and on the basis of this collectivity a collective general will can be established which legally empowers every individual to have private property. 'The owner bases himself on the innate *communal ownership* of the land and a general will which corresponds *a priori* to this and allows *private ownership* on the land. . . .'[28] Thus in a highly paradoxical manner communal property becomes the 'legal basis' for private property; total ownership 'is the only condition under which it is possible for me to exclude every other owner from the private use of the object in question. . . .'[29] No one can oblige anyone else through unilateral will to refrain from the use of an object: the private appropriation of what is universal is only possible as a legal state of affairs through the 'united will of all in total ownership'. And this 'united will' is then also the foundation of that general community which puts every individual under a universal coercive order backed by force and which takes over the defence, regulation and 'peremptory' securing of the society based on private property.

25. Ibid., p. 57. 26. Ibid., p. 54. 27. Ibid., pp. 67 and 72.
28. Ibid., p. 52. 29. Ibid., p. 64.

Thus in the origins of bourgeois society the private and general interest, will and coercion, freedom and subordination, are meant to be united. The bourgeois individual's lack of freedom under the legal authority of the rulers of his society is meant to be reconciled with the basic conception of the essentially free person by being thought of as the mutual self-limitation of all individuals which is of equally primitive origin. The formal purpose of this self-limitation is the establishment of a general community which, in uniting all individuals, becomes the real subject of social existence.

'The general community' is society viewed as the totality of associated individuals. This in turn has two connotations:

1. A *total communality* of the kind that reconciles the interests of every individual with the interests of the other individuals – so that there is really a general interest which supersedes private interests.

2. A *universal validity* of such a kind that the general interest represents a *norm equally binding* on all individuals (a law). In so far as the interests of the individuals do not prevail 'on their own', and do not become reconciled with each other 'on their own' (in a natural manner), but rather require social planning, the general community confronts the individuals as a priority and as a *demand*: in virtue of its general 'validity' it must demand recognition and achieve and safeguard this by coercion if necessary.

But now everything depends on whether the general community as the particular form of social organization does in fact represent a supersession of private interests by the general interest, and whether the people's interests are really guarded and administered in it in the best possible way. When Kant deals with social problems in the context of the 'general community', this already signifies a decisive step in the history of social theory: it is no longer God but man himself who gives man freedom and unfreedom. The unchaining of the conscious bourgeois individual is completed in theory: this individual is so free that he alone can abrogate his freedom. And he can only be free if at the same time freedom is taken away from all others: through all-round, mutual subordination to the authority of the law. The bearer of authority (in the sense of being the source of authority) is not God, or a person or a multiplicity of persons, but the general community of all (free) persons in which every individual is both the person delegated and the person delegating.

But not every general community, i.e. every actually constituted society, is truly universal. German Idealism uses bourgeois society as a model for its exposition of the concept of universality: in this sense, its theory signifies a new justification of social unfreedom. The characteristics of real universality are not fulfilled in this society. The interests of the ruling strata stand in contradiction with the interests of the vast majority of the other groups. The universally obligatory authority of the law is thus finally based not on a 'genuine' universality (in which the interests of all the individuals are common to all) but on an appearance of universality; there is an apparent universality because the particular interests of certain strata assume the character of general interests by making themselves apparently independent within the state apparatus. The true constituents of this universality are property relationships as they existed at the 'beginning' of bourgeois society and these can only be peremptorily guaranteed through the creation of a universally binding organization of social coercion.

This universality retains its 'private' character; in it the opposing interests of individuals are not transcended by the interests of the community but cancelled out by the executive authority of the law. The 'fortuitousness' of property is not eliminated by the 'elimination' of the empirical conditions under which it was appropriated: right rather perpetuates this fortuitous character while driving it out of human consciousness. The universality which comes from the combination of private possessions can only produce a universal order of injustice. Kant knew that he had constituted his theory of right for a society whose very foundations had this inbuilt injustice. He knew that 'given man's present condition . . . the good fortune of states grows commensurably with the misery of men',[30] and that it must

30. Ibid., vol. VIII, pp. 465ff.

be a 'principle of the art of education' that 'children should be educated not towards the present, but towards the future, possibly better, conditions of the human race'.[31] He has said that in this order justice itself must become injustice and that 'the legislation itself (hence also the civil constitution), so long as it remains barbarous and undeveloped, is to blame for the fact that the motives of honour obeyed by the people are subjectively incompatible with those measures which are objectively suited to their realization, so that public justice as dispensed by the state is *injustice* in the eyes of the people'.[32]

None the less Kant stuck to the view that the universality of the 'united will' was the basis of society and the foundation of authority. He drew all the resultant consequences from the unconditional recognition of the government ruling at any particular time to the exclusion of economically dependent individuals from civil rights.[33] Like Luther he maintained that right was immanent in the civil order and described rebellion against this order as the 'overthrow of all right',[34] and as 'the road to an abyss which irrevocably swallows everything',[35] the road to the destruction of social existence altogether. 'There can thus be no legitimate resistance of the people to the legislative head of state; for a state of right is only possible through submission to his universal legislative will ....'[36] His justification is in the first place purely formal: since every existing system of domination rests only on the basis of the presupposed general will in its favour, the destruction of the system of domination would mean the 'self-destruction' of the general will. The legal justification is of the same formal kind: in a conflict between people and sovereign there can be no tribunal which makes decisions having the force of law apart from the sovereign himself, because any such tribunal would contravene the 'original contract'; the sovereign is and remains, says Kant in a characteristic phrase, in sole

31. Ibid., vol. VIII, pp. 462ff.   32. *Kant's Political Writings*, p. 159.
33. Op. cit., pp. 139ff.; p. 78.   34. Op. cit., p. 162.
35. Op. cit., p. 146 (Kant's footnote to paragraph 49).
36. Op. cit., pp. 144ff.; other important passages are in op. cit., p. 143, pp. 81–2, pp. 126–7, and in *Werke*, vol. VII, pp. 179ff.

'possession of the ultimate enforcement of the public law'.[37] This is the consequence of the immanence of the law in the ruling system of authority already observed in Luther: the sovereign is his own judge and only the judge himself can be the plaintiff: 'Any alteration to a defective political constitution, which may certainly be necessary at times, can thus be carried out only by the sovereign himself through *reform*, but not by the people, and, consequently, not by *revolution*. . . .'[38]

It has been pointed out in connection with Kant's strict rejection of the right of resistance that although he does not acknowledge a (positive) 'right' of resistance as a component of any conceivable legal order, the idea of possible resistance or even of the overthrow by force of a 'defective' social order, is fully in line with his practical philosophy. The main support for this interpretation (which can be reconciled with the wording of the quoted passages of his theory of right) is Kant's apotheosis of the French Revolution in the *Contest of the Faculties*,[39] and the unconditional demand for the recognition of every new order arising from a revolution.[40] Such an interpretation strikes us as correct, as long as it does not attempt to resolve the contradiction present in Kant's position in favour of one side or the other. The transcendental freedom of man, the unconditional autonomy of the rational person, remains the highest principle in all dimensions of Kant's philosophy; here there is no haggling and calculating and no compromise. This freedom does not become a practical social force, and freedom to think does not include the 'freedom to *act*';[41] this is a feature of precisely that social order in the context of which Kant brought his philosophy to concreteness.

The internal antinomy between freedom and coercion is not resolved in the 'external' sphere of social action. Here all freedom remains a state of merely free existence under 'coercive laws', and each individual has an absolutely *equal* inborn right 'to coerce others to use their freedom in a way which harmonizes with his

37. *Kant's Political Writings*, p. 82. 38. Op. cit., p. 146.
39. Op. cit., pp. 182-5. 40. Op. cit., p. 147.
41. Op. cit., p. 59.

freedom'.[42] But mere self-subordination to general coercion does not yet provide the foundation for a generality in which the freedom of individuals is superseded. On the road from empirical to intelligible property, from the existent social universality to the Idea of an original universality, the solution of the antinomy is transferred to the transcendental dimension of Kant's philosophy. Here too the problem appears under the heading of a universality in which the freedom of the individual is realized within a general system of legislation.

In the 'external' sphere the relationship between freedom and coercion was defined in such a way that coercion was made the basis of freedom, and freedom the basis of coercion. This notion is most pregnantly expressed in the formula which Kant uses in his discussion of a 'purely republican' constitution: it is the only state form 'which makes *freedom* into the principle, indeed the *condition*, of all coercion'.[43] Just as 'legitimate' coercion is only possible on the basis of freedom, so 'legitimate' freedom itself demands coercion in order to survive. This has its rationale within the 'external' sphere: 'bourgeois' freedom (this is what is at stake here), is only possible though all-round coercion. But the result is not a supersession but a reinforcement of actual unfreedom: how then can this be reconciled with transcendental freedom?

The concept of transcendental freedom (the following discussion will be limited to this, unless otherwise indicated) appears in Kant as a concept of causality. This concept stands in opposition to that of causality in nature: it refers to causality resulting from free actions as opposed to causality resulting from necessity and its causal factors, which are of 'external' origin (i.e. causality in the sequence of temporal phenomena). People have seen in this definition of freedom as a type of causality an early derivation of the problem of freedom – a dubious transference of the categories of natural science into the dimension of human existence, and a failure to understand the 'existential' character of human freedom. But we believe that what shows the superiority of Kant's ethics over all later existential ontology is precisely this understanding

42. Op. cit., p. 76.　　　　　　43. Op. cit., p. 163.

of freedom as, from the start, a particular type of actual effectiveness in the world; freedom is not relegated to a static mode of
existence. And since the definition of causation resulting from
freedom has to meet from the outset the demand for 'universal
validity' and since the individual is placed in a universal, a general
rational realm of free persons which exists 'before' and 'over' all
natural aspects of the community, all later misinterpretations of
the organicist theory of society are refuted from the start. However, freedom is now set up as unconditional autonomy and pure
self-determination of the personal will, and the required universal
validity is posited as *a priori* and formal: here we see the impact
of the inner limits of Kant's theory of freedom (and these limits
are by no means overcome by proposing a 'material ethic of value'
as against 'formal' ethics).

Freedom for Kant is a transcendental 'actuality', a 'fact'; it is
something which man always already has if he wants to become
free. As in Luther, freedom always 'precedes' any free act, as its
eternal *a priori*; it is never the result of a liberation and it does not
first require liberation. Admittedly freedom 'exists' for Kant only
in activity in accordance with the moral law, but this activity is, in
principle, free to everyone everywhere. By the ultimate reference
of freedom to the moral law as its only 'reality', freedom becomes
compatible with every type of unfreedom; owing to its transcendental nature it cannot be affected by any kind of restriction
imposed on actual freedom. Admittedly freedom is also a liberation – man making himself free from all 'empirical' determinants
of the will, the liberation of the person from the domination of
sensuality which enters into the constitution of the human animal
as a 'created being' – but this liberation leaves all types of actual
servitude untouched.

The self-imposed and self-observed moral law of the free
person possesses 'universal validity' in itself as the reason of
knowing of its truth, but this means that it contains reference to a
'world' of universality consisting of the mutual coexistence of
individuals. Nevertheless, this universality is formal and aprioris-
tic; it may not carry over anything of the material quality of this

mutual coexistence into the law of action. Yet another 'form' is concealed in the bare 'form' of the moral law; namely the bare form of the coexistence of individuals, the form of a 'society as such'. This means that in all his actual decisions about action the individual only has the form of social existence in view: he must disregard or, so to speak, leap over the social materiality before him. Precisely to the extent that the individual acts under the law of freedom can no element of this materiality be permitted to become a determinant of his will. The fact that it is entirely excluded from the determinants of free praxis means that the individual comes up against it as a brute fact. Transcendental freedom is by its nature accompanied by social unfreedom.

The criterion for decisions concerning action under the moral law is, as already in the sphere of the theory of right, the internal coherence of maxims as a universal law: a bad maxim, if it were made into a 'universal system of legislation', would abolish the order of human coexistence; it would signify the self-destruction of social existence. It has already been shown elsewhere that this criterion cannot operate in the intended sense in a single one of the applications which Kant himself adduces.[44] It would not be the form of a social order as such which would be destroyed by 'false' maxims but always only a particular social order (Kant's ethics are by no means as formal as is claimed by the material ethics of value). Between the formal universality of the moral law and its possible universal material validity, there yawns a contradiction which cannot be overcome within the Kantian ethic. The existing order, in which the moral law is meant to become a practical reality, is not a field of real universal validity. And the alteration of this order cannot in principle serve as a maxim of free praxis, for it would in actual fact, judged according to Kant's criterion, transcend social existence as such (a universal law for the alteration of the existing order would be an absurdity).

The reversion from personal and institutional authority to the authority of the law corresponds to the justificatory reversion from the subject-matter of praxis to the form of the 'law'. This

44. *Zeitschrift für Sozialforschung*, II (1933), pp. 169ff.

'formalization' is something quite different from Luther's 'formal' recognition of the existing wordly authorities, without reference to their individual and social basis. For Kant, every personal and institutional authority has to justify itself in face of the idea of a universal law, which the united individuals have given themselves and which they themselves observe. In the 'external' sphere of social existence this law – as we have seen in the theory of right – justifies not only the authority of the actual system of 'governments' but also authority in general as a social necessity; universal voluntary self-limitation of individual freedom in a general system of the subordination of some and the domination of others is necessary for the peremptory securing of bourgeois society, which is built up on relations of private property. This is the highest rationalization of social authority within bourgeois philosophy.

But just as, with the application of the law, rationalization is brought to a standstill in face of the internal contradictions of bourgeois society, in face of its immanent 'injustice', so it is with the origin of legislation itself: 'the possibility of an intelligible property, and thus also of the external Mine and Thine, is not self-evident, but must be deduced from the postulate of practical reason.'[45] The law remains an authority which right back to its origins cannot be rationally justified without going beyond the limits of precisely that society for whose existence it is necessary.

45. Op. cit., vol. VII, pp. 57f.

Kant had introduced the antagonism between freedom and
coercion into the idea of freedom itself: there is only freedom
under the (coercive) law. The supersession of this antagonism was
sought in the unification of the individual and the general community. In the sphere of social action this appeared as the
voluntary all-round self-limitation of the united individuals
through which social existence as a world of free individuals or as
'bourgeois society' became possible for the first time.

The 'universality' which lies at the basis of bourgeois society is
by no means able to fulfil its function of replacing individual
freedom with a general freedom; this fact is the starting point for
Hegel's critique of Kant's theory of law: 'Once the principle is
adopted that what is fundamental, substantive, and primary is the
will of a single person . . . a particular individual . . . in his own
private self-will . . . , the rational can of course only come on the
scene as a restriction on the type of freedom which this principle
involves . . . and only as an external abstract universal.'[1] The
problem of freedom in Hegel remains subject to the idea of
universality:[2] individual freedom can only become real in a
'general community'. The task is to define this universality con-
ceptually and to indicate its social reality.

The description of bourgeois society in Hegel's philosophy of
law is completely based on the recognition that the universality
which has come into being in this society does not represent a
'true' universality and thus not a real form of freedom (realized
through its supersession). Moreover it *cannot* represent this, so

1. *Philosophy of Right*, trans. T. M. Knox, Oxford, 1952, para. 29.
2. *Translator's note :* German: *Allgemeinheit.* 'Universality' is the usual rendering
of this philosophical concept, but where the German refers to the concrete political
form of the concept, i.e. the mass of individuals bound together in a community or
state, the phrase 'general community' has been used.

that the realization of true freedom necessarily leads beyond bourgeois society as such.

The double 'principle' of bourgeois society is 'the concrete person, who is himself the object of his particular aims. . . . But the particular person is essentially so related to other particular persons that each establishes himself and finds satisfaction by means of the others, and at the same time purely and simply by means of the form of universality. . . .'[3] The particular person himself in this society is only a 'mixture of natural necessity and arbitrariness'; the clashing of 'selfish ends' produces a 'system of universal dependence', which may be able to 'safeguard' the subsistence, well-being and rights of the individual but as a whole continues to be governed by 'external accident and caprice'.[4] The general community is, to begin with, nothing more than the mutual dependence of 'selfish' individuals, a world of private satisfaction of needs. 'The individuals as citizens of this state are *private persons* whose end is their own interest. This end is *mediated* through the universal which thus *appears* as a *means* to its realization.'[5] The principle of this 'system of needs' only contains this universality of freedom 'abstractly, that is, as the *right of property* which, however, is no longer merely implicit but has attained its recognized actuality as the *protection of property* through the administration of justice'.[6] The highest stage of the unity of subjective particularity and universality which can be reached by such an order of universal fortuitousness and arbitrariness is thus a primary organization of coercion and interests: 'the actualization of this unity through its extension to the whole ambit of particularity, is (i) the specific function of the Police, through the unification which it effects is only relative; (ii) it is the Corporation which actualizes the unity completely, though only in a whole which, while concrete, is restricted.'[7]

Hegel sees civil society basically from the same viewpoint as Kant: as a universal coercive order for the safeguarding (of the

3. *Philosophy of Right*, para. 182.
4. Ibid., para. 185.   5. Ibid., para. 187.
6. Ibid., para. 208.   7. Ibid., para. 229.

property of) free private property owners – an order whose authority may be 'universal' (its claims being recognized by all the individuals organized within it because of their own interests) and legitimate, but which stands and falls with its own basis and presupposition: namely a social order for the peremptory safeguarding of private property. Kant saw this presupposition as necessary for any idea of a 'legitimate' social order; Hegel does not contradict him in this. But in contrast to Kant his picture of bourgeois society is coloured by its negativity. When bourgeois society is in a state of 'unimpeded activity', 'the amassing of wealth . . . is intensified on the one hand, while the subdivision and restriction of particular jobs, and thus the dependence and distress of the class tied to work of that sort, increases on the other hand'.[8] For the first time the revolutionary character of the dialectic breaks through into the dimension of civil society: the image of this society, which was still essentially static in Kant, begins to move. Despite all the 'excess of wealth', civil society is not rich enough to 'check excessive poverty and the creation of a penurious rabble';[9] through this dialectic it is 'driven beyond its own limits'.[10] Where to? The dialectic evades the real answer to this question by withdrawing into the house of the philosophical system; the relevant passages in the *Philosophy of Right* merely point to the world economic market and colonization as a way out. The systematic continuation of the dialectic is something different: it leads to the supersession of civil society by the 'state'. The idea of civil society itself constituting itself as a state is rejected; society and state are separated according to their 'principle'. This is a decisive step for the development of the problem of authority: civil society, now seen almost in its full problematic, can no longer in itself provide the basis for the social system of authority; it ceases to be the real basis of freedom and thus also of the universal community. The state confronts it as an independent totality and is thus liberated from its negativity and becomes the unconditional bearer of all social authority. The

8. Ibid., para. 243. 9. Ibid., para. 246.
10. *Early Theological Writings*, trans. by T. M. Knox, Chicago, 1948, p. 221.

thorough-going rationalization of the authoritative order is abandoned; the philosophy of absolute reason sets up a completely irrational authority on the foundations of the state. That is a rough outline of what we must now examine in detail as the form taken by the problem of authority in Hegel's philosophy of the state.

Hegel, like Kant, sees state and society in the context, first and foremost, of the idea of property. As early as 1798–99 he says with regard to Jesus's call to 'cast aside care for one's life and despise riches': 'It is a litany pardonable only in sermons and rhymes, for such a command is without truth for us. The fate of property has become too powerful for us to tolerate reflections on it, to find its abolition thinkable.' And his work on the German Constitution makes this a straight question of definition: 'A multitude of human beings can only call itself a state if it is united for the communal defence of the entirety of its property.'[11] But it is precisely here, in the inter-relationship of state and property, that the change begins: the task of legally and politically safeguarding property is taken away from the state as such and transferred to 'civil society' itself; and it is this that brings about the elevation of the state to an independent position with respect to society. 'If the state is confused with civil society and its specific end is laid down as the security and protection of property and personal freedom, then the interest of the individuals as such becomes the ultimate end of their association. . . . But the state's relation to the individual is quite different from this.'[12]

Before we look at Hegel's positive definition of this relationship, we must briefly examine the distinction which appears here. Hegel combines the basic separation of state and society with the critique of Rousseau's and Kant's 'contract theory'; since this theory understands the general will merely as the communal aspect of the individual will, the universality of the state is, as it were privatized; it is reduced to a combination of private persons, 'based on their arbitrary wills, their opinions, and their capri-

11. *Hegel's Political Writings*, trans. T. M. Knox, Oxford, 1964, p. 154.
12. *Philosophy of Right*, para. 258; cf. para. 100.

ciously given express consent; and there follow ... logical inferences which destroy the absolutely divine principle of the state, together with its majesty and absolute authority'.[13] The contract theory transfers 'the characteristics of private property into a sphere of a quite different and higher nature',[14] and such reflections must destroy the absolute authority of the 'divine' state. This is a clear indication of a new tendency to revile the genetic view that the state originates from the (material) interests and needs of individuals as being destructive of authority, and to elevate the objectivity of the state, which 'exists in and for itself' above all empirical conditions. The reasons for the authority of a 'real state', 'in so far as it has anything to do with reasons' can only be taken from 'the forms of the law authoritative within it'.[15] The fear of an historical return to the legal basis of the existing order of the state comes through clearly enough: 'In any case, however, it is absolutely essential that the constitution *should not be regarded as something made*, even though it has come into being in time. It must be treated rather as something simply existent in and by itself, as divine therefore and constant, and so as exalted above the sphere of things that are made.'[16] Faced with 'something existing in and for itself' the question of the legal basis of its authority is already meaningless. The whole series of problems which in Kant's philosophy of the state come under the title of the right of resistance no longer worries Hegel at all. 'Every nation ... has the constitution appropriate to it and suitable for it.'[17] As far as the concept of 'the people' corresponds to any reality at all, other than the general community of the 'ruled' brought together in the state, it can only be used to describe that section of the citizens 'which does *not* know what it wants'.[18]

What happens in this theory of the state at first appears to be a total reification of the social and political orders. The state, which becomes the sole bearer of the authority of this order, is deprived of any historical genesis as a preceding 'totality' and a 'reality

13. Ibid., para. 258.
15. Ibid., para. 258.
17. Ibid., para. 274.

14. Ibid., para. 75.
16. Ibid., para. 273.
18. Ibid., para. 301.

existing in and for itself', and is presented as a sphere independent of individual and society. The systematic dialectic, which merges civil society into the state, silences the historical dialectic. The 'sovereignty' of the state, freed from any personal or social basis, appears as a 'metaphysical' quality, peculiar to the state as such: it 'has its ultimate roots ultimately in the unity of the state as its simple self'.[19] This concept of the 'sovereignty of the state purely as such, without express relation to its human bearers' subsequently became the decisive theoretical weapon.[20] The elevation of the sphere of the state above bourgeois society makes it possible to subordinate all social authority to the authority of the state as such. The more obviously bourgeois society loses the appearance of 'real' universality and allows the antagonisms of class society to break through, the less this society can be claimed to be the true supersession of the freedom of the individual. Kant's practical philosophy is refuted by the history of society. It is not the least aim of Hegel's brilliant critique of the Kantian ethic[21] to show the practical impossibility of the social universality proclaimed by Kant and to discover a different, no longer social, universality as the bearer of authority and as the locus of the supersession of individual freedom. Hegel can go so far as to contend that the sphere of private property, 'the interest in proving that property must be', is the presupposition of the Kantian ethic and to use this interest as an example of the emptiness of the laws made by practical reason. For he already has the separation of civil society and the state in view, and this enables him to develop a sphere of universality which appears to be basically separated from this sphere of property. We must now show how Hegel gives a positive definition of this universality, which in his work becomes the real bearer of all authority. For this purpose it is necessary to go into Hegel's transformation of the bourgeois concept of freedom, which gives this concept its decisive form for the subsequent period.

19. Ibid., para. 278.
20. Rosenzweig, *Hegel und der Staat*, Munich, 1920, vol. II, p. 143.
21. *Schriften zur Politik und Rechtsphilosophie*, ed. Lasson, Leipzig, 1911, pp. 355f.; *Philosophy of Right*, paras 29, 135.

The undifferentiated indeterminacy of the will in the freedom of choice, the possibility of abstracting the will from every determinate state of mind, and even Kant's positive concept of the autonomy of the will, as far as this refers only to a 'formal self-activity', belong for Hegel to the merely negative or merely abstract concepts of freedom.[22] This means that the universality which comes into being through the limitation and supersession of such freedom cannot be the true universality. Hegel demands that the concept of freedom be taken out of the dimension of mere feelings, inclination and arbitrary will, and also out of the mere realm of the Ought; there is freedom only in existence, reality, known and conscious reality, 'spirit' (*Geist*). But since freedom is at the same time the substantial definition of the human will, unified with 'intelligence' in the unity of the 'theoretical and practical spirit', it follows that man can only give the existence of freedom to himself: there is freedom only in the free act of man.

The definition of freedom as reality seems to indicate that Hegel is giving the concept of freedom a strongly concrete content. But, in that freedom is still explicated as 'absolute' freedom, a change occurs: in the sphere of actual freedom everything alien, contradictory, external, fortuitous must be superseded; it is without any contradiction (for any contradiction would make it dependent) and thus also no longer has necessity pitted against it: 'freedom, shaped into the actuality of a world, receives the form of necessity'.[23] This essential unity of freedom finds its subjective fulfilment in the fact that the will is constantly 'at home with itself' and its objective fulfilment in the supersession of the tension or, as the case may be, the opposition between the 'concept and the object'. When man, with every single actual determination of his existence, freely determines himself towards this determination and freely acknowledges the necessity which he finds before him, the 'fortuitousness and limitation of the

---

22. Ibid., paras 5, 15, 29.
23. *Enzyklopädie*, vol. III; *Philosophie des Geistes* (trans. W. V. Wallace as *Hegel's Philosophy of Mind*, Oxford, 1894), para. 484; cf. *Philosophie der Weltgeschichte*, ed. Lasson, vol. I, Leipzig, 1917, p. 94.

previous practical content' are superseded.[24] The will which revolts against reality and is tensed against existence is not yet absolutely free: it is still confronted with something not yet overcome, something external; it is not yet 'with itself'. The truly free will is related to 'nothing except itself' and is thus released from any 'tie of dependence on anything else'.[25]

It is precisely this absorption of all particular individuality and restriction by the will in its state of self-identity which constitutes that 'universality' into which Hegel's theory of freedom debouches.[26] As in Kant, the concept of freedom in Hegel is linked from the outset with the concept of universality, and in the system's final form the concepts of freedom and universality mean almost the same thing.[27] We should need to return to the basis of Hegel's philosophy to unfold the concept of universality; here we must be content to point out the result. The decisive point is that 'universality' is neither a mere determination of the individual will, nor the universal content of the various combined individual wills. The concept aims rather at an objective spiritual reality, as corresponds with the situation of the problem of freedom within the philosophy of the objective spirit. 'The universal must not be simply what is thought by the individuals, it must be something existent; as such it is present in the state, it is that which is valid.'[28]

The being-with-itself of the free will and the disappearance of the contradiction between freedom and necessity is realized in a real universality in which the tension between concept and object is already discarded as the form of the objective spirit and the existent is already 'rational': in the world of 'morality', or, to be more precise, the world of the state. 'The state is the immediate and more closely defined subject of world history as a whole, and in the state freedom obtains its objectivity and lives in the enjoyment of this objectivity.'[29] The state is 'the actuality of concrete

24. *Enzyklopädie*, vol. III, para. 481.   25. *Philosophy of Right*, para. 23.
26. Op. cit., para. 24.
27. Op. cit., para. 38; *Enzyklopädie*, vol. III, para. 485.
28. *Philosophie der Weltgeschichte*, vol. I, p. 92.   29. Ibid., para. 1, p. 90.

freedom' and the idea of freedom is 'genuinely actual only as the state'.[30]

The state for its part is doubly built into Hegel's philosophy as a particular form within world-historical development and within the development of the system. As the sole locus of the 'rational existence' of man and as the 'realization of freedom', it entered reality at a relatively late stage of historical development: as the Christian-Germanic state of the West. The mode of universality realized in it is historical in its origin: human freedom has a history. But this history is complete after Christianity has brought the idea of the freedom of man as such into the world, the idea 'that man in himself is destined for the highest freedom'.[31] The state, as it is now found to exist by the individual, is the actuality of the rational, and the individual only has to acknowledge it as 'that which is valid'. The substantiality of our being is realized in the state; 'the rational has necessary existence, as being the substance of things, and we are free in recognizing it as the law'.[32]

The authority of the state is thus founded at a level quite beyond the reach of the power of the individual; it is based on the development of a 'world spirit' which has progressed on its road through the centuries up to the truth represented by the state. In the face of this, the question of the actual moral basis of authority and the correspondence of the actually given socio-political formation with the needs of man becomes meaningless: 'concept and object' are already united in the state. Freedom can no longer become objective, since it always already is: the idea of freedom is 'the actuality of men, not something which they have, as men, but which they are'.[33] If freedom has thus become actual in the universality of the state, then the freedom of the individual can only consist in the absorption of his 'arbitrary' independence by this universality; the independence of individuals is present 'only in the state'. 'The individual obeys the laws and knows that he has

30. *Philosophy of Right*, paras 260, 57.
31. *Enzyklopädie*, para. 482.
32. *Philosophie der Weltgeschichte*, vol. I, p. 94.
33. *Enzyklopädie*, vol. III, para. 482.

his freedom in this obedience.'[34] Perhaps for the first time in bourgeois philosophy *history* becomes the first and final authority, but through the closed nature of the system a particular form of historical development is posited as absolute: the 'understanding of that which is' acquires the quietistic tone of a justificatory recognition of the existing situation.

The most extreme point of the subordination of the individual to the authority of the state, which, in its universality, continues according to Hegel to 'correspond' to him, has its counterpart on the other side, at the very summit of the state, in a completely 'groundless' and 'unmediated' authority: the authority of the monarch. The ultimate self in which the will of the state is concentrated, 'raised above all particularity and conditions', no longer bases its authority on history but on – 'Nature'. This concept contains the 'definition of naturalness': the dignity of the monarch is determined 'in an immediate natural fashion, through his birth in the course of nature'.[35] Hegel simply piles up characteristics which emphasize the irrational nature of the hereditary monarchy: 'the will's ungrounded self', the 'ungrounded immediacy' and the ultimate 'being in itself' which does not risk being drawn down 'into the sphere of capricious argument' and which, precisely because of its irrational naturalness, is excluded from the conflict of factions around the throne and 'from the enfeeblement and overthrow of the power of the state'.[36] The recourse to ungrounded naturalness as the last protection of authority is not the only place in which irrationality breaks into this system of reason. Before we return to this point, we must examine another tendency of Hegel's philosophy of the state which is important for the problem of authority.

The (subjective) basis of Hegel's philosophy of the state and society is – as already in Kant – the human will: bourgeois society is dealt with as the sphere of existence of the free will, and the state as its completed actuality. The construction of the state out of the will of individuals ended with the free subordination of

34. *Philosophie der Weltgeschichte*, vol. I, p. 99.
35. *Philosophy of Right*, para. 280.   36. Ibid., para. 281.

the individual will to the general will of the state. It demands in its turn what might be called a subjective preparation: the building up of a state-upholding sentiment in the psyche of the individual; the authority of the state must be rooted in the basic psychological attitude of the citizen. We shall follow this process in its more important stages, for it can almost be taken as a sketch of the development of the authoritarian consciousness.

The 'institutions' of the state essentially have the effect of producing and continually keeping alive the 'political attitude' which forms the subjective foundation of the state. 'The political sentiment, patriotism pure and simple . . . and a volition which has become habitual, are purely a product of the institutions subsisting in the state. . . .'[37] The institutions of the state, however, which the individual always finds before him in their finished form, are not enough to make this state-upholding volition habitual. The preparation goes further back into the history of the individual: through the state of the 'corporations' to the 'family'. 'As the family was the first, so the corporation is the second ethical root of the state, the one planted in civil society.'[38] In particular, notions of civil qualifications, orderliness and efficiency, and 'rank and dignity' are ways in which the individual is tied to the general community. 'Unless he is a member of an authorized corporation . . . an individual is without rank or dignity.'[39] His civil 'recognition' within the general community presupposes that he himself recognizes the universality of that community's institutions. The significance of that other, prior 'root' of the state – the *family* – is even more basic. We must, however, guard against the misunderstanding to the effect that Hegel assumed a genetic development of the state out of the family (like some sociological theories). Rather the family is for him the 'ethical' root of the state: it brings out characteristics through which the individual can become a part of the state which represents 'objective' morality; it is the first, still direct and natural form of the objective universality which supersedes

37. Ibid., para. 268.   38. Ibid., para. 255.
39. Ibid., para. 253.

'subjective particularity'; it is the 'ethical spirit' in its immediate and natural form.

The features which qualify the family for such a function are: the direct unification of individuals into a general community without the person as such being negated; the real character of this general community of which the individuals are constantly aware in their everyday existence; and the actual communal nature of needs and interests which, since they concern an actual universality, are raised from the sphere of mere selfishness and 'moralized'. But all these features of the family are only realized in that centre around which all features of the family are grouped in Hegel: in the specific relationship between *family* and *property*. The family not only has its 'external reality' in property, but also the existence of its 'substantial personality'. Only in and through the family is property transformed from the 'arbitrary expression of the particular need' to a 'permanent and secure asset', and the 'selfishness of greed' is transformed into 'something ethical, into labour and care for a common possession'.[40]

From this we can see the full significance of the family on the road from individual to state, from egoism to a state-orientation. The individual as an existing person for Hegel is basically – a private owner. Only in property does the person 'become merged with himself',[41] only in property does he possess the 'external sphere of his freedom'. So essential is the inter-relationship of personal freedom and property that property is not only a means for satisfying needs but 'from the standpoint of freedom, property is the first embodiment of freedom and so is in itself a substantive end'.[42] But as long as the individual remains tied to the 'arbitrariness' of private property, it is not possible to realize that actual universality which the socio-political order must possess for its authority. Since the idea of the non-existence of private property (after property has once been proclaimed as 'destiny') cannot even be discussed, a relationship between the individual and the general community must be established in and through property

40. Ibid., para. 170. 41. *Enzyklopädie*, vol. III, para. 490.
42. *Philosophy of Right*, para. 45.

itself: property must in a certain manner be stripped of its merely 'private' and egoistic character without thereby losing the character of property. It is essentially the family which accomplishes this, or more exactly, the right of inheritance of the family. Since the family as a whole, and not the individual, becomes the actual subject of property, coming into inheritance only means entering into the ownership of 'assets which are themselves communal'.[43] The universality of property is safeguarded particularly from the arbitrary will of the person himself, through a characteristic limitation on the arbitrariness of the freedom of bequest. Since property is anchored in the family and guaranteed in the right of inheritance through successive generations, the individual receives his property, as it were, from the general community itself, by force of an eternal natural order, in trust for, and in the service of, the general community. It is the specific function of the family in moralizing and eternalizing property which justifies the elevation of the state above the sphere of property, as revealed in the separation between the state and civil society. Society and state are relieved of the task of the primary 'peremptory' safeguarding of property, since this has already been taken over by the family.[44] In the subsequent period the family, with these functions, enters bourgeois sociology as the basis of the state and society.

In the return from the 'finished' socio-political order, the family is not the final stage on which this order is constructed and the individual integrated into the general community. The further stage of this return leads back to earlier levels of Hegel's philosophy which in the completed system have lost some of their original importance. At these earlier levels, the historical-social world is not yet seen in the later quietistic-justificatory manner: the dialectic has not yet been forced from its ground through

43. Ibid., para. 178.

44. Cf. Rosenzweig's accurate formulation (op. cit., vol. II, p. 118): 'The family's right of inheritance, based on the communal nature of the family income, serves to uphold the necessary connection between person and property without necessitating the direct intervention of the state and society. It is the first and decisive line of demarcation by which Hegel's thesis of property as a necessity for every individual differentiates itself in advance from communism.'

being enclosed into a system, and it thus reveals its full force. We shall pass over the significance of the family in the *Phenomenology of Mind*, and pursue the question of the building up and the anchoring of the authoritative socio-political order back to the genesis of the *Phenomenology*. Here we find the family in close proximity to the relationship of *domination* (*Herrschaft*) and *servitude* (*Knechtschaft*) in which Hegel discerns mutual 'recognition' as the basis of social existence. In his *Jenenser Realphilosophie* of 1805–6, the establishment of the family immediately follows the struggle for property ending in the recognition of property as a general right: and in the *System of Morality* of 1802 the family is the 'external, openly manifested' element of the relationship between domination and servitude in its 'indifference'.[45]

Within the world of the 'spirit', which is the historical-social world, human existence is firstly 'self-consciousness'. But self-consciousness is 'in and for itself' only because it is in and for itself through another, which means 'only in being something recognized'.[46] If recognition is thus placed at the beginning of social order, this concept does not refer merely to the voluntary subordination, somehow deriving from insight, of one person to another which occurs over and above direct force (we shall show how this happens below), but to the justification of such recognition in the material sphere of society: it occurs in Hegel, after a 'life and death struggle', in the realm of appropriation and property, work and service, fear and discipline. The way in which the domination of the master is constituted (and here we put together the expositions of the *Phenomenology* and the stages of the system preceding it) is 'greed' for the 'enjoyment' of things, 'appropriation' as the 'sensuous acquisition of property', through which the other is 'excluded' from ownership, and the binding of the subordinated person through the 'work' which is forced upon

45. For the interpretation of the dialectic of domination and servitude and its systematic place in Hegel's philosophy, cf. H. Marcuse, *Hegels Ontologie und die Grundlegung einer Theorie der Geschichtlichkeit*, Frankfurt, 1932, pp. 291ff. We must limit ourselves here to an outline of this work's conclusions.

46. *The Phenomenology of Mind*, trans. J. B. Baillie, London, 1966, p. 255.

him, in which the servant 'works on' and 'forms' things for the enjoyment of the master. The servitude of the servant is constituted by his material powerlessness, his 'absolute fear' of the master, his constant 'discipline' of service and above all his being chained to his work, whereby he becomes 'dependent' on things and through them on the master who owns these things. The decisive insight is that domination and servitude only become possible through a particular form of the labour process: in the labour process existence for the servant becomes the 'chain from which he cannot abstract in the struggle'; the labour process is the cause and the safeguard of his 'dependence', just as, conversely, it is the cause and safeguard of the independence of the master.

Hegel's analysis of domination and servitude not only contains the justification of the authority of domination in the sphere of the social struggle: it also provides the *dialectic* of this authority. The immanent development of the relationship between domination and servitude not only leads to the recognition of servitude as the real 'truth' of domination, but also to the servant's own insight into the lord's real power and thus into its (possible) supersession; it is shown that the authority of the lord is, in the last analysis, dependent on the servant, who believes in it and sustains it.

Only through the labour performed in servitude does domination become real as a recognized power over the realm in which things are at its disposal. 'The truth of independent consciousness is accordingly the consciousness of the bondsman. . . . But just as domination shows its essential nature to be the reverse of what it wants to be, so, too, servitude will, when completed, pass into the opposite of what it immediately is. Being a consciousness repressed into itself, it will enter into itself, and transform itself into true independence.'[47] 'Fear' and 'service' (discipline and obedience), the features of the most extreme powerlessness and dependence, themselves become the productive forces which drive servitude out of its state of dependence. In the fear of 'absolute power' the consciousness of the servant is thrown back

47. Op. cit., p. 237.

on the 'simple essence of consciousness of himself', on his pure being for himself. And fear of the master becomes the 'beginning of wisdom': it forces the servant into the labour-process, in which his real power will reveal itself and in which he will come 'to himself'. Through the servant's work the immediate form of things is superseded by the only form in which they can be enjoyed and used. In the labour-process the 'subordinate consciousness' puts itself 'as such into the element of permanence; and thereby becomes for itself something existing for itself'. The form which it has given things, although it is 'put out' into the world of objects, does not become something alien or other: it is the manner of existence of its 'truth'; 'thus through this rediscovery of itself through itself, it acquires its *own meaning*, precisely in labour, where there seemed to be merely an *alien* meaning'.[48] And the real lever of further development, the supersession of the domination-servitude relationship, is not the dominating but the 'serving consciousness' which has acquired its true form in the labour-process.

This analysis of the relationship of domination and servitude doubtless marks the profoundest breakthrough of German Idealism into the dimension in which the social existence of man is built up as an authoritative order of domination. It is not absolute reason but absolute force which stands at the beginning of the 'objective spirit': the 'life and death struggle' for the recognition of property, the constitution of domination through the enslavement of the subordinated person in the labour-process. It is a long road to the total justification of the state by the absolute truth of the 'concept' – a road which nevertheless remains the prisoner of its origin. The young Hegel knew this: 'The concept . . . carries with it so much self-mistrust that it has to be validated by force, and only then does man submit to it.'[49]

48. Op. cit., p. 239.
49. *Hegel's Political Writings*, p. 242.

A. COUNTER-REVOLUTION

The theory of the counter-revolution emerged simultaneously
with the French Revolution: Burke's *Reflections on the Revolution
in France* appeared in 1790, Bonald's *Théorie du Pouvoir* and de
Maistre's *Considérations sur la France* in 1796. Gentz, Friedrich
Schlegel and Adam Müller undertook the propagation of their
theories in Germany, and a straight line of social and ideological
development leads from them to Friedrich J. Stahl's theory,
elaborated under the Restoration in Germany. In the counter-
revolution's philosophy of the state and society the theory of
authority which subsequently becomes increasingly predominant
is worked out for the first time – a consciously irrationalist and
traditionalist theory. While the French use it clearly and tren-
chantly, mostly cynically, as a brilliant weapon in the political and
social struggle, in the Germans it appears in an almost complete
isolation from its actual basis; in the following we shall con-
centrate predominantly on its original form.

The theory of the counter-revolution initially fought for the
feudal and clerical groups against the bourgeoisie as bearer of the
revolution. In its long history it undergoes a decisive change of
function: it is ultimately adapted for use by the ruling strata of
the bourgeoisie. The bourgeoisie changes from object to subject
of the theory. It is the finest example in modern times of the
justification and defence of a threatened social order. The change
of function of the theory accompanies the change in the history of
the bourgeoisie from the struggle of a rising class against the
remnants of a social organization which has become a fetter on it,
to the absolute domination of a few privileged strata against the
onslaught of all progressive forces; it also accompanies the

alienation of the bourgeoisie from all the values which it had proclaimed at the time of its rise. It becomes clear precisely from the theory of the counter-revolution, in particular with regard to the problem of authority, how strong were the progressive tendencies in the bourgeois philosophy of the state and society.

This already emerges from a basic thesis common to the whole theory of counter-revolution,[1] which is directed against the bourgeois construction of state and society out of the rational will of man. If, in the face of this, state and society are now viewed, indirectly or directly, as divine institutions whose authority beyond this is derived either from its mere existence or mere permanence, or from a mystical *âme nationale* (de Maistre), this signifies the elevation of the existing system of domination above any possibility of justification *vis-à-vis* the insight and needs of individuals. The authoritative order embracing state and society is at once the 'divine and natural' order of things. 'Society is not the work of man, but the immediate result of the will of the Creator, who willed it that man should be what he has been always and everywhere.'[2]

Far from being able to constitute a state and a society by his own power, man can only 'retard the success of the efforts' made by a society in order to arrive at its 'natural constitution'. The political and religious constitutions of society 'result from the nature of human beings': 'they could not be anything other than they are, without colliding violently with the nature of the beings who compose each society'.[3] It is not the business of men to give society its constitution:[4] social organization can never be the subject of rational and deliberate human planning. That is the counter-attack not only against all bourgeois 'counter theories' (Rousseau's *Contrat social* is the initial target of the attack of counter-revolutionary theory), but also against any connection between state and society and the categories of 'reason': Hegel's

1. Carl Schmitt, *Politische Romantik*, 2nd edn, Munich, 1925, p. 153.
2. de Maistre, *Oeuvres complètes*, Lyon, 1891–2, vol. I, p. 317.
3. Bonald, *Oeuvres complètes* (ed. Migne), Paris, 1864, vol. I, pp. 121ff.
4. Ibid., p. 123.

theory of the state, too, is later attacked by the theory of the Restoration in the context of this main idea.

The civil constitution of the peoples is never 'the result of a discussion';[5] instead of this, God has given the people their government in two ways: he either leaves it to no one, 'as insensibly as a plant', or he uses 'rare men', 'truly chosen men to whom he entrusts his powers'.[6] The main motifs of the counter-revolutionary theory of authority are here united: the (theological-) *naturalist* and *personalist* justification of authority. A decisive tendency of the bourgeois theory of authority was the separation of office and person, the detachment of authority from its current personal bearer: basically it is not the (fortuitous) person who could justify the authority of the office but an order and legality which is somehow objective. That is now changed. Government becomes a charisma which is given by God to the current governing person as such and this charisma radiates out from the person of the ruler to the whole political and social order which culminates in him. This order is essentially personal and 'by nature' is centred on a single, indivisible personality: the monarch. 'In a situation where all men, having equal wills and unequal powers, necessarily wish to attain mastery, it is necessary that one man should be the master, otherwise all men would destroy each other.'[7]

This leads on the one hand to the irrational establishment of authority as an absolute: to the doctrine of the 'infallibility of the sovereign', and on the other to the total rejection of any attempt to change the prevailing rule of authority: to traditionalism. 'All possible sovereignties necessarily act in an infallible manner; for all government is absolute.'[8] Sovereignty is unconditionally 'valid', independently of its performance, its suitability, or its success; the ruler rules, because he possesses the 'royal spirit'. This is most clearly expressed in de Maistre's formula: 'It is generally believed that a family is royal because it reigns; on the contrary, it reigns because it is royal.'[9] (The German philosophy

5. Ibid., p. 346.   6. Ibid., p. 344.   7. Bonald, op. cit., p. 151.
8. de Maistre, op. cit., vol. II, p. 2; cf. vol. I, p. 417.   9. Ibid., vol. II, p. 421.

of the Restoration then disguised this clear-cut doctrine: C. L. von Haller endeavoured to show, with pages of argument, that in all areas of political and social life the rulers 'according to a universal law of nature', are also the most worthy.[10]

What, then, is the basis for the social life-process taking place in an order in which by far the greatest part of the people are subordinated to the unconditional domination of a few charismatically gifted persons? The divine order is at the same time the 'natural' order in the state of concupiscence, and the natural order is necessarily an order of classes: 'In all societies, consisting of different classes, certain classes must necessarily be uppermost. The apostles of equality therefore only change and pervert the natural order of things.'[11] 'Man, in his quality of being at once moral and corrupted, pure in his understanding and perverse in his wishes, must necessarily be subject to government.'[12] This appeal to the 'nature of man' leads back to the particular *anthropology* which underlies the theory of the counter-revolution as its most essential component.

It is an image of man which is drawn in terms of hate and contempt, but also of worldly wisdom and power: man who has fallen from God is an evil, cowardly, clumsy, half-blind animal which, if left on its own, only brings about dirt and disorder, which basically desires to be ruled and led and for which total dependence is ultimately the best thing. 'Sovereignty' originated with society itself: 'society, and sovereignty were born together'.[13] Whoever really knows the 'sad nature' of man knows also that 'man in general, if he is left to himself, is too wicked to be free'.[14] The natural wickedness of man corresponds to his natural weakness: the theory of the counter-revolution sanctions the total dependence of men on a few 'sovereigns' by engaging in a total defamation of human reason. 'Human reason, if we rely

10. C. L. von Haller, *Restauration der Staatswissenschaft*, Winterthur, 1820, vol. I, pp. 355ff.

11. Burke, *Reflections on the Revolution in France*, ed. H. P. Adams, London, 1927, p. 50.

12. de Maistre, op. cit., vol. II, p. 167.

13. Ibid., vol. I, p. 323. 14. Ibid., vol. II, p. 339.

solely on its innate powers, is nothing but a beast, and all its strength is reduced to the power of destruction.'[15] It is 'as much a nullity for the happiness of states as for that of the individual'. All great institutions derive their origin and their preservation from elsewhere; 'human reason . . . only involves itself in them in order to pervert and destroy them'.[16]

A similar tendency towards the devaluation of reason was already discernible in Luther and there too it was a part of his justification of worldly authorities. Here, however, in the theory of counter-revolution, every quietistic eschatological feature is obliterated: anti-rationalism is consciously wielded as an instrument in the class struggle, as an effective means of domination over the 'mass'; it has an explicitly political and activist character. One need only read the classic chapter: 'How will the counter-revolution be achieved, if it happens?', in de Maistre: *Considérations sur la France.*[17] And the most important element of this theory of domination over the masses is the theory of the social importance of *authority*.

'Men never respect what they have done':[18] this sentence indicates the basic motif. Since respect for the *status quo* is the psychological basis for the social order of domination, but this attitude is necessarily lacking in relation to works done by purely human might (what I have made, I can also destroy), state and society must be presented as something exceeding all human power: 'Every Constitution . . . is a creation in the full meaning of the expression, and every creation goes beyond the powers of man.'[19] The principle which upholds state and society is not the truth as arrived at through human insight, but faith: prejudice, superstition, religion and tradition are celebrated as the essential social virtues of man. Burke sings a hymn in praise of prejudice: 'Prejudice is of ready application in the hour of emergency. . . . It previously engages the mind in a steady course of wisdom and virtue. . . . Prejudice renders a man's virtue his habit. . . . Through just prejudice, his duty becomes part of his nature.'[20] De Maistre

15. Ibid., vol. I, p. 735.   16. Ibid., p. 367.   17. Ibid., vol. I, pp. 113ff.
18. Ibid., p. 353.   19. Ibid., p. 373.   20. Burke, op. cit., p. 90.

is even clearer: for man 'there is nothing so important . . . as prejudices'; they are 'the real elements of his happiness, and the watchdogs of empire'; without them there is 'neither religion, nor morality, nor government'. And he gives this instruction for the maintenance of every religious and political 'association': 'In order to conduct himself properly, man needs not problems but beliefs. His cradle should be surrounded with dogmas; and when his reason awakens, he should find all his opinions ready-made, at least on everything which relates to his behaviour.'[21] The true legislators knew why they intertwined religion and politics, 'so that the citizens are believers whose loyalty is exalted to the level of faith, and whose obedience is exalted to the level of enthusiasm and fanaticism'.[22]

The second form of domination over the masses as unquestioned subordination of 'individual reason' to universal prejudices is 'patriotism': 'the absolute and general reign of national dogmas, that is to say, useful prejudices.' The government is a 'true religion' which has its dogmas, mysteries and priests. 'Man's first need is that his dawning reason should be curbed beneath this double yoke, that it should obliterate itself, lose itself in the national reason.'[23] This conception of 'national soul' (*âme nationale*) and 'national reason' (*raison nationale*) here appears as an authority-producing factor in an anti-rationalist theory of domination over the masses; this is clearly very different from Hegel's concept of the people's spirit which, as the fulfilment of subjective and objective reason, was still linked with the rational will of individuals: the anti-bourgeois theory of the counter-revolution does not coincide with the philosophy of state originating in the rising bourgeoisie, even where their respective concepts have the most affinity. In the latter philosophy, the 'generality' into which the freedom of the individual was incorporated was meant at least in theory to fulfil the values and needs of the individuals in their 'superseded' form; the theory of the

---

21. de Maistre, op. cit., vol. I, p. 375.
22. Op. cit., p. 361. Burke calls religion 'the basis of civil society' (op. cit., p. 93).
23. Ibid., p. 376.

counter-revolution simply places the generality above all such values and needs. It stands above all human reason, beyond criticism and insight; for the individual it does not signify fulfilment but 'abnegation', 'annihilation'. The generality now stands in a negative relationship to the rational voluntariness of the individual: it simply demands his subordination. The apologia for religion and patriotism as the basis of society thus directly becomes the apologia of subordination and of an authority rising above all insight. After de Maistre has celebrated 'faith and patriotism' as the great 'healers of this world', he continues: 'they only know two words: *submission* and *faith*; with these two levers they raise the universe; their very errors are sublime.'[24]

If the social order is elevated as something divine and natural above the rational will and the plan-making insight of individuals, and if its authority is constantly held beyond the reach of critical insight by the psychological levers of religion, patriotism, tradition, prejudice, etc., this is meant to prevent the will of the 'mass of the people' from drawing conclusions from their perceptions, and undertaking to destroy an order of which they already know the origin and effect. This is not an interpretation, but the literal meaning of the texts of de Maistre and others. We quote the main passage from de Maistre's *Étude sur la Souveraineté* here, because in a few lines it indicates the arguments behind this whole theory of authority: 'To put it briefly, the mass of the people has absolutely no part in any political creation. It only respects the government itself because the government is not its own work. This feeling is engraved deeply into its heart. *It bends beneath the sovereign power because it feels that this is something sacred which it can neither create nor destroy.* If it succeeds in extinguishing from itself this preservative sentiment, owing to corruption and traitorous suggestions, if it has the misfortune to believe it is called, *en masse*, to reform the state, all is lost. This is why it is of infinite importance, even in the free states, that the men who govern should be separated from the mass of the people by the personal factor which results from birth and wealth: *for if the*

24. Ibid., p. 377.

opinion of the people does not place a barrier between itself and authority, if the power is not out of its reach, if the crowd who are governed can believe they are the equal of the small numbers who actually govern, *government no longer exists*: thus the aristocracy is the sovereign, or the ruling authority by its essence; and the principle of the French Revolution is in head-on conflict with the eternal laws of nature.'[25] The derivation of the decisive social relationships from authority is a central feature of the theory of the counter-revolution. Bonald endeavours to show that language, the first medium of socialization, is only received by the individual through authoritative communication.[26] The same goes for the law, science, art, methods of work, etc. 'Thus the initial means of all understanding is the word accepted on faith and without examination, and the initial means of education is authority.'[27] And, consistently with this, he defines the relationship between authority and reason in such a way that 'authority forms man's reason, by enlightening his spirit with the knowledge of the truth; authority placed the seeds of civilization in society . . .'.[28] The 'people' in particular, that is 'those whose purely mechanical and repetitious occupations keep them in a habitual state of childhood', are counted, along with women and children, among that class of people who because of their natural 'weakness' do not actively belong to society at all, but have to be protected by it. 'The people's reason must consist of *feelings*: we have to direct them, and form their *heart* rather than their *intellect*.' They have, then, to be kept in the state of weakness which is theirs by nature: reading and writing have to do with neither their physical nor moral happiness, are, in fact, not even in their interest.[29]

When authority is thus referred to as the 'seed of civilization', Bonald does not have in mind its 'domesticating' function in the sense of the regulation of the production process or the disposition of social labour with a view to the greatest possible exploitation of productive forces, but its *power of conservation and preservation*. The theory of the counter-revolution creates modern *tradi-*

25. Ibid., pp. 354ff. (my italics). 26. Bonald, op. cit., p. 1212.
27. Ibid., p. 1175.   28. Ibid., p. 1199.   29. Ibid., p. 747.

tionalism as a rescue operation for the endangered social order. The 'discovery of history' as the 'supreme master of politics', played off against the revolution 'without a history' has a purely reactionary character from this point onwards and right up to Moeller van den Bruck and 'existential philosophy': the historical, without regard for its material content, becomes an absolute force, which unconditionally subordinates man to the *status quo* as something which has always been and always will be; it even serves to 'destroy the category of time'.[30] History is only the preservation and handing on of what has existed in the past: 'every important and really constitutional institution never establishes anything new; it does nothing but proclaim and defend rights anterior to it.'[31] The 'new' is already in itself a sin against history. The binding and crippling power of such an attitude, if – as all the theorists of counter-revolution demand – it is impressed on the people from the cradle upwards through public and private education, is clearly recognized. For Burke, 'to be attached to the subdivision, to love the little platoon we belong to in society, is the first principle (the germ, as it were) of public affections'.[32]

But all this does not yet adequately describe the function of this irrationalist theory of authority. Its whole emotional effect was derived from its contemporary struggle against the French Revolution, in which (in Gentz's words) it saw the 'ultimate crime'. The divine and natural sanction of the social system of domination applies also, and to no small extent, to the inequality of property relations, and authority is to a considerable degree the authority of property. De Maistre gave this away by unquestioningly equating 'birth' and 'wealth', and Burke made the point openly: 'As property is sluggish, inert, and timid, it never can be safe from the invasions of ability, unless it be, out of all proportion, predominant in the representation. It must be represented too in great masses of accumulation, or it is not rightly protected. The characteristic essence of property formed out of the combined principles of its acquisition and conservation, is to be *unequal*.

30. H. J. Laski, *Authority in the Modern State*, New Haven, 1927, p. 127.
31. Bonald, op. cit., p. 373.   32. Burke, op. cit., p. 47.

The great masses therefore which excite envy, and tempt rapacity, must be put out of the possibility of danger. Then they form a natural rampart about the lesser properties in all their gradations.'[33] The decisive place of the family within the social system of authority also comes into view in the property context: 'The power of perpetuating our property in our families is one of the most valuable and interesting circumstances belonging to it, and that which tends the most to the perpetuation of society itself.'[34]

The idea of the inheritance of property is one of the most effective factors through which the family is tied to the order of state and society which protects it, and the individual is tied to the family; however, this is not the only reason why the family becomes a matter of life and death to the state. Authoritarian traditionalism knows very well that it is precisely in the family that the 'dogmas and prejudices' which it proposes as the basis of society are originally handed down: 'we know the morality that we have received from our fathers as an ensemble of dogmas or useful prejudices adopted by the national reason.'[35] The family is the basic image of all social domination, and although de Maistre does not wish to assert any 'exact parity between the authority of the father and the authority of the sovereign' he does say that 'the first man was the king of his children'.[36] Burke ascribes the stability of the English constitution to the fact that 'we took the fundamental laws into the womb of our families'; the authoritarian family becomes one of the key bulwarks against revolution: 'Always acting as if in the presence of canonized forefathers, the spirit of freedom . . . is tempered with an awful gravity.'[37] And to the ideal constitution of the family is added the genetic: Bonald claims that the 'political society' arose out of the struggle between 'proprietary families'.[38]

33. Op. cit., p. 52.
34. Loc. cit.
35. de Maistre, op. cit., vol. I, p. 400.
36. Ibid. p. 323.
37. Burke, op. cit., p. 34.
38. Bonald, op. cit., p. 1242.

B. RESTORATION

The spread of the theory of the counter-revolution in Germany and its transformation into the theory of the restoration took shape in two broad currents of thought: the first centred around 'political romanticism', beginning with Gentz's translation of Burke (1793) and reaching its peak in the time before and during the Vienna Congress (Friedrich Schlegel, Adam Müller, Baader, Görres); the second, the Restoration's theory of the state, was consolidated in Stahl's *Rechtsphilosophie* (the first edition of this book appeared at the time of the July Revolution, and it was given its final form in 1854). Von Haller's *Restauration der Staatswissenschaft* (from 1816 to 1834) represents, as it were, a link between the two currents. While, in France, the bourgeoisie was fighting to defeat the counter-revolution of the feudal aristocracy and after the July revolution consolidating its own political domination, the weaker economic development of the bourgeoisie in Germany led nowhere to real political power. The German theory of counter-revolution thus lacks all immediacy, trenchancy and aggressiveness; it isn't fighting against a revolution at all; the actual social antagonisms appear only fragmentarily through endless mediations. There is not a single decisive motif, for our context, which was not already present in the French theory of counter-revolution. But the situation has changed at the end of this process of development: the feudal monarchies are faced with the revolution. Stahl's theory of the authoritarian-theocratic state now becomes a welcome weapon in the open struggle.

The preface to the third edition (the second edition appeared a year after the revolt of the Silesian weavers and three years before the March Revolution in Germany) appeals to philosophy to come quickly to the aid of the threatened authorities in state and society; it is a convincing document on the justificatory and conservative function of philosophy in Germany.

'For one and a half centuries philosophy has not based government, marriage and property on God's order and providence but on the will of men and their contract, and the peoples were merely following its teachings when they raised themselves above their governments and all historically ordained orders and ultimately above rightfully existing property.'[1] This reproach is aimed not only at Rousseau and Kant, but also at Hegel, who may have proclaimed the 'sanctity of the concept' in place of the sovereignty of the will, but then 'who is afraid of this concept and who respects it?' It is precisely fear and respect which matter: philosophy must implant and sustain 'guilty obedience to authority'. Stahl exclaims anxiously: 'Should one leave the question "what is property?" only to the Proudhons?'[2] Philosophy should take over the great task of 'nurturing respect for all orders and governments which God has set over men, and for all conditions and laws, which have come into being in an orderly way under his directions'.[3]

Stahl's system (in its basis, not in its fully elaborated form, which reveals many concessions to bourgeois-liberal tendencies) is the first purely authoritarian German philosophy of the state, in so far as the social relations of people and the meaning and purpose of the political organization of society are from first to last directed towards the preservation and strengthening of an unassailable authority. The 'norms of civil order' are not taken from the real needs of the people, or from the general wish for the constitution of a true 'generality', or from a recognition of the progress of historical 'reason', but from the conception of a 'moral realm' whose cardinal feature is 'the necessity for an authority completely elevated above the people', that is, the necessity 'for a claim to obedience and respect which applies not only to the law but to a real power outside them – the government (state power)'. And since none of the theories which take the rational will of men as their starting point can ever arrive at an 'absolutely superior real authority', they are all, 'in their innermost foundations, revolutionary'.[4]

In the closer definition of this authority, the same tendencies converge as those already played off by the theory of the counter-

---

1. Stahl, *Rechtsphilosophie*, 3rd edn, Heidelberg, 1854–6, vol. II, 1, p. x.
2. Ibid., p. xvii.   3. Ibid., p. xxii.   4. Ibid., vol. II, 2, pp. 3ff.

revolution against the characteristics of the bourgeois social order; we have summarized them under the heading of the irrational personalization and the traditionalist stabilization of the existing (feudal-aristocratic) system of domination. The right of functioning authorities is freed from any justification through success and performance, and they are thus elevated charismatically above any control by society. To the removal of authority's material-objective character, through its fixation on the person who is 'gifted' with it, there corresponds on the other hand an (irrational) assertion of independence on the part of the state apparatus controlled by the persons in authority. Since the charismatic sanction can only consecrate a person and not an apparatus, the state as such must become a person: an independent 'organism', outlasting social changes, which, directly ordained by God, has its life outside the realm of individual and general aspirations. The irrational personalization of authority is transformed here, in Stahl's state-absolutism, into the most extreme form of reification: into the authority of the state seen as the supreme thing-in-itself. 'As the institution for the control of the entire condition of the human community the state is the *one, supreme and sovereign power* on earth. People and their aspirations, other institutions and communities, even the church, as far as its external existence is concerned, are subordinated to it. It judges them, without being judged by them or being able to be called to account by them, for there is no authority and no judge above it.'[5] This reified state-absolutism was alien to the French counter-revolution: their image of domination was based too much on the nobility's personal pride and hate and personal contempt for the mass of the people to permit such a depersonalization. The independence of the state apparatus leaves open the possibility of replacing the bearers of authority, while retaining the supporting relations of production; the state philosophy of restoration leaves room for a compromise with the advancing bourgeoisie. There is a further indication of this in the connection between the absolute state and the 'soul of the people', with the people as an 'originally

5. Ibid., vol. II, 2, pp. 154f.

given unity'[6] in whose consciousness the state has its roots. This is no longer the 'national soul' of the counter-revolution, which was ultimately nothing more than an amalgamation of 'useful prejudices'. Stahl's concept of the soul of the people and of the people already clearly reflects a real participation by the dominated classes in their domination: the 'natural, organic community of the people' is meant to replace the social generality arising from the rational will of individuals which the bourgeois philosophy of the state had up till then required.

But the pure irrationality of the state-authority emerges again and again through the layer of ethical and organicist concepts which conceals it; this kind of authority can only demand obedience but cannot give a reason for it. The prestige of the state 'rests on its mere existence as such. It is an immanent, original prestige, and the subjects thus have the immediate duty to obey. . . . This obedience is not voluntary or dependent on consent but necessary; it is similar to one's duty towards one's parents. . . .'[7] Love and justice now acquire their real meaning as sanctions of the existing social system of authority. Love is based on obedience, which is 'the first and indispensable moral motive', and without which all love is merely 'pathological'.[8] And justice is defined as the 'inviolability of a given order . . . without regard to its content'.[9]

The ideological function of the law is proclaimed here with naïve openness. The organicists were aware why they placed such value on the traditional 'constancy' of the law: 'Through such constancy of the law the original simplicity of the people's consciousness is preserved, so that what is existing law is taken as just, and what is just as existing. Its effect is that law in itself is not known in any form other than the form of the law of the fatherland. . . . Hence the existing law is regarded as, by and large, what is necessary, and cannot be otherwise.'[10] Law and positive law become 'equivalent concepts'; there is no natural law or rational law which could be played off against the positive law.[11]

6. Ibid., pp. 234, 241.   7. Ibid., pp. 179ff.   8. Ibid., vol. II, 1, pp. 106ff.
9. Ibid., p. 163.   10. Ibid., p. 227.   11. Ibid., pp. 221ff.

The law regulates a social organization which is based on the triple pillars of 'the protection of the person', 'assets' and 'the family'.[12] It is the characteristic trinity which we have already met in bourgeois theory. Stahl too sees property as an 'original right of the personality', as the 'material for the revelation of the individuality of the man',[13] and lets the 'moral conservation' of property take place through the family; he rejects any attempt to base property on the will of men and traces it back directly to the providence of God. The social theory of the restoration is already confronted with a developed socialist theory: Stahl polemicizes against Considérant, Fourier and Proudhon. He knows that 'if the providence of God is not recognized as the legal basis of all property', there will be no reason for a private right to what is a means for the enjoyment and sustenance of all. 'Communism is thus correct as opposed to the philosophy of law from Grotius to Hegel, which bases property merely and finally on the will of man, and would be right as opposed to the present society if society itself would be prepared to free itself from God.'[14] Hence the necessity for a return from the human to the divine institution. But for the actual state of property relations an actual tribunal which can deputize for God is after all necessary. And here the anti-bourgeois character of the restoration breaks through again: 'the beginning of property among the people . . . is not appropriation by individuals but allocation by the government.' The historical legal basis for the distribution of property must not, under any circumstances, be founded – as in the bourgeois theory – on individual success and individual achievement. Property is to be based *'not on personal initiative but on authority*, not something gained through struggle but something received'.[15] It is the monarchical, feudal structure of authority which is expressed here: the authority of property does not depend on the individual property-owner, or on the general law safeguarding the individual property-owners, but on an ultimate 'government' from which the

12. Ibid., p. 310. 13. Ibid., p. 351.
14. Ibid., p. 375.
15. Ibid., p. 360 (my italics).

individuals receive their property as a 'fief' – although this distribution then becomes 'irrevocable'.[16]

In the course of the feudal-traditionalist theory of property the importance of the *family* for the stabilization of the authoritarian state is also recognized and defined. Only because it serves 'the revelation of individuality and the care of the family' does 'the moral consecration of property' take place.[17] It was precisely this function of the family which Hegel had already heavily emphasized in the finished form of his system and it is found at the same time in Riehl's typically bourgeois theory of the family. The theories of the Feudal Restoration and the liberal bourgeoisie meet in the celebration of the family as the material and moral foundation of society: the authoritarian and constitutionalist theories unite on the common ground of the protection of the family and of the order of property.

'The family is the centre of human existence, the link between the individual and the communal life', for in being 'the satisfaction of the individual' it is at the same time the means through which the civil and religious community 'comes into being both physically and morally and intellectually (through upbringing)'.[18] The political and social organization of the feudal monarchy as described by Stahl is so authoritarian in its construction that education towards authority in the family does not have to be particularly urged. Instead of this there is an emphatic indication that the endurance and the stability of the existing class order is largely due to the restriction of inheritance to within the family, which over many generations implants an interest in the continuity of this order in the individual consciousness: '. . . In this succession of families and of the wills modelled on them, there lies *order* and *continuity*, for the whole human race. Through this, mankind possesses property throughout a succession of generations, thus uninterruptedly controlling it as a substratum of the consciousness and the will, and preserving the legal groupings of people drawn up with respect to this property and through them

16. Ibid.
17. Ibid., vol. II, 2, p. 93.   18. Ibid., vol. II, 1, p. 424.

the connection between the generations.'[19] With regard to the material basis of the family community, Stahl recognizes that it is only through property that the 'goods of the earth' can become the instrument of 'family ties and family life'.[20] And he states that although 'in its most important aspect' the educational power has as its sole aim the 'advancement of the child', in addition to this, 'since the whole relationship also serves the satisfaction of the parents, it equally involves a domination of the children for the parents' own benefit: i.e. disposal of their services and labour'.[21]

19. Ibid., pp. 500ff.   20. Ibid., p. 352.   21. Ibid., p. 487.

On the road from Luther to Hegel bourgeois philosophy had increasingly dealt with the authority relationship as a social relationship of domination. It had thereby moved essentially from the centre to the periphery: the fixed centre was the Christian (inner, transcendental) freedom of the person, and the social order only appeared as the external sphere of this freedom. With values apportioned in this manner it was not difficult to accommodate the fact that the external sphere was primarily a realm of servitude and unfreedom, for this did not, after all, affect 'actual' freedom. Liberation always referred only to the inner realm of freedom: it was a 'spiritual' process, through which man became what he had always been in actuality. Since internal freedom always remained the eternal presupposition, or *a priori*, of unfreedom, external unfreedom could never close this gap: it was eternalized along with its opposite pole.

Since the eighteenth century there has been no lack of movements within bourgeois philosophy which have protested against this conception. The French Enlightenment made the concern for worldly freedom and the worldly happiness of men into a subject of philosophy: its limits were the limits of social order, which it could not essentially transcend. The only possibility of overcoming this whole conception lay beyond this order.

Behind the bourgeois concept of freedom with its unification of inner freedom and outer unfreedom Marx saw the Christian 'cult of the abstract man'; Christian freedom did not affect the social praxis of the concrete man (it was rather the unconditional authority of the 'law' or the worldly government which ruled there), but its actual 'inner' being as distinguished from its external existence. Thus the sphere in which men produced and reproduced their life appeared as a sphere of actual unfreedom and antagonisms, in which men were only counted free and equal as 'men' or as 'persons' without regard to their material existence. This image corresponds to bourgeois society as a society of commodity producers, in which men do not confront each other as concrete individuals but as abstract buyers and sellers of commodities and in which 'private labour' is expressed as abstract 'equal human labour', measurable in abstract social labour-time.[1] And a decisive presupposition of this society is the freedom of labour, in which all the features of the Christian bourgeois concept of freedom are realized. Freedom from all worldly goods here means that the worker has become 'free and independent' of all the things which are necessary for the preservation of his life; freedom of man to himself here means that he can freely dispose of the only thing which he still possesses, his labour-power; he has to sell it in order to live.[2] As far as he can sell it, he relates to it as to his 'property'. Bourgeois philosophy had taught that the freedom of the person could only be realized in free property. In this reality of bourgeois society one's own person has itself become property which is offered for sale on the market.

This revealing irony exposes the double truth which underlies the bourgeois categories: what this society has made of man, and what can be made out of him. The ground is laid bare on which the lever of transforming praxis can be put into operation in the direction of both poles. According to Marx the cultural values as well as the physical and psychological powers of men have become commodities under the capitalist mode of production. The situation of the labour market is what directly determines the freedom of men and the possibilities of life, and is itself always dependent on the dynamics of society as a whole.

Bourgeois philosophy's formulation of the problem was thus inverted; the same thing happened with the doctrine of the two realms of freedom and necessity and the dialectical relationship between them. The sphere of material production is and remains a 'realm of necessity': a perpetual struggle with nature determined by 'need and external requirement' and dependent on the

1. Marx, *Capital*, vol. I, Moscow, 1954, p. 73.   2. Op. cit., p. 169.

'more or less abundant conditions of production' in which it takes place.[3] But the realm of necessity also has its freedom; admittedly not 'transcendental' freedom, which leaves necessity behind and is satisfied with an 'inner' process. Marx had already traced the concept of necessity back to its content by including in it the real distress of men and their struggle with nature for the preservation of their life; he now did the same with the concept of freedom. 'Freedom in this field can only consist in socialized man, the associated producers, rationally regulating their interchange with nature, and bringing it under their common control instead of being ruled by it as if by a blind force; and achieving this with the minimum expenditure of energy and under conditions which are the most favourable to them and the most worthy of their human nature.'[4] Here for the first time freedom is understood as a mode of real human praxis, as a task of conscious social organization. The worldly happiness of men has been included in its content under the heading of 'the most adequate and the most worthy' conditions of human nature: the supersession of 'external' distress and 'external' servitude belong to the sense of this concept of freedom.

And yet there is still a 'higher' freedom: a 'development of human forces' which is not spurred on by need and external expediency, but 'is an end itself'. It only begins 'beyond' the sphere of material production, which will 'always remain a realm of necessity'. But its prerequisite is the rational organization of society: 'The true realm of freedom' can 'only blossom forth with that realm of necessity as its base. . . . The shortening of the working day is its basic prerequisite.'[5]

'The shortening of the working day is its basic prerequisite.' This sentence points to the injustice committed over a centuries-long development and gathers together the suffering and yearning of generations. The achievement of freedom is now recognized as one of the purposes of the organization of the social labour process and the appropriate form or organization has been determined:

3. *Capital*, vol. III, Moscow, 1959, p. 799.
4. Op. cit., vol. III, p. 800.   5. Loc. cit.

with this we are shown the road from the realm of necessity to the realm of freedom, a freedom which, although it is still something Beyond, is no longer the transcendental Beyond which eternally precedes man, or the religious Beyond which is meant to supersede their distress, but the Beyond which men can create for themselves if they transform a social order which has become rotten. The complete inversion of the problem of freedom, through which the realm of freedom as a particular 'worldly' organization of society is now founded on the realm of necessity, is only one aspect of the general inversion, in which the material relations of production of society are understood as the basis of the whole political and cultural 'superstructure' and its corresponding forms of consciousness.

In this connection, Marx also deals with the social bearing of the *problem of authority*. He confronts authority as a relationship of dependence in the capitalist process of production. His analysis is therefore concerned less with authority as such than with authority as a factor within a given society's relations of production. Only if we contrast this specific authority with the forms of authority prevalent in other societies do the more general functions of authority become visible.

Authority is a manifestation of the relationship of domination and servitude as a social relationship of dependence. However, the relationship of domination and servitude, 'as it grows directly out of production itself', is determined by the 'specific economic form in which unpaid surplus labour is pumped out of the immediate producers'.[6] The specific form of the capitalist labour process determines the form of the authority relationships predominant in capitalist society. This labour process[7] requires the 'cooperation of many wage-labourers' first in cottage industry and later in the factory, and 'social or communal labour on a larger scale'. Such labour necessarily has to have a management which unites the individual activities, caused by the division of labour,

6. Op. cit., vol. III, p. 324.
7. The quotations in the following three paragraphs are from *Capital*, vol. I, pp. 330ff.

into a 'productive overall body': it mediates, supervises and leads. Since the means of production and the immediate conditions of production were in the possession of capital, this function of management necessarily fell to the capitalist: originally the 'command of capital over labour' appeared to be 'only a formal consequence of the fact that the worker works, not for himself, but for the capitalist and therefore under the capitalist'. In so far as the dominating authority of the capitalist is a 'direct requirement for the carrying out of the labour process' it is a real requisite of production: the capitalist's command on the field of production is as indispensable as the general's command on the field of battle.

But this is only one side of authority. The capitalist production process aims for the greatest possible production of surplus value, i.e. for the greatest possible exploitation of the labour power of the wage labourer. The greater their number grows and the more their resistance to their economic situation increases, the fiercer the pressure of the dominating authority of capital. 'The management of the capitalist is not only a function which springs from the social labour process and which particularly appertains to him, it is at the same time a function of the exploitation of a social labour process and thus dependent on the inevitable antagonisms between the exploiter and the raw material of his exploitation.' This is the second side of authority. And in this two-sidedness it now determines the specific form which the relationships of domination and dependence assume in capitalist society.

There now grows out of the dialectic of the labour relationship what Marx has called the 'despotic form' of capitalist management. It comes into being when, in the development of production, the following two functions of management directly coincide: the function which springs from the communal labour process, and the function which springs from the process of the realization of capital, that is, authority as a condition of production, and authority as exploitation. The 'office' of management is not the result of the material rational organization of the labour process, but appears as an adjunct to the ownership of the means of production: it becomes the prerogative of the capitalist. 'The capitalist is not a capitalist because he is an industrial commander but becomes an industrial commander because he is a capitalist.' The division of labour is reified and stabilized so that it becomes a 'natural' division between the disposition and the execution of labour; the 'labour of overall supervision hardens into its exclusive function'.

This whole process is constantly reproduced under the compulsion of economic necessity; it runs its course as it were behind the backs of the men who are subject to it. The authority which springs from economic power appears to them as the personal authority of the capitalist, as the 'power of an alien will, which submits its activity to his purposes'. Reification is transformed into a false personalization: whoever happens to be the manager of the labour process is always ready in possession of an authority which, properly speaking, could only emerge from the actual prior management of the labour process. The capitalist possesses and uses his authority *vis-à-vis* the workers essentially as the 'personification of capital; his personal authority *vis-à-vis* the workers' is only the 'personification of the conditions of labour *vis-à-vis* labour itself'.[8]

This analysis of the authority relationship as it has grown directly out of the production process also shows how the irrational personalization of authorities typical of the later period is anchored in the essence of the capitalist production process. It further shows that the existence side-by-side of an authoritarian and an anti-authoritarian attitude, which we have been able to follow right through bourgeois philosophy, similarly springs from the peculiar character of this process.[9]

While the division of labour within the workshop or factory uniformly subjects the cooperating workers to the unconditional authority of the capitalist and creates a purposeful and despotic form of management, the social division of labour itself, as a whole, is still left to an arbitrariness following no rules: 'chance and caprice have full play in distributing the producers and their

8. Op. cit., vol. III, p. 418.
9. What follows is based on *Capital*, vol. I, p. 355.

means of production, among the various branches of social labour.' Without a plan regulating the overall process of production, the independent commodity producers confront each other without 'acknowledging any authority other than that of competition, of the coercion exerted by the pressure of their mutual interests'. The more the anarchy which permeates the whole social process spreads, the more despotic will the authority of the capitalist over the immediate producers become in the labour process itself. In capitalist society 'anarchy in the social division of labour and despotism in that of the workshop mutually condition each other'. In a retrospective glance at pre-capitalist social organizations Marx differentiates between the anarchic-despotic authority structure just described and the authority relationships predominant in those earlier societies.[10] The relationship between the social and 'factory-type' division of labour is there exactly reversed: while the overall social division of labour is subjected to a 'planned and authoritative organization', the division of labour in the workplace is not at all developed or only undergoes a 'dwarf-like' development. Marx points to the example of the small Indian communities: the specialization of trade develops 'spontaneously' out of the given forces and conditions of production and crystallizes into a legal system, authoritatively and systematically regulating the community's relations of production; while within the individual trades each artisan works, although exactly according to tradition, 'independently and without acknowledging any authority'. Here too the law of the overall social division of labour has 'the irresistible authority of a law of nature'; but this 'law of nature' is comprehensible to the people there who are subject to it, and to a great extent it is a 'natural' law which regulates the reproduction of society according to the natural and historical conditions of production; whereas in capitalist society it is opaque and operates as an alien force resistant to the possibilities already available.

In summary Marx lays down the distinction between the

10. *Capital*, vol. I, pp. 357–9, and *The Poverty of Philosophy*, Moscow, 1966, p. 118.

distribution of authority in capitalist and in precapitalist societies as a 'general rule': 'the less authority presides over the division of labour inside society, the more the division of labour develops inside the workshop, and the more it is subjected to the authority of a single person. Thus authority in the workshop and authority in society, in relation to the division of labour, are in *inverse ratio* to each other.'[11]

The dialectical and two-sided character of the authority relationship is also the determining factor in the establishment of a *positive concept of authority*; this became a particularly central preoccupation in the debate with the anti-authoritarian anarchies of the followers of Bakunin. A small essay by Engels, *On the Principle of Authority*, summarizes the principal points of this discussion.[12]

In contrast to the undialectical rejection of all authority, emphasis is first laid on the dialectical character of the authority relationship: it is an 'absurdity' to present the principle of authority as absolutely bad and the principle of autonomy as absolutely good. There is a kind of authority which is inseparably linked with all 'organization', a kind of subordination, based on functional-rational assumptions, to genuine management and performance-labour discipline. Such functional authority is necessary in every social organization as a condition of production; it will also play an important role in a future society. Admittedly this society will only allow authority to exist within the bounds 'inevitably drawn by the relations of production'. The features of the authority structure determined by class society will disappear, in particular the function of exploitation and the political appropriation of 'management' in the capitalist system of domination. Public function will lose this political character and change into 'simple administrative functions'; those who fulfil these functions will watch over the social interests of the whole society.

11. *The Poverty of Philosophy*, p. 118.
12. Engels, *Von der Autorität*, Marx-Engels Werke, Berlin, 1960, vol. 18, pp. 305–308 (originally written in Italian for the *Almanacco Repubblicano per l'anno 1874*).

Engels holds up another decisive function of genuine authority as an objection against the anti-authoritarian: the role of leadership and the leading party in the revolution. 'A revolution is certainly the most authoritarian thing there is, an act in which one part of the population forces its will on the other with muskets, bayonets and cannons, which are all very authoritarian means.' Revolutionary subordination in one's own ranks and revolutionary authority towards the class enemy are necessary prerequisites in the struggle for the future organization of society.

This progressive function of authority was more closely defined by Lenin in the context of his struggle against 'economism'. The authority of rational leadership is separated off by Lenin from anarchism on the one hand and the theory of spontaneity on the other. The worship of the spontaneous mass movement which pursues its aim unaided, and the related disparagement of the initiative of the leaders signifies 'converting the working-class movement into an instrument of bourgeois democracy'.[13] The 'conscious element' is a decisive factor in the movement; to weaken it means to strengthen bourgeois and in particular petty-bourgeois influence. 'Class political consciousness can be brought to the workers only *from without*, that is, only from outside the economic struggle, from outside the sphere of relations between workers and employers.'[14] From the importance of the conscious element there emerges the necessity for a strict, centralist organization with a proven and schooled leadership at its head. Lenin claims that 'no revolutionary movement can endure without a stable organization of leaders maintaining continuity' and that 'the broader the popular mass drawn spontaneously into the struggle, which forms the basis of the movement and participates in it, the more urgent the need for such an organization'.[15]

In Marx the starting-point for the analysis of authority was the interest which a particular society had in subordinating people to a directing will within the material process of production and reproduction. In capitalist society this interest is first and last the

13. *What is to be Done?*, Moscow, 1969, p. 194.
14. Op. cit., p. 78.   15. Op. cit., p. 121.

interest of the ruling class, an interest growingly antagonistic to the interest of the great majority, even if – thanks to the double-edged character of the authority relationship in this case – to a certain (and increasingly problematic) degree, the interest of the whole of society was thereby served. The material root of the authority relationship described was the specific form of the capitalist production process: 'The immediate relationship of the owners of the conditions of production to the immediate producers.' But the social function of authority is by no means exhausted in this immediate relationship and its immediate consequences. Through numerous mediations it extends from this point to embrace the entire compass of human social organization. Marx followed the main directions of these mediations: he dealt with the problem under the most varied headings (state, law, tradition, history, etc.) and let it lead into the ultimate question of the reality of the social freedom of man. In the following we shall only point to some of the questions which are directly relevant to the problem of authority.

First we must remember that the 'domination–servitude relationship, as it grows directly out of production itself . . . in turn has a determining effect on the latter'.[16] It is one of those social relationships which, once they have come into being at a particular stage of the production process, build up a powerful resistance to the development of this process, harden into their acquired form and in this hardened form influence the material life process of society. This mechanism, by which an authoritative relationship of domination, originally made possible through the labour process, extends and stabilizes itself beyond its origins, this 'reification' of authority, occurs partly 'by itself', partly as the praxis of the ruling groups. The reification occurs by itself when the basis of an existing state of social production is constantly reproduced and assumes a regulated and ordered form (regulation and order are themselves an 'indispensable element in every mode of production'). It occurs as the praxis of the ruling group, because it is in their interest to 'sanctify as law' the existing state of

16. *Capital*, vol. III, p. 324.

affairs, in which they have risen to a position of domination. It is the authority of *tradition*, in which Marx here reveals the same double-edged quality as exists in the authority of the director of labour: the private appropriation of a social interest and its transformation into an instrument of economic and psychological domination.

Marx discovered the same double-edged duality, determined by the material relations of production in capitalist society, in those authority relationships which have the most 'general' character: in the political organization of society. Bourgeois philosophy had essentially understood the problem of social unfreedom as the problem of the unification of the individual and the generality (the supersession of individual freedom in the generality); Marx, in investigating this generality in a historical materialist way, shows its character as *appearance* in previous history and reveals the mechanism which turns the appearance into a real force.

What is the importance of the general in the social existence of men? Firstly, nothing other than the 'mutual interdependence of the individuals among whom the labour is divided',[17] their common neediness, their common reliance on the available productive forces and conditions of production. The general interest is the reproduction of the whole society under the best exploitation of the productive forces available, for the greatest possible happiness of the individuals. In every society in which labour is divided and appropriated according to class, in which the acquisition of surplus value occurs at the cost of the immediate producers, a contradiction necessarily appears between the general interest and the interest of the ruling class. And 'precisely from this contradiction between the particular and the general interest' the *state* assumes an apparently independent form. The process tending towards the independence and consolidation of the general as an alien and independent power, separated from the wishes and acts of the individuals, is one of the decisive elements in the universal reification which was already present in the

17. *The German Ideology*, Moscow, 1968, p. 44.

authority of the 'management' of labour. And here too the process is double-edged. On the one hand the ruling class, in order to justify its dominating position in the process of production, has to make the particular interest of its class seem valid as the general interest, 'that is expressed in ideal form, to give its ideas the form of universality, and represent them as the only rational, universally valid ones'.[18] Thus far, the general is merely a 'creation' of individuals who are defined as private people and the contradiction between the general and the private interest, like the independence of the general, is only an 'appearance',[19] which is produced again and again in history and destroyed again and again. On the other hand the independence of the apparently general is based on a very real power: the state in all its institutions as genuine force. The perpetually conflicting activity, the perpetual struggle between 'opposed particular interests' requires, if the reproduction of the anarchically producing society is to be safeguarded, a universal apparatus which is equipped with all the material and intellectual instruments of coercion: it 'makes practical intervention and control necessary through the illusory "general" interest in the form of the state'.[20]

The analysis of the concrete social character of the generality, of its nature as an appearance which is nevertheless real, now also leads to the critique of the bourgeois concept of freedom.

The personal freedom, which bourgeois society did in fact develop in contrast to the personal bondage of feudalism, is the expression of the free competition of commodity producers. Freedom of labour, freedom of movement, freedom of occupation, freedom of profit – all these varieties of bourgeois freedom express the 'accidental nature of the conditions of life', which the capitalist production process has brought forth in general competition and in the general struggle of individuals amongst each other.[21] Such freedom is merely fortuitous – in fact, the personality itself becomes something fortuitous and fortuitousness becomes a personality.[22] And what asserts itself in the overall

18. Op. cit., p. 62.   19. Op. cit., p. 272.
20. Op. cit., p. 46.   21. Op. cit., p. 95.   22. Op. cit., p. 421.

society in the form of this fortuitousness is only that anarchic form of its reproduction. It is on this and particularly on the transformation into wages of the value and the price of labour power (obscuring the real relationship) that 'all the illusions of freedom' in bourgeois society are based.[23] Its freedom is only the phenomenal form of general unfreedom, powerlessness in relation to the social production process, which for these people becomes a 'material force' by which they are ruled instead of ruling it. Freedom is only possible in the general community: that was the correct answer of bourgeois philosophy. But the general community which makes freedom possible is a quite particular form of organization of the whole society which can only be realized through the supersession of its bourgeois organization. The latter was an 'apparent' universality in which the unification of the individuals signified general unfreedom. In a genuine universality 'the individuals obtain their freedom in and through their association'.[24] 'In place of the old bourgeois society . . . we shall have an association in which the free development of each is the condition for the free development of all.'[25]

We have pursued the authority problem down to its most general formulations because only thus could we show that for Marx it is entirely a social problem, which can only be tackled by a particular social praxis at a particular stage of historical development. Marx's work is not a description of social conditions, but the theory of tendencies of social development. The supersession of capitalist by socialist society is an historical tendency which is itself at work in the given social situation. 'The "Idea" always disguised itself insofar as it differed from the "Interest".'[26] The decisive authority is not the idea (not even the idea of a just and free society), but *history*. Only in history can there originate the 'interest' which is needed by the idea for its realization.

The materialist analysis of the tendencies of the capitalist

23. *Capital*, vol. I, p. 540. 24. *The German Ideology*, p. 93.
25. *The Manifesto of the Communist Party*, in Marx-Engels, *Selected Works*, vol. I, Moscow, 1956, p. 109. 26. *The Holy Family*, Moscow, 1956, p. 109.

production process now also attacks an element of bourgeois theory which had been of decisive importance ever since Luther: the idea of the *family* as the moral foundation of the social system of domination. The concept of the family is an indifferent abstraction (which none the less makes good ideological sense as the perpetuation and generalization of a particular form of the family); it is the form of the patriarchal, monogamous, nuclear family which, in the long historical development beginning at a particular stage of the social life process, obtains objective status as an important element in this process.[27] Marx distinguishes the ideological appearance of the bourgeois family from its material reality; existing theories had so far put the two together.[28]

The reality of the bourgeois family is determined, like all forms of life under capitalism, by the character of the commodity economy; as a 'property' with its specific costs and expenses, profit and surplus value, it is entered into the general account. Economic interests govern not only the choice of partner (mostly prescribed by the father) but also the production and upbringing of the children. Like the physiological functions, the spiritual values are also tied to the economic interests; in their accustomed and comfortable form they govern day to day cohabitation. 'The bourgeoisie historically gives the family the character of the bourgeois family, in which boredom and money are the binding link.'[29] On this basis there now appear the phenomena characterized by Marx as the apparent dissolution of the bourgeois family by the bourgeoisie itself: the breaking of monogamy through 'secret adultery', the hidden 'community of married women', prostitution, etc. While on the one hand the bourgeoisie has 'torn away from the family its sentimental veil, and has reduced the family relation to a mere money relation',[28] this 'dirty existence' of the family has its counterpart on the other hand in the 'holy concept of it in official phraseology and universal

27. We shall not here go into the historical-genetic theory of the family developed by Engels.
28. On this distinction, see especially *The German Ideology*, pp. 195–8.
29. Op. cit., p. 195.
30. *The Manifesto of the Communist Party*, p. 37.

hypocrisy'.[31] For the bourgeoisie has a vital interest in the continued existence of the family because marriage, property and the family are 'the practical basis on which the bourgeoisie has erected its domination, and because in their bourgeois form they are conditions which make the bourgeois a bourgeois'.[32] This is the materialist formulation of the relationship, idealized after Marx by bourgeois theory, in which the family of private property-owners is made into the moral foundation of society. The bourgeois family continues to exist because its existence 'has been made necessary by its connection with the mode of production that exists independently of the will of bourgeois society'.[33] While its dissolution is only an apparent one, this mode of production leads on the opposite side – in the proletariat – to a real dissolution of the family. Marx has portrayed the terrible destruction of the proletarian family by large-scale industry from the middle of the nineteenth century:[34] the exploitation of the labour of women and children dissolved the economic base of the old family; to the increased general exploitation was added the as it were additional exploitation of wife and children by the father, who was driven to the selling of both.

If capitalism thus actually perverted all apparently 'eternal' and 'natural' family relationships, it was nevertheless precisely through this that it made visible the social determination of the existing form of the family and the way to overcome it. Large-scale industry 'by assigning as it does an important part in the process of production, outside the domestic sphere, to women, to young persons, and to children of both sexes, creates a new economical foundation for a higher form of the family and of the relations between the sexes'.[35] The functions fulfilled by the bourgeois family will be freed from their connections with the characteristics of the capitalist production process: authority will be separated from the interest of exploitation, the education of

31. *The German Ideology*, p. 195.
32. Loc. cit.
33. Op. cit., p. 196.
34. *Capital*, vol. I, pp. 480ff.
35. Op. cit., p. 490.

children from the interest of private property. This will result in the destruction of the two bases of marriage so far: 'the dependence of the woman on the man and of the children on their parents through private property.'[36]

36. *Marx-Engels Gesamtausgabe*, part 1, vol. VI, p. 519.

The transformation of the bourgeois theory of authority into the theory of the totalitarian state (Sorel and Pareto)

A good deal of the history of bourgeois society is reflected in the bourgeois theory of authority. When the bourgeoisie had won political and economic domination in Western and Central Europe the contradictions within the society it organized were obvious. As the ruling class the bourgeoisie could hardly retain its interest in the theory with which it had been linked as a rising class and which was in crying contradiction with the present. This is why the actual bourgeois theory of society is to be found only before the real domination of the bourgeoisie, and the theory of the dominant bourgeoisie is no longer bourgeois theory. Comte was the last man in France, Hegel was the last man in Germany to discuss the problems of social organization within a comprehensive theory as tasks for rational human praxis.

Problems of the organization of state and society, once they have broken away from the supporting foundation of the comprehensive theory, fall to the business of the specialist discipline of *sociology*. A brief survey will be given elsewhere[1] of the forms assumed by the problem of authority in the various tendencies of bourgeois sociology. They are symptomatic of certain stages and streams within the development of society, but none offers a new interpretation of social domination and none consciously expresses a new overall social constellation.[2] The real bourgeois theory

1. Cf. my essay *Autorität und Familie in der deutschen Soziologie bis 1933*, Paris, 1936.

2. We omit here the theory of the 'Basel Circle', particularly of Nietzsche and Burckhardt, which contains decisive insights into the development of society. Their concrete social importance has not yet been recognized. They have had no effect up to the present: their current derivations stand in total contradiction to their actual content. Cf. references to this state of affairs in *Zeitschrift für Sozialforschung*, IV (1935), pp. 15ff.

continues in a weak and, as regards content, an increasingly thin line (the neo-Kantian philosophy of law); the more the liberal bourgeoisie transforms itself and goes over to anti-liberal forms of domination, the more abstract becomes the theory of the state (the theory of the formal legal state) which still clings to the liberalist foundations.

Only at the present time of preparation for world war do the elements of a new theory of social domination corresponding to a new overall situation come together. This theory has taken on a firm shape simultaneously with the abolition of democratic and parliamentarian forms of government in Central and Southern Europe. The bourgeoisie has retained its domination by retaining the leadership of the smallest, economically most powerful, groups. The total political apparatus is built up under the most severe economic crises. Social relationships of authority assume a new form. Theory as a whole attains a different significance: it is consciously 'politicized' and made into the weapon of the total authoritarian state.

The unity of bourgeois theory at this stage is *negative*: it rests exclusively on the united front against liberalism and Marxism. It is the enemy who prescribes the position of the theory. It has no ground of its own from which the totality of social phenomena could be understood. All its basic concepts are counter-concepts: it invents the 'organic' view of history in opposition to historical materialism, 'heroic realism' in opposition to liberal idealism, 'existentialist philosophy' in opposition to the rationalist social theory of the bourgeoisie, and the totally authoritarian 'Führer-staat' in opposition to the rational state. The material social content of the theory, i.e. the particular form of the relations of production, for the maintenance of which it functions, is obscured.

This determines a basic characteristic of the theory: its *formalism*. This may seem strange, since it is precisely material contents (like race, people, blood, earth) which are brought into the field against the formal rationalism of the old theory of state and society. But where these concepts are not yet in the forefront (as in Pareto) or represent a later disguise (as in Carl Schmitt) the formal character of the theory becomes obvious. We will illustrate this directly with reference to the concept of authority.

Seen from the previous stage of its development, the relationship of authority and domination is defined in such a way that authority is not seen as a function of domination, a means of dominating, etc., but as the basis of domination. Authority as power over voluntary recognition and over the voluntary subordination to the will and insight of the bearer of authority, is a 'quality' which certain people have 'by birth'. This seems at first sight to be merely a revival of the charismatic justification of authority; but this is not the case, for the charisma of authority is itself in turn 'justified' (without direct recourse to God). Its prerequisite is that the bearer of authority should belong to a given 'people' (*Volkstum*) or a given 'race': his authority rests on the genuine 'identity of origin' of the leader and the led.[3] This very broad biological basis makes it possible to extend charismatic authority at will to any number of people throughout all social groups. How can the hierarchy of authorities necessary for social domination within a total-authority system be built on such a formation, if social development has made every 'generally valid' rational and material criterion for the necessity of the required system of authority impossible?

After every possible rational and material content of authority has fallen away only its mere form remains: authority as such becomes the essential feature of the authoritarian state.[4] The absolute activity and the absolute decision of the leading men obtain a value independent of the social content of their acts and decisions. The absolute acceptance of their decision, the 'heroic' sacrifice of the led, becomes a value independent of insight into its social purpose. According to this theory society is not divided into rich and poor, nor into happy and miserable, nor into progressive and reactionary, but with the cancellation of all these material contradictions, into leaders and led. And the specific hierarchy of such an authority system hangs (since the merely

3. Carl Schmitt, *Staat, Bewegung, Volk*, Hamburg, 1933, p. 42.
4. Koellreutter, *Allgemeine Staatslehre*, Tübingen, 1933, p. 58.

biological identity of origin on human society does not create any hierarchical gradations) in thin air: the leading 'élites' can be changed at will according to the requirements of the power groups standing behind them.

The formalism of the authoritarian theory of the state is the thin veil which reveals more than it conceals of the actual constellation of power. It shows the distance which separates the new theory from the genuine bourgeois philosophy of state and society. Quite unjustifiably it invokes Hegel's idea of the 'organic' state, to which its anti-rationalism is in utter contradiction. And not only that: Hegel's philosophy is entirely 'material' in these dimensions. It measures the rationality of the state by the material progress of society and is, as one can imagine, unsuited for the defence of the total-authoritarian state. And those of its defenders who make the struggle against German Idealism a heart-felt test of 'heroic realism' are here guided by a more accurate instinct.[5]

We shall not go into the theory of the totally authoritarian state;[6] we shall merely deal briefly with the theory of Sorel and Pareto as the transition to the present-day conception of authority.

A. SOREL

In Sorel's work (from 1898, the year in which *L'avenir socialiste des syndicats* appeared) the changed social situation, which necessitates changed tactics in the social struggle, is announced for the first time in sociological literature. Sorel's anarcho-syndicalism, his myth of the eschatological general strike, and of the proletarian violence which will 'unalterably' destroy the bourgeois order, seem a long way from the theory of the authoritarian state.

5. E.g. Ernst Krieck, in his essays in the periodical *Volk im Werden*, 1933, and in his book *Nationalpolitische Erziehung*.
6. Some of the connections between the total-authoritarian theory of the state and the problem discussed here are presented in *Zeitschrift für Sozialforschung*, III (1934), pp. 161ff.; trans. J. J. Shapiro and printed in Marcuse, *Negations*, Boston, 1968, pp. 3–42.

Sorel's position and influence is ambiguous;[7] we shall not attempt a new categorization here. We shall merely seek to bring out a few features of his work which pave the way for the theory of the authoritarian state.

Sorel's work is a typical example of the transformation of an abstract anti-authoritarian attitude into reinforced authoritarianism. Sorel struggles against organized centralism under the guidance of the party leadership, against the political organization of the proletariat as a 'power formation'; he demands a 'loosened, federalized world of proletarian institutions and associations'; an 'acephalous' socialist movement.[8] This anti-authoritarian anarchism is closely tied to the freeing of socialism from its economic basis: to its transformation into a 'metaphysics of morals'.[9] Materialism is abandoned at one of its decisive points: 'Socialism as the promise of sensual happiness is destruction'[10] – a sentence which is not made less significant even by Sorel's attacks on the Idealists.

The failure to recognize the meaning of authority as a condition of all (even socialist) 'organization' is only an expression of the removal of the socialist base just referred to. Proletarian 'violence', which along with the myth of the general strike is engaged in the final struggle with the bourgeois order, is separated from its economic and social purpose; it becomes an authority in itself. If its criterion no longer lies in material rationality and greater happiness in the social life-process towards which this force is directed, then there is no rational explanation whatsoever as to why proletarian should be 'better' than bourgeois violence. In its effect, Sorel's work, with its strong attacks on soggy liberalism, the degeneration of parliament, the cowardly willingness to compromise, the pre-eminence of intellectuals, etc., could just as easily be taken as a call to the bourgeoisie openly to use the power which it clearly factually possesses: 'It is here that the role of violence in history appears to us as singularly great, for it can, in

7. M. Freund, *Georges Sorel*, Frankfurt (1932), contains a good compilation of the material.
8. Ibid., p. 105.   9. Ibid.   10. Ibid., p. 104.

an indirect manner, so operate on the middle class as to awaken them to a sense of their own class sentiment.'[11]

In a decisive context Sorel himself emphasized the central importance of authority in the revolutionary movement: in connection with the question, on the basis of what authority the workers would be kept to increased labour-discipline in the production process after the struggle had been won.[12] The authority problem here appears under the heading of revolutionary 'discipline': Sorel establishes a basic distinction between the 'discipline which imposes a general stoppage of work on the workers, and the discipline which can lead them to handle machinery with greater skill'. He separates this positive authority from any external coercion and seeks its basis in a new 'ethics of the producers', a free integration of the individual into the collective. The 'acephaly' of socialism is transformed into the theory of revolutionary 'élites': social revolution gives birth to new 'social authorities' which 'grow organically' out of social life and take over the disciplinary leadership of the production process. The élite as bearer of future 'social authority' is an élite of 'social merit': it consists of 'groups, which enjoy a moral hegemony, a correct feeling for tradition and in a rational manner care for the future'.[13]

Direct lines of development have been drawn from Sorel's concept of social élites to both the proletarian 'avant-garde' of Leninism and to the élite 'leaders' of Fascism. Freed from the connection with a clear economic base and elevated into the 'moral' sphere, the conception of the élite tends towards formalistic authoritarianism. We shall now examine this tendency and briefly look at the form which the concept of the élite assumed in Pareto's sociology.

11. *Reflections on Violence*, trans. T. E. Hulme and J. Roth, London, 1970, p. 90. Cf. the apology for violent and cunning capitalists, op. cit., pp. 86ff.
12. Op. cit., p. 237.   13. Freund, op. cit., p. 215.

B. PARETO

Pareto's concept of the élite is part of a rationalist-positivist social theory which for the most part constructs the social 'equilibrium', especially the stability of domination and being dominated, on irrational factors: on the functioning of certain psychological mechanisms and their derivations. This sociology has achieved the ideal state of a complete 'freedom from values': with overt cynicism it dispenses with any 'moral' standpoint at all towards social processes. But it also dispenses with any standpoint towards their material content. The economic matter of social production and reproduction is of no interest to it: it only describes what is meant to have occurred on a given material base in all times and in all places. Nevertheless there is no doubt here as to the social groups in whose interest its formalism functions.

Society, which is necessarily and by nature heterogeneous, falls for Pareto into two strata: 'a lower stratum, the *non-élite*, and a higher stratum, the *élite*, which is divided into two: (a) a governing *élite*; (b) a non-governing *élite*.'[1]

The ruling élite is constituted on the basis of the degree of 'capacity' through which the individual distinguishes himself in his 'profession'. The 'profession' itself is not immediately relevant. The great courtesan and the great capitalist, the great confidence trickster and the great general, the great poet and the great gambler in this manner belong to the superior class, the élite,[2] and, if they somehow succeed in obtaining influence on the ruling group, also the 'governing élite'. To get 'on top' and be able to stay 'on top' becomes the only criterion of the élite, where 'on top' is defined purely formally as opposed to 'below': as the power and disposal over other people and things (no matter in which areas and for which ends this power is used).

In this conception of the élite there are still strong *liberal*

1. V. Pareto, *The Mind and Society: A Treatise on General Sociology*, trans. A. Bongiorno and A. Livingstone, New York, 1935.
2. Op. cit., para. 2027.

elements: the elbow-room of the aspiring bourgeoisie, the pure 'ideology of success', the individual possibility for everyone of rising from every social position. These are reinforced even more by the theory of the 'circulation of élites': new and refreshing streams from the *lower class* penetrate the *higher class* which in its constitution otherwise becomes increasingly rigid or flabby: 'The governing class is restored . . . by families which rise from the lower classes and bring with them the vigour and the proportions of residues necessary to keep it in power.'[3] Revolution, as a sudden and forceful replacement of one élite by another, is as it were only a disturbance in the normal circulation process.[4] It is a decisive feature of this theory that it replaces the material division of society into classes by a formal division, which itself in turn fluctuates, going diagonally through classes according to 'abilities' (*capacité*) – it interprets social domination as a system 'open' on all sides, into which elements from all social groups can be admitted. This interpretation, obscuring the real state of affairs, has become a central part of the authoritarian theory.

Even in the year in which Pareto's sociology appeared, the concept of the open system of domination only applied to a thin upper layer of social reality. From the point of view of the economic base the system of domination had long ago become closed along class lines, and the circulation of élites as he described it was only a peripheral feature of the social mechanism. But this made it all the easier for the ruling groups to adopt the theory of élites: against the firm background of the class-hierarchy a gentle circulation of élites was quite permissible; the economic and political apparatus was strong enough to regulate it within certain limits. What Pareto gave to the political disciples of his theory was above all the ability to grasp the central importance of certain psychological constants and mechanisms and to see the value of irrational, 'non-logical' actions for the stabilization of social domination. 'Ruling classes, like other social groups, perform both logical and non-logical actions, and the chief element in what happens is in fact the order, or system, not the conscious

3. Op. cit., para. 2054.   4. Op. cit., para. 2057.

will of individuals, who indeed may in certain cases be carried by the system to points where they would never have gone of deliberate choice.'[5] Pareto is the first to grasp and deal with the *psychological* problem of class domination in the monopolistic phase of capitalism; he is also the first to introduce authority into this social context.

It is the 'residues' which determine the organization of society; but the rationalized form of that organization is determined by the 'derivations' plus the 'appetites and interests' of which the 'residues' are the expression.[6] 'Residues' are certain socially effective psychological constants, which 'correspond' to certain simple instincts (appetites, tastes, inclinations) and interests possessed by men[7] and which constitute the real core of the 'non-logical actions' which are socially so relevant. The derivations can be described more or less as the rationalizations of the residues; they draw all their social strength from the residues which they transform into firm complexes of ideas.[8] If the residues are a 'manifestation of the emotions', the derivations are a 'manifestation of the need to reason'.[9] They function primarily for the maintenance of the 'social balance', or more concretely (as Pareto once says with regard to the social sciences): 'to persuade men to act in a certain manner considered useful to society.'[10]

The decisive feature is that these psychological constants and their rationalizations are now built into a theory of social domination. The stability and continuity of domination depend on the existence and effect of the 'residues' and 'derivations', and the particular proportion existing between the two elements. It is true that all domination rests on force and on the rationalization

5. Op. cit., para. 2254.   6. Op. cit., paras 861, 2205.
7. Op. cit., paras 850, 851.   8. Op. cit., para. 1397.   9. Op. cit., para. 1401.
  10. Op. cit., para. 1403. For the sake of clarification, we shall quote the general division into *residues* and *derivations* in Pareto (paras 888, 1419). RESIDUES: (1) Instinct for combinations; (2) Persistence of aggregates (and particularly religious and family feelings); (3) Need to express sentiments by external acts; (4) Residues connected with sociality (particularly the need for uniformity; pity and cruelty and the sentiments of social rank); (5) Integrity of the individual and his appurtenances; (6) The sex residue. DERIVATIONS: (1) Assertion; (2) Authority; (3) Accords with sentiments or principles; (4) Verbal proofs.

of force, but these can never on their own guarantee the stability and continuity of domination: the more or less voluntary consent (*consentement*) of the dominated is required: 'everywhere there is a governing class which is small in numbers and which maintains itself in power partly by force, and partly with the consent of the governed class, which is much more numerous.'[11] And this consent rests basically on the presence of the residues and the derivations in the right proportions and on the ability of the governing class to employ them as a 'means of government'. Pareto elaborated the ideological character of these means of domination, pointing out that their social value derives not from their truth content but from their 'social usefulness' in obscuring the real background to social organizations and evoking 'sentiments' which provide a psychological anchorage for and perpetually reproduce the existing structure of domination. 'To sum up, these derivatives express above all the feeling of those who are firmly in possession of power and wish to retain it, and also the much more general feeling of the usefulness of social stability.'[12] They serve 'to calm' the governed: it is impressed upon them that all power comes from God, that any rebellion is a crime and that to achieve what is just only 'reason' and never 'force' may be used. 'This derivative has the main aim of preventing the governed from giving battle on a terrain which is favourable to them.'[13] But all derivations are in turn dependent on the psychological constants which lie deeper down in the layer of the subconscious and the irrational: '. . . the policies of governments are the more effective, the more adept they are at utilizing existing residues.'[14] Pareto recognizes that the relatively slow change in these psychological constants, and their resistance to the more rapid upheavals of social phenomena, are of decisive importance for the continuity of the social life-process: 'it is that also which assures continuity in the history of human societies, since the category (a) [the residues] varies slightly or slowly.'[15]

This also gives us our definition of the authority problem. It

11. Op. cit., paras 2244, 2251.   12. Op. cit., para. 2184.
13. Op. cit., para. 2192.   14. Op. cit., para. 2247.   15. Op. cit., para. 2206.

appears firstly as derivation, in its rationalized, manifest shape, and secondly as residue: as the feeling which underlies this manifestation. Under the heading of derivation Pareto is really only describing various relationships of authority;[16] he points to the particular 'pertinacity' of the phenomenon of authority: 'the residue of authority comes down across the centuries without losing any of its vigour.'[17] More important are the residues of which the authority relationship is the derivation: as its psychological basis we must consider above all the class of sentiments grouped under the heading 'persistence of aggregates'.[18] Once again those sentiments among them which have their roots in the family are in the foreground: relationships of family and kindred groups, relations between the living and the dead, relations between a dead person and the things that belonged to him in life, etc. Pareto saw the importance of the family in the preparation, maintenance and transmission of authority; on several occasions he emphasized that any weakening of this persistence of aggregates would directly threaten the stability of social domination. The second psychological anchorage of authority he sees in the sentiments of inferiors: subordination, affection, reverence, fear. 'The existence of these sentiments is an indispensable condition for the constitution of animal societies, for the domestication of animals, for the ordering of human societies.'[19] Here too Pareto gives a 'value-free' description of the phenomena, but the social function of the phenomena described becomes clearly evident precisely though this open description, which foregoes any moral or intuitive concepts and focuses completely on the usefulness of the psychological constants and mechanisms as a means of government. Much more clearly, indeed, than in Sorel, who at some points preceded Pareto in the discovery of unconscious psychological realms as the ground for social stabilization.

Above all, Sorel drew attention to the role of the family in the realization of social '*valeurs de vertu*'. The family is the 'mysterious

16. Op. cit., paras 1434–63.
17. Op. cit., para. 1439.
18. Op. cit., para. 1434.   19. Op. cit., para. 1150.

region . . . whose organization influences all social relations';[20] in it the values most prized by current society are realized, as for example, 'respect for the human person, sexual fidelity, and devotion to the weak'.[21] But, in contrast to Pareto, Sorel gives the family a moral and sentimental consecration: he praises the monogamous family as the 'administrator of the morality of mankind' without recognizing its connection with bourgeois society. Owing to his use of an intuitionist method, with its tendency towards making a general survey of the whole rather than dissecting it analytically, Sorel here completely misses the dialectical character of social objects. He sees the family statically, in the manner of either-or, and he has the same manner of viewing authority. His only way, beyond the alternatives of authority in the class state and lack of authority in anarchy, is to escape into metaphysical-moral dimensions.

Pareto's positivist analysis has a much greater affinity to the dialectics of social reality. It also allows him to reveal the double-edged character of the authority relationship which behind the backs of the bearers of authority, as it were, works also in the interests of those subject to authority. 'Nor can it be said that the subject class is necessarily harmed when a governing class works for a result that will be advantageous to itself regardless of whether it will be beneficial, or the reverse, to the former. In fact there are very numerous cases where a governing class working for its own exclusive advantage has further promoted the welfare of a subject class.'[22]

Pareto did not investigate the dynamic of the double-edged character of this relationship any further; he mechanically placed the positive and the negative element side by side. However, it is this dynamic which characterizes history.

20. *Reflections on Violence*, p. 180.   21. Op. cit., p. 261.
22. Pareto, op. cit., para. 2249.

Sartre's Existentialism

[1948]

Publisher's note : This essay was written in English and first published in *Philosophy and Phenomenological Research,* vol. VIII, no. 3, 1948. The version printed below follows the original, except for the Postscript which was rewritten as a separate section by Marcuse for the essay's republication in German in his *Kultur und Gesellschaft,* vol. 2, Frankfurt, 1965. The translations from the French are those prepared by Beatrice Braude for Marcuse in 1948.

'The following pages deal with the sentiment of absurdity which prevails in our world.' This opening sentence of Albert Camus's *Le Mythe de Sisyphe* conveys the climate in which Existentialism originates. Camus does not belong to the existentialist school, but the basic experience which permeates his thought is also at the root of Existentialism. The time is that of the totalitarian terror: the Nazi regime is at the height of its power; France is occupied by the German armies. The values and standards of western civilization are co-ordinated and superseded by the reality of the fascist system. Once again, thought is thrown back upon itself by a reality which contradicts all promises and ideas, which refutes rationalism as well as religion, idealism as well as materialism. Once again, thought finds itself in the Cartesian situation and asks for the one certain and evident truth which may make it still possible to live. The question does not aim at any abstract idea but at the individual's concrete existence: what is the certain and evident experience which can provide the foundation for his life here and now, in this world?

Like Descartes, this philosophy finds its foundation in the self-certainty of the Cogito, in the consciousness of the Ego. But whereas for Descartes the self-certainty of the Cogito revealed a rational universe, governed by meaningful laws and mechanisms, the Cogito now is thrown into an 'absurd' world in which the brute fact of death and the irretrievable process of Time deny all meaning. The Cartesian subject, conscious of its power, faced an objective world which rewarded calculation, conquest, and domination; now the subject itself has become absurd and its world void of purpose and hope. The Cartesian *res cogitans* was opposed by a *res extensa* which responded to the former's knowledge and action; now the subject exists in an iron circle of frustration and failure. The Cartesian world, although held together by its own rationality, made allowance for a God who cannot deceive; now the world is godless in its very essence and leaves no room for any transcendental refuge.

The reconstruction of thought on the ground of absurdity does not lead to irrationalism. This philosophy is no revolt against reason; it does not teach abnegation or the *credo quia absurdum*. In the universal destruction and disillusion, one thing maintains itself: the relentless clarity and lucidity of the mind which refuses all shortcuts and escapes, the constant awareness that life has to be lived 'without appeal' and without protection. Man accepts the challenge and seeks his freedom and happiness in a world where there is no hope, sense, progress and morrow. This life is nothing but 'consciousness and revolt', and defiance is its only truth. Camus's *Mythe de Sisyphe* recaptures the climate of Nietzsche's philosophy:

Absurd man envisages a burning and icy universe, transparent and limited, where nothing is possible but everything is given, beyond which is extinction and the void.[1]

Thought moves in the night, but it is the night

of desperation which remains lucid, polar night, eve of the mind out of which will perhaps rise that white and integral clarity which designs every object in the light of the intellect.[2]

The experience of the 'absurd world' gives rise to a new and extreme rationalism which separates this mode of thought from all fascist ideology. But the new rationalism defies systematization. Thought is held in abeyance between the 'sentiment of absurdity' and its comprehension, between art and philosophy. Here, the ways part. Camus rejects existential philosophy: the latter must of necessity 'explain' the inexplicable, rationalize the absurdity and thus falsify its reality. To him, the only adequate expression is living the absurd life, and the artistic creation, which refuses to rationalize ('raisonner le concret') and which 'covers with images that which makes no sense' ('ce qui n'a pas de raison'). Sartre, on the other hand, attempts to develop the new experience into a philosophy of the concrete human existence: to elaborate the structure of 'being in an absurd world' and the ethics of 'living without appeal'.

1. A. Camus, *Le Mythe de Sisyphe*, Paris, 1946, pp. 83ff.   2. Ibid., pp. 89ff.

The development of Sartre's Existentialism spans the period of the war, the Liberation, and reconstruction. Neither the triumph nor the collapse of fascism produces any fundamental change in the existentialist conception. In the change of the political systems, in war and peace, before and after the totalitarian terror – the structure of the 'réalité humaine' remains the same. 'Plus ça change, plus c'est la même chose.' The historical absurdity which consists in the fact that after the defeat of fascism the world did not collapse, but relapsed into its previous forms, that it did not leap into the realm of freedom but restored with honour the old management – this absurdity lives in the existentialist conception. But it lives in the existentialist conception as a metaphysical, not as a historical fact. The experience of the absurdity of the world, of man's failure and frustration, appears as the experience of his ontological condition. As such, it transcends his historical condition. Sartre defines Existentialism as a doctrine according to which 'existence precedes and perpetually creates the essence'.[3] But in his philosophy, the existence of man, in creating his essence, is itself determined by the perpetually identical ontological structure of man, and the various concrete forms of man's existence serve only as examples of this structure. Sartre's existential analysis is a strictly philosophical one in the sense that it abstracts from the historical factors which constitute the empirical concreteness: the latter merely illustrates Sartre's metaphysical and meta-historical conceptions. In so far as Existentialism is a philosophical doctrine, it remains an idealistic doctrine: it hypostatizes specific historical conditions of human existence into ontological and metaphysical characteristics. Existentialism thus becomes part of the very ideology which it attacks, and its radicalism is illusory. Sartre's *L'Être et le Néant*, the philosophical foundation of Existentialism, is an ontological-phenomenological treatise on human freedom and could as such come out under the German occupation (1943). The essential freedom of man, as Sartre sees it, remains the same before, during,

3. In *Les lettres françaises*, 24 November, 1945. Cf. also Sartre, *L'existentialisme est un humanisme*, Paris, 1946, p. 17 (henceforth referenced in text thus: EH).

and after the totalitarian enslavement of man. For freedom is the very structure of human being and cannot be annihilated even by the most adverse conditions: man is free even in the hands of the executioner. Is this not Luther's comforting message of Christian liberty?

Sartre's book draws heavily on the philosophy of German idealism, in which Luther's Protestantism has found its transcendental stabilization. At the outset, Sartre's concept of the free subject is a reinterpretation of Descartes's Cogito, but its development follows the tradition of German rather than French rationalism. Moreover Sartre's book is in large parts a restatement of Hegel's *Phenomenology of Mind* and Heidegger's *Sein und Zeit*. French Existentialism revives many of the intellectual tendencies which were prevalent in the Germany of the twenties and which came to naught in the Nazi system.

But while these aspects seem to commit Existentialism to the innermost tendencies of bourgeois culture, others seem to point in a different direction. Sartre himself has protested against the interpretation of human freedom in terms of an essentially 'internal' liberty – an interpretation which his own analysis so strongly suggests – and he has explicitly linked up his philosophy with the theory of the proletarian revolution.[4]

Existentialism thus offers two apparently contradictory aspects: one the modern reformulation of the perennial ideology, the transcendental stabilization of human freedom in the face of its actual enslavement; the other the revolutionary theory which implies the negation of this entire ideology. The two conflicting aspects reflect the inner movement of existentialist thought[5] which reaches its object, the concrete human existence, only where it ceases to analyse it in terms of the 'free subject' and describes it in terms of what it has actually become: a 'thing' in a reified world. At the end of the road, the original position is reversed: the realization of human freedom appears, not in the

4. 'Matérialisme et Révolution' in *Les Temps modernes*, I, 9 and 10, Paris, June and July 1946 (henceforth referenced in text thus: TM, 9, 10).
5. Unless otherwise stated, 'existentialist' and 'Existentialism' refer only to Sartre's philosophy.

res cogitans, the 'Pour-soi', but in the *res extensa*, in the body as thing. Here, Existentialism reaches the point where philosophical ideology would turn into revolutionary theory. But at the same point, Existentialism arrests this movement and leads it back into the ideological ontology.

The elucidation of this hidden movement requires a critical restatement of some of the basic conceptions of *L'Être et le Néant*.

I

L'Être et le Néant starts with the distinction of two types of being – Being-for-itself (Pour-soi; consciousness, cogito) and Being-in-itself (En-soi). The latter (roughly identical with the world of things, objectivity) is characterized by having no relation to itself, being what it is, plainly and simply, beyond all becoming, change, and temporality (which emerge only with the Pour-soi), in the mode of utter contingency. In contrast, the Being-for-itself, identical with the human being, is the free subject which continually 'creates' its own existence; Sartre's whole book is devoted to its analysis. The analysis proceeds from the question as to the 'relationship' (*rapport*) between these two types of being. Following Heidegger, subjectivity and objectivity are understood, not as two separate entities between which a relationship must only be established, but as essential 'togetherness', and the question aims at the full and concrete structure of this togetherness.

The concrete can be only the synthetic totality of which consciousness as well as phenomenon (Being-in-itself) constitute but moments. The concrete – that is man in the world. . . .[6]

The question thus aims at the full and concrete structure of the human being as being-in-the-world (*la réalité humaine*).

In order to elucidate this structure, the analysis orients itself on certain typical 'human attitudes' (*conduites exemplaires*). The first

6. *L'Être et le Néant*, Paris, 1943, p. 38 (henceforth referenced in text thus: EN).

of these is the attitude of questioning (*l'attitude interrogative*), the specific human attitude of interrogating, reflecting on himself and his situation at any given moment. The interrogation implies a threefold (potential) negativity: the not-knowing, the permanent possibility of a negative answer, and the limitation expressed in the affirmative answer: 'It is thus and not otherwise.' The interrogative attitude thus brings to the fore the fact that man is surrounded by and permeated with negativity:

It is the permanent possibility of not-being, outside of us and in us, which conditions our questions about being (EN, p. 40).

However, the negativity implied in the interrogative attitude serves only as an example and indication of the fundamental fact that negativity surrounds and permeates man's entire existence and all his attitudes:

The necessary condition which makes it possible to say 'no' is that the not-being is perpetually present, in us and outside of us, is that the void haunts being (EN, p. 47).

Negativity originates with and constantly accompanies the human being, manifesting itself in a whole series of negations (*néantisations*) with which the human being experiences, comprehends, and acts upon himself and the world. The totality of these negations constitutes the very being of the subject: man exists 'as perpetually detaching himself from what is' (EN, p. 73); he transcends himself as well as his objects toward his and their possibilities, he is always 'beyond' his situation, 'wanting' his full reality. By the same token, man does not simply exist like a thing (*en soi*) but makes himself and his world exist, 'creates' himself and his world at any moment and in any situation.

This characterization of the 'réalité humaine' (which is hardly more than a restatement of the idealistic conception of the Cogito or Selfconsciousness, especially in the form in which the *Phenomenology of Mind* develops this conception) furnishes the fundamental terms of Sartre's Existentialism – the terms which guide the subsequent development of his philosophy. There is first of all the identification of the human being with liberty. The series of negations by which man constitutes himself and his world at the same time constitutes his essential freedom:

[Liberty] arises with the negation of the appeals of the world, it appears from the moment when I detach myself from the world where I had engaged myself so that I perceive myself as consciousness (EN, p. 77).

Human freedom thus conceived is not one quality of man among others, nor something which man possesses or lacks according to his historical situation, but is the human being itself and as such:

That which we call liberty is therefore indistinguishable from the being of the 'human reality'. Man does not first exist in order to be free subsequently, but there is no difference between his being and his free-being [being-free] (EN, p. 61).

Secondly, from the identification of the human being with freedom follows the full and unqualified responsibility of man for his being. In order to concretize his idea of freedom and responsibility, Sartre adapts Heidegger's emphasis on the *Geworfenheit* of man into a pre-given 'situation'. Man always finds himself and his world in a situation which appears as an essentially external one (the situation of his family, class, nation, race, etc.). Likewise, the objects of his environment are not his own: they were manufactured as commodities; their form and their use are pre-given and standardized. However, this essential 'contingency' of man's situation is the very condition of life of his freedom and responsibility. His contingent situation becomes 'his' in so far as he 'engages' himself in it, accepts or rejects it. No power in heaven or on earth can force him to abdicate his freedom: he himself, and he alone is to decide and choose what he is.

Thirdly, man is by definition (that is to say, by virtue of the fact that he is, as 'être-pour-soi', the permanent realization of his possibilities) nothing but self-creation. His Being is identical with his activity (action), or rather with his (free) acts. 'L'homme est ce qu'il fait', and, vice versa, everything that is is a 'human enterprise'.

Man engages in his life, designs its shape, and outside this shape, there is nothing. . . . Man is nothing else but a series of enterprises (undertakings), he is the sum total, the organization, the ensemble of the relationships which constitute these enterprises (EH, pp. 57ff.).

Human existence is at any moment a 'project' that is being realized, freely designed and freely executed by man himself, or, man's existence is nothing but his own fundamental project. This dynamics is based on the fact that man's actual situation never coincides with his possibilities, that his Being is essentially being-in-want-of (*manque*). However, the want is not want of something, so that the want would disappear with its satisfaction; it is the manifestation of the basic negativity of the human being:

Human reality is not something which first exists in order to want for this or that later; it exists as want and in close synthetic union with what it wants. . . . In its coming into being, (human) reality is cognizant of itself as an incomplete being. . . . Human reality is a perpetual reaching for a coincidence which is never accomplished (EN, pp. 132ff).

The existentialist dynamics is thus not an aimless and senseless one: the 'projet fondamental' which is man's existence aims at the ever lacking coincidence with himself, at his own completeness and totality. In other words, the *Pour-soi* constantly strives to become *En-soi*, to become the stable and lasting foundation of his own being. But this project, which would make the *Pour-soi* an *En-soi* and vice-versa, is eternally condemned to frustration, and this ontological frustration shapes and permeates the entire Being of man:

Human reality suffers in its being because it emerges into existence as though perpetually haunted by a totality which it is without being able to be it, since in effect it cannot attain Being-in-itself without losing Being-for-itself. It is therefore essentially unhappy consciousness (EN, p. 134).

Sartre's ontological analysis has herewith reached its centre: the determination of the human being as frustration, *Scheitern*, 'échec'. All fundamental human relationships, the entire 'human enterprise' are haunted by this frustration. However, precisely because frustration is permanent and inevitable (since it is the ontological characteristic of the human being), it is also the very foundation and condition of human freedom. The latter is what it is only in so far as it 'engages' man within his contingent situation, which in turn, since it is a pregiven situation, prevents him once and for all from ever becoming the founder of his own Being-for-himself. The circle of ontological identifications is thus closed: it combines Being and Nothing, freedom and frustration, self-responsible choice and contingent determination. The *coincidentia oppositorum* is accomplished, not through a dialectical process, but through their simple establishment as ontological characteristics. As such, they are transtemporally simultaneous and structurally identical.

The ontological analysis of the *l'ê tre-pour-soi* furnishes the framework for the interpretation of the *l'existence d'autrui*, of the Other. This transition presents a decisive methodological problem. Sartre has followed so closely the idealistic conception of Self-Consciousness (*Cogito*) as the transcendental origin and 'creator' of all Being that he constantly faces the danger of transcendental solipsism. He takes up the challenge in an excellent critique of Husserl and Heidegger (and Hegel), in which he shows that their attempts to establish the Being of the Other as an independent ontological fact fail, that in all of them the existence of the Other is more or less absorbed into the existence of the Ego (EN, pp. 288ff.). Sartre himself renounces all efforts to derive ontologically the existence of the Other:

The existence of the Other has the nature of a contingent and irreductible fact. The Other is encountered; he is not constituted (by the Ego) (EN, p. 307).

However, he continues, the Cogito provides the only point of departure for the understanding of the existence of the Other because all 'fait contingent', all 'nécessit de fait' is such only for and by virtue of the Cogito:

The *Cogito* (examined once again) must cast me outside of itself onto the Other.... We must ask the Being-for-itself to give us the Being-for-another; absolute immanence must cast us back into absolute transcendence (EN, pp. 308ff.).

The experience of the Cogito which establishes the independent existence of the Other is that of 'being-looked-at by another [man]'. The relation of being-seen by another (man) constitutes, for the Cogito, 'l'existence d'autrui':

My perception of the Other in the world as probably being (a) man relates to my permanent possibility of being-seen-by-him. . . . On principle, the Other is he who looks at me (EN, p. 315).

'Le regard d'autrui' becomes constitutive of the fundamental inter-human relationships. Sartre illustrates this by the example of a jealous lover who peeps through a keyhole. In this situation, he suddenly feels himself seen by another man. With this glance, he becomes somebody whom another (man) knows in his innermost being, who *is* that which the other sees. His own possibilities are taken away from him (he cannot hide where he intended to hide, he cannot know what he desired to know, etc.); his entire world at once has a new, different focus, structure, and meaning: it emerges as the other's world and as a world-for-the-other. His being thus emerges, in a strict sense, as being 'at the liberty' of the other: from now on,

it is a question of my being as it is inscribed in and through the liberty of the Other. Everything occurs as though I possessed a dimension of being from which I was separated by a profound void, and this void is the liberty of the Other (EN, p. 320).

The other's glance turns me into an object, turns my existence into 'nature', alienates my possibilities, 'steals' my world.

By the very emergence of his existence, I have an appearance, a nature; the existence of the Other is my original sin (EN, p. 321).

The appearance of the Other thus transforms the world of the Ego into a world of conflict, competition, alienation, 'reification'. The Other, that is 'la mort cachée de mes possibilités'; the Other, that is he who usurps my world, who makes me an 'object of appreciation and appraisal', who gives me my 'value'.

Thus, being seen constitutes me as being without any defence against a liberty which is not my liberty. In this sense we may consider ourselves as 'slaves' in so far as we appear to the Other. But this bondage is not the historical and surmountable result of the life of an abstract consciousness (EN, pp. 391ff.).

This conception of the Other as the irreconcilable antagonist of the Ego now serves as the basis for Sartre's interpretation of the interhuman relationships. They are primarily corporal relationships (as already indicated by the constitutive role attributed to the '*regard*'). However, the body enters these relationships not merely as a physical-biological 'thing' but as the manifestation of the individuality and contingency of the Ego in his 'rapport transcendant' with the world (EN, pp. 391ff.). The original experience of the Other as the source of alienation and reification calls for two fundamental reactions which constitute the two fundamental types of interhuman relationships: (1) the attempt, on the part of the Ego, to deny the liberty and mastery of the Other and to make him into an objective thing, totally dependent on the Ego; or, (2) to assimilate his liberty, to accept it as the foundation of the Ego's own liberty and thereby to regain the free Ego (EN, p. 430). The first attitude leads to Sadism, the second to Masochism. But the essential frustration which marks all existential 'projects' of the Ego also characterizes these attempts: the complete enslavement of the Other transforms him into a thing, annihilates him *as* the (independent) Other and thus annihilates the very goal which the Ego desired to attain. Similarly, the complete assimilation to the Other transforms the Ego into a thing, annihilates it as a (free) subject and thus annihilates the very freedom which the Ego desired to regain. The frustration suffered in the sadistic attitude leads to the adoption of the masochistic attitude, and vice versa:

Each of them implies the death of the other, that is, the failure of one motivates the adoption of the other. Therefore, my relations with the Other are not dialectical but circular, although each attempt is enriched by the failure of the other (EN, p. 230).

The two fundamental human relationships produce and destroy themselves 'en cercle' (EN, p. 431).

The only remaining possible attitude toward the Other is that which aims directly at his utter destruction, namely, hate. However, this attitude too fails to achieve the desired result: the liberation of the Ego. For even after the death of the Other (or the

Others), he (or they) remain as 'having been' and thus continue to haunt the Ego's conscience.

The conclusion: since

all the complex attitudes of men toward each other are only variations of these two attitudes (and of hate) (EN, 477)

there is no breaking out of the circle of frustration. On the other hand, man *must* 'engage' in one of these attitudes because his very reality consists in nothing but such 'engagement'. Thus, after the failure of each attempt,

there is no alternative left for the Being-for-itself but to return into the circle and to be tossed about indefinitely from one to the other of these two fundamental attitudes (EN, p. 484).

Here, the image of Sisyphus and his absurd task appears most naturally as the very symbol of man's existence. Here, too, Sartre deems it appropriate to add in a footnote that 'these considerations do not exclude the possibility of a morality of liberation and salvation'; however, such a morality requires a 'radical conversion, which we cannot discuss in this place'.

II

The main ontological argument is concluded by this analysis of the fundamental interhuman relationships; the remaining part of the book is taken up by a synopsis of the 'réalité humaine' as it has emerged in the preceding interpretation. The synopsis is guided by the concept of freedom. The ontological analysis had started with the identification of Ego (Cogito) and freedom. The subsequent development of the existential characteristics of the Ego had shown how his freedom is inextricably tied up within the contingency of his 'situation', and how all attempts to make himself the free foundation of his existence are eternally condemned to frustration. The last part of Sartre's book resumes the discussion at this point in order to justify finally, in the face of these apparent contradictions, the ontological identification of human being and freedom.

For Sartre, the justification cannot be that which is traditionally featured in idealistic philosophy, namely, the distinction between transcendental and empirical freedom. This solution cannot suffice for him because his analysis of the Ego does not remain within the transcendental-ontological dimension. Ever since his Ego, in the Third Part of his book, had to acknowledge the existence of the Other as a plain 'nécessité de fait', his philosophy had left the realm of pure ontology and moved within the ontic-empirical world.

Sartre thus cannot claim that his philosophy of freedom is a transcendental-ontological one and therefore neither committed nor equipped to go into the (empirical) actuality of human freedom. Quite in contrast to Heidegger (whose existential analysis claims to remain within the limits of pure ontology), Sartre's philosophy professes to be an '-ism', Existentialism, that is to say, a *Weltanschauung* which involves a definite attitude toward life, a definite morality, 'une doctrine d'action' (EH, p. 95). Sartre must therefore show the actuality of the entire 'existentialist' conception of man. The last part of *L'Être et le Néant* is chiefly dedicated to this task.

Sartre attempts to demonstrate that the ontological definition actually defines the 'réalité humaine', that man is in *reality* the free being-for-himself which the existential ontology posits.

We have seen that, according to Sartre, man, as a Being-for-itself that does not simply exist but exists only in so far as it 'realizes' itself, is essentially act, action, activity.

Man is free because he is not merely himself but present to himself. The being which (merely) is what it is cannot be free. Freedom is, actually, the void which is in man's heart and which forces the human reality to *create itself* rather than to *be* (EN, p. 516).

This 'se faire' applies to every single moment in man's life: whatever he does or does not do, whatever he is or is not – he himself has 'chosen' it, and his choice was absolutely and perfectly free:

Our existence is actually our original choice (EN, p. 539).

As against this proclamation of the absolute freedom of man, the objection arises immediately that man is in reality determined by his specific socio-historical situation, which in turn determines the scope and content of his liberty and the range of his 'choice'.

'La réalité humaine', that is, for example, a French worker under the German occupation, or a sales clerk in New York. His liberty is limited, and his choice is prescribed to such an extent that their interpretation in the existentialist terms appear like mere mockery. Sartre accepts the challenge and sets out to prove that even in a situation of extreme determinateness, man is and remains absolutely free. True, he says, the worker may live in a state of actual enslavement, oppression, and exploitation, but he has freely 'chosen' this state, and he is free to change it at any moment. He has freely chosen it because 'enslavement', 'oppression', 'exploitation' have meaning only for and by the 'Pour-soi' which has posited and accepted these 'values' and suffers them. And he is free to change his condition at any moment because these values will cease to exist for him as soon as he ceases to posit, accept, and suffer them. Sartre understands this freedom as a strictly individual liberty, the decision to change the situation as a strictly individual project, and the act of changing as a strictly individual enterprise.

The fact that for the individual worker such individual action would mean loss of his job and probably lead to starvation, imprisonment, and even death, does not invalidate his absolute freedom, for it is again a matter of free choice to value life and security higher than starvation, imprisonment, and death. The existentialist proposition thus leads inevitably to the reaffirmation of the old idealistic conception that man is free even in chains, or, as Sartre formulates it: 'but the executioner's tools cannot dispense us from being free' (EN, p. 587).

However, Sartre does not want to have this proposition interpreted in the sense of a merely 'internal' freedom. The slave is literally and actually free to break his chains, for the very meaning ('sens') of his chains reveals itself only in the light of the goal which he chooses: to remain a slave or to risk the worst in order to liberate himself from enslavement.

If, for example, he chooses to revolt, slavery, far from being first an obstacle to this revolt, takes its meaning and its coefficient of adversity only from this revolt (EN, p. 635).

All adversities, obstacles, limitations to our liberty, are thus posited by and emerge ('surgir') with ourselves; they are parts of the free 'project' which is our existence (EN, pp. 562, 569).

The coefficient of adversity of things . . . cannot be an argument against our freedom because it is *through us*, that is, through the preliminary setting of a goal that this coefficient of adversity emerges. The very rock which displays profound resistance if I wish to change its position, will, on the other hand, be a precious help to me if I wish to climb it in order to contemplate the countryside (EN, p. 562).

Sartre does not hesitate to push this conception to its last consequences. Being a Frenchman, a Southerner, a worker, a Jew – is the result of the 'Pour soi's' own 'making'. By the same token, all the restrictions, obstacles, prohibitions which society places upon the Jew 'exist' only because and in so far as the Jew 'chooses' and accepts them:

'No Jews allowed here', 'Jewish restaurant, Aryans forbidden to enter', etc., can only have meaning on and through the foundation of my free choice (EN, p. 607).

It is only by recognizing the liberty . . . of the anti-Semites and by assuming this being-Jewish which I represent to them, that being-Jewish will appear as the external objective limit of my situation. If, on the other hand, it pleases me to consider them simply as objects, my being-Jewish disappears immediately to give way to the simple consciousness of being a free transcendence (EN, p. 610).

The treatise on human freedom has here reached the point of self-abdication. The persecution of the Jews, and 'les tenailles du bourreau' are the terror which is the world today, they are the brute reality of unfreedom. To the existentialist philosopher, however, they appear as examples of the existence of human freedom. The fact that Sartre's demonstration is ontologically correct and a time-honoured and successful feature of idealism only proves the remoteness of this demonstration from the 'réalité humaine'. If philosophy, by virtue of its existential-ontological concepts of man or freedom, is capable of demonstrating that the persecuted Jew and the victim of the executioner are and remain absolutely free and masters of a self-responsible choice, then these philosophical concepts have declined to the level of a mere ideology, an ideology which offers itself as a most handy justification for the persecutors and executioners – them-

'Pour-soi', *qua* 'Pour-soi', is and remains free in the hands of the selves an important part of the 'réalité humaine'. It is true that the numerous executioners who provide the numerous opportunities for exercising existential freedom, but this freedom has shrunk to a point where it is wholly irrelevant and thus cancels itself. The free choice between death and enslavement is neither freedom nor choice, because both alternatives destroy the 'réalité humaine' which is supposed to be freedom. Established as the locus of freedom in the midst of a world of totalitarian oppression, the 'Pour-soi', the Cartesian Cogito, is no longer the jumping-off point for the conquest of the intellectual and material world, but the last refuge of the individual in an 'absurd world' of prostration and failure. In Sartre's philosophy, this refuge is still equipped with all the paraphernalia which characterized the heydays of individualistic society. The 'Pour-soi' appears with the attributes of absolute autonomy, perpetual ownership, and perpetual appropriation (just as the Other appears as the one who usurps, appropriates, and appraises my world, as the 'thief' of my possibilities). Behind the nihilistic language of Existentialism lurks the ideology of free competition, free initiative, and equal opportunity. Everybody can 'transcend' his situation, carry out his own project: everybody has his absolutely free choice. However adverse the conditions, man must 'take it' and make compulsion his self-realization. Everybody is master of his destiny. But in the face of an 'absurd world' without meaning and reward, the attributes of the heroic period of bourgeois society assume naturally an absurd and illusory character. Sartre's 'Pour-soi' is closer to Stirner's *Einziger und sein Eigentum* than to Descartes's *Cogito*. In spite of Sartre's insistence on the Ego's *Geworfenheit* (being thrown into a pregiven contingent situation), the latter seems to be wholly absorbed by the Ego's ever-transcending power which posits, as its own free project, all the obstacles encountered on its way. True, man is thrown into a 'situation' which he himself has not created, and this situation may be such that it 'alienates' his freedom, degrades him into a thing. The process of 'reification' appears in manifold forms in Sartre's philosophy: as the subordination of the 'Pour-soi' to the standardized technics of everyday life (EN, pp. 495ff., 594), and as the interchangeability of the individual (EN, p. 496). But to Sartre reification as well as its negation are only obstacles on which man's freedom thrives and feeds itself: they become parts of the Cogito's existential project, and the whole process once again serves to illustrate the perpetual liberty of the 'Pour-soi' which finds only itself in the most alienated situation.

The Self-consciousness that finds itself in its Being-for-Others: Sartre's Existentialism thus revives Hegel's formula for the free and rational condition of man. To Hegel, however, the realization of this condition is only the goal and end of the entire historical process. Sartre takes the ontological shortcut and transforms the process into the metaphysical condition of the 'Pour-soi'. Sartre accomplishes this transformation by a trick: the term 'Pour-soi' covers the We as well as the I; it is the collective as well as the individual self-consciousness.

le Pour-soi 'fait qu'il soit daté par ses techniques' . . . . (EN, p. 604).

. . . se fait Français, meridional, ouvrier (EN, p. 606).

Thus, the 'Pour-soi' creates nation, class, class distinctions, etc., makes them parts of his own free 'project', and, consequently, is 'responsible' for them. This is the fallacious identification of the ontological and historical subject. While it is a truism to say that the *ideas* 'nation', class', etc., arise with and 'exist' only for the 'Pour-soi', 'nation', 'class', etc., are not created by the 'Pour-soi', but by the action and reaction of specific social groups under specific historical conditions. To be sure, these groups are composed of individuals who may be ontologically characterized as 'Pour-soi', but such characterization is totally irrelevant to the understanding of their concreteness. The ontological concept of the 'Pour-soi', which defines equally the wage earner and the entrepreneur, the sales clerk and the intellectual, the serf and the landlord, prejudices the analysis of their concrete existence: in so far as the different existential situations are interpreted in terms of the realization of the 'Pour-soi', they are reduced to the abstract denominator of a universal essence. In subsuming the various historical subjects under the ontological idea of the 'Pour-soi', and making the latter the guiding principle of the existential philosophy, Sartre relegates the specific differences which constitute the very concreteness of human existence to mere manifestations of the universal essence of man – thus offending against his own thesis that 'existence creates the essence'. Reduced to the role of examples, the concrete situations cannot bridge the gap between the terms of ontology and those of existence. The ontological foundation of Existentialism frustrates its effort to develop a philosophy of the concrete human existence.

The gap between the terms of ontology and those of existence is concealed by the equivocal use of the term 'is'. Sartre's 'is' functions indiscriminately and without mediation as the copula in the definition of the essence of man, and as the predication of his actual condition. In this twofold sense, the 'is' occurs in proposition like 'Man is free', 'is his own project', etc. The fact that, in the empirical reality, man is not free, not his own project, is obliterated by the inclusion of the negation into the definition of 'free', 'project', etc. But Sartre's concepts are, in spite of his dialectical style and the pervasive role of the negation, decidedly undialectical. In his philosophy, the negation is no force of its own but is *a priori* absorbed into the affirmation. True, in Sartre's analysis, the development of the subject through its negation into the self-conscious realization of its project appears as a process, but the process-character is illusory: the subject moves in a circle.

Existentialist freedom is safe from the tribulations to which man is subjected in the empirical reality. However, in one respect, the empirical reality does not affect Sartre's concept of human liberty. Although the freedom which is operative as the very being of the 'Pour-soi' accompanies man in all situations, the scope and degree of his freedom varies in his different situations: it is smallest and dimmest where man is most thoroughly 'reified', where he is least 'Pour-soi'. For example, in situations where he is reduced to the state of a thing, an instrument, where he exists almost exclusively as body, his 'Pour-soi' has all but disappeared. But precisely here, where the ontological idea of freedom seems to evaporate together with the 'Pour-soi', where it falls almost entirely into the sphere of things – at this point a new image of human freedom and fulfilment arises. We shall now discuss the brief appearance of this image in Sartre's philosophy.

III

In illustrating the permanent transcendence of the 'Pour-soi' beyond every one of its contingent situations (a transcendence which, however free, remains afflicted with the very contingency it transcends), Sartre uses the term 'jouer à être'. He introduces the term in describing the behaviour of a 'garçon de café'. The waiter's behaviour exemplifies the manner in which man has to 'make himself what he is' (EN, p. 98): every single one of the waiter's motions, attitudes, and gestures shows that he is constantly aware of the obligation to be a waiter and to behave as a waiter, and that he is trying to discharge this obligation. He 'is' not a waiter, he rather 'makes' himself a waiter. Now 'being a waiter' consists of a set of standardized and mechanized motions, attitudes, and gestures which almost amount to being an automaton. Such a set of behaviour patterns is expected from a waiter, and he tries to live up to this expectation: he 'plays' the waiter, he 'plays' his own being. The obligation to be what he is thus becomes a play, a performance, and the freedom of the 'Pour-soi' to transcend his contingent condition (being-a-waiter) shows forth as the freedom to play, to perform.

Can the example be generalized so that the transcendence of the *Cogito*, the realization of its freedom, shows forth as a permanent and ubiquitous play, a 'jouer à être'? Sartre strongly suggests such generalization, although he does not make the concept of 'jouer a l'être' the guiding idea of his analysis. But at least at one decisive place, he does link it with the general condition of man. The essential contingency of human existence coagulates in the fact that man is and remains his past, and that this past prevents him once and for all from freely creating his being.

[The past is] the fact which cannot determine the content of my motivations but which passes through them with its contingence because they can neither suppress nor change it. The past is rather that which the motivations necessarily carry with them and modify.... This is what causes me, at each instant, *not to be* a diplomat or a sailor, but rather a professor, although I can only play this being without ever being able to rejoin it (EN, pp. 162ff.).

But if man can only play his being, then the freedom of the 'Pour-soi' is in reality nothing but his ability to act a prescribed role in a play in which neither his part nor its interpretation is of his own free choosing. The *Cogito*'s transcendence, instead of showing forth as the very root of man's power over himself and his world, would appear as the very token of his being for others. Moreover, and most important, his liberty would lie, not in the 'free' transcendence of the *Cogito* but rather in its negation: in the cancellation of that performance in which he has to play permanently the 'Pour-soi' while actually being-for-others. But the negation of the 'Pour-soi' is the 'En-soi', the negation of the *Cogito* is the state of being a thing, nature. The analysis is thus driven into the sphere of reification: this sphere seems to contain the possibility of a freedom and satisfaction which are quite different from that of the *Cogito* and its activity.

The state of reification as the lever for the liberation of man appears in Sartre's philosophy on two different levels: (1) on the level of the individual existence as the 'attitude of (sexual) desire', (2) on the socio-historical level as the revolutionary attitude of the proletariat. Sartre does not establish the link between these two levels: whereas the first is intrinsically connected with the main philosophical argument, the second remains extraneous to it and is developed only outside *L'Être et le Néant*, in the article 'Matérialisme et Revolution'.

According to Sartre, 'le désir' is essentially 'le désir sexuel'. To him, sexuality is not 'un accident contingent lié à notre nature physiologique', but a fundamental structure of the 'Pour-soi' in its being-for-others (EN, pp. 452ff.). He had previously described the two chief types of human relations in terms of sexual relations (sadism and masochism); now sexuality becomes the force which cancels the entire apparatus of existentialist freedom, activity, and morality.

'Le désir' becomes this force first by virtue of the fact that it is the negation of all activity, all 'performance': 'Le désir n'est pas désir de *faire*' (EN, p. 454).

Whatever activity the desire may engender, all 'technique amoureuse', accrues to it from outside. The desire itself is 'purement et simplement désir d'un objet transcendant', namely, 'désir d'un corps'. And this object is desired purely and simply as what it is and appears, in its brute 'facticité'.

In describing the 'désir sexuel' and its object, Sartre emphasizes the characteristics which make this relation the very opposite of the 'Pour-soi' and its activity:

... in sexual desire consciousness is as though dulled; one appears to let oneself be pervaded by the mere facticity (of one's existence as body), to cease fleeing from it, and to glide into a passive ascent to desire (EN, p. 457).

This is the coming-to-rest of the transcending *Cogito*, the paralysis of its freedom, 'projects' and performances. And the same force which cancels the incessant performance of the 'Pour-soi' also cancels its alienation. The 'désir sexuel' reveals its object as stripped of all the attitudes, gestures, and affiliations which make it a standardized instrument, reveals the 'corps comme chair' and thereby 'comme révélation fascinante de la facticité' (EN, p. 458). Enslavement and repression are cancelled, not in the sphere of purposeful, 'projective' activity, but in the sphere of the 'corps vécu comme chair', in the 'trame d'inertie' (EN, p. 458). By the same token, the image of fulfilment and satisfaction is, not in the ever transcending 'Pour-soi', but in its own negation, in its pure 'être-là', in the fascination of its being an object (for itself and for others). Reification itself thus turns into liberation.

The 'désir sexuel' accomplishes this negation of the negation not as a mere relapse into animal nature, but as a free and liberating human relation. In other words, the 'désir sexuel' is what it is only as activity of the 'Pour-soi', an activity, however, which is rather the negation of all activity and which aims at the liberation of the pure presence to its object. This activity is 'la caresse':

Desire expresses itself through caress as thought does through language (EN, p. 459). The breaking of the reified world, the revelation of the 'Chair . . . comme contingence pure de la présence' is only brought about by the 'caresse':

Caress causes the Other to be born as flesh for me and for himself. . . . Caress reveals the flesh by divesting the body of its action, by isolating it from the possibilities which surround it . . . (EN, p. 459).

It is thus in complete isolation from its possibilities, oblivious of its freedom and responsibility, divested of all its performances and achievements, in being a pure 'object' ('corps vécu comme chair') that the *Ego* finds itself in the Other. The relationships among men have become relationships among things, but this fact is no longer concealed and distorted by societal fetishes and ideologies. Reification no longer serves to perpetuate exploitation and toil but is in its entirety determined by the 'pleasure principle'.

Moreover, the fundamental change in the existential structure caused by the 'désir sexuel' affects not only the individuals concerned but also their (objective) world. The 'désir sexuel' has, according to Sartre, a genuinely cognitive function: it reveals the (objective) world in a new form.

If my body . . . is no longer felt to be the instrument which can be used by any other instrument, that is, as the synthetic organization of my acts in the world, if it is lived as flesh, it is then, as reverberation of my flesh, that I seize

the objects in the world. This means that I make myself passive in relationship to them.... A contact as caress means that my perception is not
utilization of an object and not the transcending of the present with a view
to a goal. To perceive an object, in the attitude of desire, is to caress myself
with it (EN, p. 461).

The 'attitude désirante' thus releases the objective world as well
as the *Ego* from domination and manipulation, cancels their
'instrumentality', and, in doing so, reveals their own pure
presence, their 'chair'.

We have seen that the fixation on the property relation permeates Sartre's entire book: not only the relation between the
'Pour-soi' and 'En-soi', but also the fundamental relationships
between the 'Pour-soi' and 'l'autrui', the inter-human relationships are eventually interpreted in terms of 'appropriation'.
Finally, the 'désir sexuel' is the attempt to appropriate freely the
liberty of the Other. That all these appropriations turn out to be
futile and self-defeating only renews and perpetuates the attempt
to appropriate. And the one point, the one moment which appears
as fulfilment, possession, is where and when man becomes a
thing: body, flesh; and his free activity becomes complete inertia:
caressing the body as thing. The *Ego*, thus far separated from the
'things' and therefore dominating and exploiting them, now has
become a 'thing' itself – but the thing, in turn, has been freed to
its own pure existence. The Cartesian gap between the two
substances is bridged in that both have changed their substantiality. The *Ego* has lost its character of being 'Pour-soi', set
off from and against everything other-than-the *Ego*, and its object
have assumed a subjectivity of their own. The 'attitude désirante'
thus reveals (the possibility of) a world in which the individual is
in complete harmony with the whole, a world which is at the same
time the very negation of that which gave the *Ego* freedom only to
enforce its free submission to necessity. With the indication of
this form of the 'réalité humaine', Existentialism cancels its own
fundamental conception.

In the sphere of the individual existence, the cancellation is
only a temporary one: the free satisfaction afforded in the 'attitude

désirante' is bound to end in new frustration. Confined within the circle of sadistic and masochistic relationships, man is driven back into the transcending activity of the 'Pour-soi'. But the image which has guided Sartre's analysis to seek the reality of freedom in the sphere of reification and alienation also leads him into the socio-historical sphere. He tests his conception in a critical discussion of Historical Materialism.

IV

In Sartre's interpretation of the socio-historical sphere, the reification of the subject (which, in the private sphere, appeared as the 'corps vécu comme chair') manifests itself in the existence of the industrial worker. The modern entrepreneur tends to

reduce the worker to the state of a thing by assimilating his behaviour to [that of] properties (TM, 10, p. 15).

In view of the brute mechanization of the worker and his work, in view of his complete subjugation to the capitalistic machine process, it would be ridiculous to preach him the 'internal' liberty which the philosophers have preached throughout the centuries:

The revolutionary himself . . . distrusts freedom. And rightly so. There has never been lack of prophets to proclaim to him that he was free, and each time in order to cheat him (TM, 10, p. 14).

Sartre mentions in this connection the Stoic concept of freedom, Christian liberty, and Bergson's idea of freedom:

They all come back to a certain internal liberty which man can preserve in any situation whatsoever. This internal liberty is nothing but an idealistic mystification . . . (TM, 10, p. 14).

It would seem that Sartre's own ontological concept of freedom would well be covered by this verdict of 'idealistic mystification', and *L'Être et le Néant* provides little ground for evading it. Now he recognizes the fact that, in the empirical reality, man's existence is organized in such a way that his freedom is totally 'alienated', and that nothing short of a revolutionary change in the social structure can restore the development of his liberty (TM, 9, pp. 15–16). If this is true, if, by the organization of society, human freedom can be alienated to such an extent that it all but ceases to exist, then the content of human freedom is determined, not by the structure of the 'Pour-soi', but by the specific historical forces which shape the human society. However, Sartre tries to rescue his idea of freedom from Historical Materialism. He accepts the revolution as the only way to the liberation of mankind, but he insists that the revolutionary solution presupposes man's freedom to *seize* this solution, in other words, that man must be free '*prior*' to his liberation. Sartre maintains that this presupposition destroys the basis of materialism, according to which man is wholly determined by the material world. But according to Historical Materialism, the revolution remains an act of freedom – in spite of all material determination. Historical Materialism has recognized this freedom in the important role of the maturity of the revolutionary consciousness. Marx's constant emphasis on the material determination of the consciousness in all its manifestations points up the relationships between the subject and his world as they actually prevail in the capitalist society, where freedom has shrunk to the possibility of recognizing and seizing the necessity for liberation.

In the concrete historical reality, the freedom of the 'Pour-soi', to whose glorification Sartre devotes his entire book, is thus nothing but one of the preconditions for the possibility of freedom – it is not freedom itself. Moreover, isolated from the specific historical context in which alone the 'transcendence' of the subject may become a precondition of freedom, and hypostatized into the ontological form of the subject as such, this transcendental liberty becomes the very token of enslavement. The anti-fascist who is tortured to death may retain his moral and intellectual freedom to 'transcend' this situation: he is still tortured to death. Human freedom is the very negation of that transcendental liberty in which Sartre sees its realization. In *L'Être et le Néant* this negation appeared only in the 'attitude désirante': it was the loss of the 'Pour-soi', its reification in the 'corps vécu comme chair' which suggested a new idea of freedom and happiness.

Similarly, in Sartre's interpretation of the socio-historical sphere, it is the existence, not of the free but of the reified subject which points the way toward real liberation. The wage labourer, whose existence is that of a thing, and whose activity is essentially action on things, conceives of his liberation naturally as a change in the relationship between man and things. Sartre interprets the process between capital and wage labour in terms of the Hegelian process between master and servant. The labourer, who works in the service of the entrepreneur on the means of production, transforms, through his labour, these means into the instruments for his liberation. True, his labour is imposed upon him, and he is deprived of its products, but 'within these limitations', his labour confers upon him 'la mâitrise sur les choses':

The worker sees himself as the possibility of modifying endlessly the form of material objects by acting on them in accordance with certain universal rules. In other words, it is the determinateness of matter which offers him the first view of his freedom. . . . He transcends his state of slavery through his action on things, and things give back to him, by the very rigidity of their bondage, the image of a tangible freedom which consists of modifying them. And since the outline of tangible freedom appears to him shackled to determinism, it is not surprising that he visualizes the relationship of man to man, which appears to him as that of tyrannic liberty to humbled obedience, replaced by a relationship of man to thing, and finally, since, from another point of view, the man who controls things is in turn a thing himself, by the relationship of thing to thing (TM, 10, pp. 15-16).

Sartre maintains that the materialistic conception of freedom is itself the victim of reification in so far as it conceives the liberated world in terms of a new relationship among things, a new organization of things. As the liberation originates in the process of labour, it remains defined by this process, and the liberated society appears only as 'une entreprise harmonieuse d'exploitation du monde' (TM, 10, p. 17). The result would simply be 'a more rational organization of society' (TM, 10, p. 21) – not the realization of human freedom and happiness.

This critique is still under the influence of 'idealistic mystifications'. The 'more rational organization of society', which Sartre belittles as 'simplement', is the very precondition of freedom. It means the abolition of exploitation and repression in all their forms. And since exploitation and repression are rooted in the material structure of society, their abolition requires a change in this structure: a more rational organization of the relationships of production. In Historical Materialism, this organization of the liberated society is so little 'defined by labour' ('définie par le travail') that Marx once formulated the Communist goal as the 'abolition of labour', and the shortening of the working day as the precondition for the establishment of the 'realm of freedom'. The formula conveys the image of the unfettered satisfaction of the human faculties and desires, thus suggesting the essential identity of freedom and happiness which is at the core of materialism.

Sartre notes that throughout history, materialism was linked with a revolutionary attitude:

No matter how far back I go, I find it [materialistic faith] linked with the revolutionary attitude (TM, 9, pp. 15–16).

Indeed, the materialist faith was revolutionary in so far as it was materialistic, that is to say, as it shifted the definition of human freedom from the sphere of consciousness to that of material satisfaction, from toil to enjoyment, from the moral to the pleasure principle. The idealistic philosophy has made freedom into something frightening and tyrannic, bound up with repression, resignation, scarcity, and frustration. Behind the idealistic concept of freedom lurked the demand for an incessant moral and practical performance, an enterprise the profits of which were to be invested ever again in the same activity – an activity which was really rewarding only for a very small part of the population. The materialistic conception of freedom implies the discontinuation of this activity and performance: it makes the reality of freedom a pleasure. Prior to the achievement of this 'utopian' goal, materialism teaches man the necessities which determine his life in order to break them by his liberation. And his liberation is nothing less than the abolition of repression.

Sartre hits upon the revolutionary function of the materialistic principle in his interpretation of the 'attitude désirante': there, and only there, is his concept of freedom identical with the abolition of repression. But the tendencies which make for the destruction of his idealistic conception remain confined within the framework of philosophy and do not lead to the destruction of the ideology itself. Consequently, in Sartre's work, they manifest themselves only as a disintegration of the traditional philosophical 'style'. This disintegration is expressed in his rejection of the 'esprit de sérieux' (seriousness).

V

According to Sartre, the 'esprit de sérieux' must be banned from philosophy because, by taking the 'réalité humaine' as a totality of objective relationships, to be understood and evaluated in terms of objective standards, the 'esprit de sérieux' offends against the free play of subjective forces which is the very essence of the 'réalité humaine'. By its very 'style' philosophy thus fails to gain the adequate approach to its subject. In contrast, the existentialist style is designed to assert, already through the mode of presentation, the absolutely free movement of the *Cogito*, the 'Pour-soi', the creative subject. Its 'jouer à être' is to be reproduced by the philosophical style. Existentialism plays with every affirmation until it shows forth as negation, qualifies every statement until it turns into its opposite, extends every position to absurdity, makes liberty into compulsion and compulsion into liberty, choice into necessity and necessity into choice, passes from philosophy to *belles lettres* and vice versa, mixes ontology and sexology, etc. The heavy seriousness of Hegel and Heidegger is translated into artistic play. The ontological analysis includes a series of 'scènes amoureuses', and the existentialist novel sets forth philosophical theses in italics.

This disintegration of the philosophical style reflects the inner contradictions of all existential philosophy: the concrete human existence cannot be understood in terms of philosophy. The contradiction derives from the historical conditions under which Western philosophy has developed and to which it remained committed throughout its development. The separation of the intellectual from the material production, of leisure and the leisure class from the underlying population, of theory from practice caused a fundamental gap between the terms of philosophy and the terms of existence. When Aristotle insisted that philosophy presupposed the establishment of the arts directed to the necessities of life, he defined not only the situation of the philosopher but of philosophy itself. The content of the basic philosophical concepts implies a degree of freedom from the necessities of life which is enjoyed only by a small number of men. The general concepts which aim at the structures and forms of being transcend the realm of necessity and the life of those who are confined to this realm. Their existence is not on the philosophical level. Conversely philosophy does not possess the conceptual instruments for comprehending their existence, which is the concreteness of the 'réalité humaine'. The concepts which do adequately describe this concreteness are not the exemplifications and particularizations of any philosophical concept. The existence of a slave or of a factory worker or of a sales clerk is not an 'example' of the concept of being or freedom or life or man. The latter concepts may well be 'applicable' to such forms of existence and 'cover' them by their scope, but this coverage refers only to an irrelevant part or aspect of the reality. The philosophical concepts abstract necessarily from the concrete existence, and they abstract from its very content and essence; their generality transcends the existence *qualitatively*, into a different *genus*. Man as such, as 'kind', is the genuine theme of philosophy; his *hic et nunc* is the ὕλη (matter, stuff) which remains outside the realm of philosophy. Aristotle's dictum that man is an ultimate indivisible kind (ἔσχατον ἄτομον; ἄτομον εἶδος; ἄτομον τῷ γένει), which defies further concretization pronounces the inner impossibility of all existential philosophy.

Against its intentions and efforts, Existentialism demonstrates the truth of Aristotle's statement. We have seen how, in Sartre's philosophy, the concept of the 'Pour-soi' vacillates between that of the individual subject and that of the universal *Ego* or consciousness. Most of the essential qualities which he attributes to the 'Pour-soi' are qualities of man as a *genus*. As such, they are *not* the essential qualities of man's concrete existence. Sartre makes reference to Marx's early writings, but not to Marx's statement that man, in his concrete historical existence, is not (yet) the realization of the *genus* man. This proposition states the fact that the historical forms of society have crippled the development of the general human faculties, of the *humanitas*. The concept of the *genus* man is thus at the same time the concept of the abstract-universal and of the *ideal* man – but is *not* the concept of the 'réalité humaine'.

But if the 'réalité humaine' is not the concretization of the *genus* man, it is equally indescribable in terms of the individual. For the same historical conditions which crippled the realization of the *genus* man also crippled the realization of his individuality. The activities, attitudes, and efforts which circumscribe his concrete existence are, in the last analysis, not his but those of his class, profession, position, society. In this sense is the life of the individual indeed the life of the universal, but this universal is a configuration of specific historical forces, made up by the various groups, interests, institutions, etc., which form the social reality. The concepts which actually reach the concrete existence must therefore derive from a theory of society. Hegel's philosophy comes so close to the structure of the concrete existence because he interprets it in terms of the historical universal, but because he sees in this universal only the manifestation of the Idea he remains within the realm of philosophical abstraction. One step more toward concretization would have meant a transgression beyond philosophy itself.

Such transgression occurred in the opposition to Hegel's philosophy. Kierkegaard and Marx are frequently claimed as the origins of existential philosophy. But neither Kierkegaard nor Marx wrote existential philosophy. When they came to grips with the concrete existence, they abandoned and repudiated philosophy. Kierkegaard comes to the conclusion that the situation of man can be comprehended and 'solved' only by theology and religion. For Marx, the conception of the 'réalité humaine' is the critique of political economy and the theory of the socialist revolution. The opposition against Hegel pronounces the essential inadequacy of philosophy in the face of the concrete human existence.

Since then, the gap between the terms of philosophy and those of existence has widened. The experience of the totalitarian organization of the human existence forbids to conceive freedom in any other form than that of a free society.

POSTSCRIPT

Existentialism 'leads men to understand that reality alone counts, that dreams, expectations, and hopes only permit the definition of a man as a deceived dream, an abortive hope, useless expectation. . .' (EH, p. 58). These phrases are frighteningly ambivalent. 'Reality alone counts' – as what? Such a statement could be the motto of total conformism; or worse: of a healthy acceptance of reality. But it can also show the direction which Sartre's own thought has since taken: the way of radical contradiction. For this direction reality is what must be overthrown so that human existence can begin.

It was said in a note to *L'Être et le Néant* that a morality of liberation and deliverance was possible, but that it would require a 'radical conversion'. Sartre's writings and the stands he has taken over the last two decades are a conversion of this kind. In Sartre's concept pure ontology and phenomenology recede before the invasion of real history, the dispute with Marxism and the adoption of the dialectic. Philosophy becomes politics because no philosophical concept can be thought out and developed without incorporating within itself the inhumanity which is today organized by the rulers and accepted by the ruled. In this politicized philosophy the basic existentialist concept is rescued through the consciousness which declares war on this reality – in the knowledge that the reality will remain victor. For how long? This question, which has no answer, does not alter the validity of the position which is today the only possible one for the thinking person. In his famous Preface to Fanon's *Wretched of the Earth*, in his declarations against the colonial wars in Vietnam and San Domingo, Sartre has fulfilled his promise of a 'morality of liberation'. If, as he fears, he has become an 'institution', then it would be an institution in which conscience and truth have found refuge.

Karl Popper
and the Problem of
Historical Laws

[1959]

Publisher's note: This essay was written in English and first published as 'Notes on the Problem of Historical Laws' in *Partisan Review*, vol. 36, no. 1, New York, 1959.

I

Karl R. Popper's *The Poverty of Historicism* is dedicated to the 'memory of the countless men and women of all creeds or nations or races who fell victim to the fascist and communist belief in Inexorable Laws of Historical Destiny'.

The concern with the role of political violence, expressed in this Dedication, appears in Popper's book in the framework of a discussion of historical and social theory. In the course of the discussion, certain theories emerge to which the tendency to violence seems to be germane, namely, those which believe in inexorable and predictable laws of history. Some of these theories – Popper calls them 'holist' – couple this belief with the notion that the State, Society, or the Nation are 'totalities' over, above, and other than the mere sum total of their component parts, governed by laws of their own, to which the individuals are subordinated. The notion of totality in turn implies, in these theories, the possibility of totalitarian control over all individual relationships, specific events, institutions, etc. Popper thus stipulates a connection between methodological and political totalitarianism: the former provides, as it were, the logical and philosophical justification for the latter. Consequently, a logical refutation of the former would prove the factual impossibility of the latter. Political totalitarianism would then be shown as 'Utopian' – and this is indeed the result of Popper's argument – an argument which, as we shall see, does not involve much ingenuity. As an antidote against totalitarianism, Popper recommends a pluralistic, gradualistic, and 'piecemeal' approach to history and society, which refrains from 'holist' notions so conducive to holist policies and holist sacrifices to 'historical destiny'.

Before examining Popper's argument further, I wish to discuss briefly the context in which it appears. It is a philosophical, more exactly, a methodological context in which the application of wholesale violence is explained in terms of a specific philosophy of history and society. Moreover, responsibility is assigned to the philosophy of historical law and destiny (although perhaps not the entire responsibility), which includes, undifferentiated by Popper, the fascist ideology and the communist theory. And the same philosophy is held to be logically faulty, unscientific, and in this sense irrational. I wish to raise the question whether the philosophical context in which historical violence is discussed does not develop the problem on a level of misplaced abstractness, thus diverting attention from the real factors of violence, from its societal function, and from the historical means of combating it.

Now it is certainly true that a philosophy of history has frequently been used to justify the liquidation of countless individuals who, by their faith or origin, by their position in society, by their opinions and actions, were considered as standing in the way of historical destiny. Examples may be adduced from Robespierre's Republic of Virtue to the Stalinist terror. One might not stress unduly the concept of historical destiny if one goes further back and adds practically all crusades, inquisitions, religious wars – even those declared in the name of toleration and religious freedom. It is also true that Marxian theory contains the notion of inexorable laws of society – although here it is precisely the *abolition* of these *oppressive* laws which is the aim and the rationale of the socialist revolution. It is much less certain whether the fascist ideology has the idea of inexorable laws of history – rather the denial of history, acting against history, regression to 'nature' are characteristic of fascism. But this is largely irrelevant to the question whether, in all these cases, belief in historical destiny really explains terror. I propose that it does not: where it was prevalent, it was derivative from and conditional upon other factors in such a sense that a discussion which neglects these factors abstracts from the essential and suggests an incorrect interpretation of the causes, the function, and the prospects of historical violence. If these factors are present (I shall presently try to indicate them), there is no philosophy of history which may not lend itself to the systematic use of violence. As the history of liberalism from the seventeenth to the present century shows, the gradualist and pluralist approach is no exception – be it only because of its incapacity to prevent violence and by its readiness (with good conscience) to meet violence with violence.

I admit that this last point can be conceded only if the indictment of mass extermination is not from the beginning restricted and made to conform with the standards and criteria of the society from whose position the indictment is levelled. In Popper's case, these standards call for a fundamental distinction between legal and extra-legal mass extermination: between war and civil war, invasion and police action, in a successful and in a failing revolution, by a legally constituted and a not yet thus constituted government.

But does not acceptance of these distinctions imply recognition that there are historically very different forms and functions of mass violence, which – while all morally repugnant and condemnable – have very different causes and aims? The question has direct bearing on Popper's analysis: because he abstracts from the real factors of mass violence, he arrives at a false generalization, obliterating the political features of terror in the contemporary period and minimizing its scope and prospect.

The real factors of mass violence are those which, in the respective society, make for the suspension of the 'normal' controls and of normal law and order. The facts are well known and a brief reminder will suffice. In the case of fascism, the expansionist policy of 'rectifying' the peace settlements of 1919 and of gaining more *Lebensraum* for the defeated states could no longer be pursued within the framework of the established democratic system and its large labour opposition. The unprecedented degree of violence corresponded to the extent of sacrifices and costs imposed upon the population. The people must be tied to the regime with all conceivable means: share in the spoils and share in the guilt; they must also be compensated for their victimization. Here is perhaps the ground on which the 'irrational' forces are released: sadistic cruelty, destructiveness, and stupidity – revenge against whatever and whomever can be blamed for the old and the new misery of the underlying population. Compared with these factors, the philosophy of 'historical destiny' seems to be negligible. Indeed, rarely has an ideology been a more transparent rationalization, a more expendable by-product.

In the case of communism, the basic factors of the terror are of a very different nature. The mass exterminations accompanying the first Five Year Plan occurred in the course of the violent collectivization and industrialization, undertaken against a backward, apathetic, or hostile population. Even if one stretches the Marxian notion of inexorable laws of historical development to the extent that it stipulates advanced industrialization as an indispensable precondition for socialism, it will be hard to maintain that this notion played any decisive role in Stalinist policy. Rapid building up of the economic and military potential of Soviet society in order to enable it to withstand the 'threat of capitalism' and especially of fascism appears as the driving force behind this policy, and no 'holist' philosophy is required to explain it. The theoretical discussion was crushed, not consummated, by the Stalinist plan. As to the purges of the middle and late thirties and then again of the late forties: I cannot see how they are attributable to a philosophical concept by any stretch of the imagination.

These brief comments may serve to indicate one of the major defects of Popper's book. A philosophical analysis which remains abstract to the extent that it never reaches the historical dimension in which mass violence emerges and operates is of little value in explaining and combating it. I shall attempt to show that Popper's generalizations are theoretically untenable – but they also do violence to the empirical facts and events. To be sure, terror is and remains in all its forms and circumstances a crime against humanity – an instrument of domination and exploitation. This does not change the fact that terror has had very different historical functions and very different social contents: it has been used for the preservation of the status quo and for its overthrow, for the streamlining of a declining society and for the release of new political and economic forces. Understanding the historical function of terror may be an indispensable weapon for combating it. The horror of slaughter does not wipe out the difference between the Jacobin terror and that of the post-Thermidorian reaction, between the terror of the dying Commune and that against it, between the Red and the White terror – a difference which is *not* a subtle philosophical point but a struggle of opposing political forces that changed the course of history.

II

Popper's analysis of totalitarianism is part of his sweeping critique of historicism. The meaning which Popper gives to this term is strikingly unusual:

... I mean by 'historicism' an approach to the social sciences which assumes that *historical prediction* is their principal aim, and which assumes that this aim is attainable by discovering the 'rhythm' or the 'pattern,' the 'laws' or the 'trends' that underlie the evolution of history. ... And I have not hesitated to construct arguments in its support which have never, to my knowledge, been brought forward by historicists themselves. I hope that, in this way, I have succeeded in building up a position really worth attacking.

The last statement deserves some attention before we take a closer look at this notion of historicism. What a strange method: to build up a position really worth attacking and then to attack it! Why does the critic have to construct the target of his attack? I would have passed over the statement as a mere manner of speech if I did not believe that this method is characteristic of much of contemporary philosophical analysis. In reading Popper's book, I often stopped and asked: against what is he really arguing? who has actually maintained what he is so efficiently destroying? And often I was unable to identify the attacked theory (especially since Popper is extremely sparing with references).

In the philosophical tradition, 'historicism' has become a well defined term, referring to those schools of thought which emphasize the historical uniqueness and 'equivalence' of cultures. Historicism thus implies a rather high degree of pluralism and relativism, perhaps most characteristically epitomized in Ranke's phrase that all historical periods are '*unmittelbar zu Gott*'. Neither predictability nor the idea of historical 'laws' plays a central role in these theories. Certainly, it would be entirely unjustified to insist on conformity with lexicographical usage. However, I think that such a strange deviation from usage should have firmer grounds than a construction built from disparate elements of disparate theories. Popper's construction is general enough to include practically all theories which take history seriously, which see in it the 'fate' of mankind: his opposition to historicism is in the last analysis opposition to *history*. And the construction is selective enough to enable him to establish a link between historicism and totalitarianism.

The book divides the whole of what is called 'historicism' into two main types of theory: pro-naturalistic doctrines, which claim that the methods of physical science can, at least to a large extent, be applied to the social sciences, and anti-naturalistic doctrines, which deny such applicability and insist on a scientific method germane to the social sciences. Popper presents and criticizes both types of theories and concludes that neither one can lay claim to a rational and scientific theory of history allowing predictability. He sums up his main argument against the predictability of history as follows: the course of history is 'strongly influenced' by the growth of human knowledge, but we cannot predict, by 'rational or scientific methods', the future growth of scientific knowledge; consequently, we cannot predict the future course of history. By the same token, there cannot be a social science or a 'theoretical history' corresponding to theoretical physics; there 'can be no scientific theory of historical development serving as a basis for historical prediction'. The fundamental aim of historicist method is therefore 'misconceived; and historicism collapses'. Popper's dictum of collapse seems to be somehow premature. He argues that a 'theoretical history' corresponding in method and aim to theoretical physics is impossible – a statement which few 'historicists' would contest. The essential difference between the method of the historical and that of the physical sciences has been one of the major points in the philosophical discussion since the nineteenth century, but one looks in vain for a discussion (or even mentioning) of those theoretical efforts which were decisive for the foundation, development, and critique of historicism: Droysen, Dilthey, Simmel, Windelband, Rickert, Troeltsch – to mention only a few. These are not merely additional names or references which may or may not be there; their analysis of conceptualization in the social and physical sciences and of the 'rationality' of history has direct bearing on Popper's arguments. Failure to face their positions in full strength may account for much of the thinness and abstractness of Popper's discussion.

But apart from this failure, Popper's argument against historical predictability seems in itself inconclusive. To be sure, the growth of human knowledge has 'strongly influenced' the course of history. However, as such a factor, it has in turn been historically conditioned. It seems that scientific knowledge has really influenced the course of history only as *accepted* knowledge, that is to say, if and when it corresponded to the needs and capabilities of society. The latter are facts and forces which operate in any given society as observable trends and tendencies, and these provide the ground for historical predictability – which is never more than projection of tendencies.

There are other theories which posit historical predictability and more rigid and sweeping 'laws' of historical development. They are mostly cyclical theories, assuming a return of the pattern of the past. Ultimately, they are derived from the idea of the basic unchangeability of human nature, which asserts itself through all variations and innovations. Thucydides and Machiavelli, Vico, Spengler and Toynbee may serve as examples. Their conception is fundamentally different from that according to which the laws of historical development all but preclude a return of the pattern of the past – so much so that they almost appear as the laws of human freedom, circumscribing the conditions for the exercise of human freedom, for the possibilities of change. Popper's presentation and critique obliterates the decisive difference between these types of theories by submerging both in the constructed syndrome of 'historicism'. We shall presently return to this point, after a further brief examination of the syndrome.

III

Popper's abstract methodological discussion comes to life when it reveals its concrete political implications. His most telling arguments against historicism are in the last analysis political arguments, and his own position is in the last analysis a political position. The political dimension is not merely superimposed upon the methodological: the latter rather reveals its own political content. The awareness of this relationship and its outspoken development is a rewarding feature of Popper's book.

The political implications of the critique of historicism centre on the notion of 'holism'. (The word itself seems to revolt against its formation!) According to this notion (which Popper attributes to the anti-naturalistic doctrines),

social groups must never be regarded as mere aggregates of persons. The social group is *more* than the mere sum total of its members, and it is also *more* than the mere sum total of the merely personal relationships existing at any moment between any of its members.

Thus far this is a very harmless notion, and one may doubt whether even the most radical empiricist would seriously deny it. Popper goes on to distinguish two meanings of the word 'whole': (1) those properties or aspects of a thing which make it appear an organized structure rather than a mere 'heap', and (2) 'the totality of *all* the properties or aspects of a thing, and especially of *all* the relations holding between its constituent parts' (my italics). The first meaning, used in Gestalt theory, is acceptable to Popper, while he rejects the second as entirely inapplicable to the social sciences. It is rejected because a whole in this sense can never be described and observed, since 'all description is necessarily selective'. Nor can such a totality ever be the object 'of any activity, scientific or otherwise'. Popper links methodological and political totalitarianism: 'It is for many reasons quite impossible to control all, or "nearly" all' the relationships embraced by society, if only 'because with every new control of social relations we create a host of new social relations to be controlled'. 'In short, the impossibility is a *logical* impossibility' (my italics); logically impossible because the attempt would lead to an 'infinite regression' – as it would in the study of society as a whole. Popper himself seems to be somewhat uneasy; he adds a footnote which says that 'Holists may hope that there is a way out of this difficulty by denying the validity of logic which, they think, has been superseded by dialectic' and he says that he has tried to 'block this way' in his article 'What is Dialectic' (*Mind*, vol. 49 N.S., pp. 403ff.). I do not know who the 'holists' might be that entertain such hope and that 'may' deny the validity of logic, but the reference to the dialectic suggests that Popper is thinking of Hegel and the Marxists who are thus charged with an illogical 'totalitarian intuition' – although even the 'holist' Stalin emphatically asserted the validity of (traditional) logic. At stake is not the validity of logic but the adequacy of the logic applied. But the notion that society is more than the mere aggregate of its parts and relations does not imply that all or 'nearly all' public and private relations within society must be analysed in order to comprehend the 'structure' of a society. On the contrary, the hypothesis that such a structure prevails and asserts itself in and through all institutions and relations (defining and determining them) does not preclude but calls for a 'selective' analysis – one which focuses on the *basic* institutions and relations of a society (a distinction which must, of course, be demonstrated and justified logically as well as empirically). Similarly, for the totalitarian control of society it is not necessary to control directly *all* or 'nearly all' relations because control of the *key* positions and institutions assures control of the whole. Certainly, every new control creates new social relations to be controlled, but far from being an impossible infinite regression, this constellation perpetuates and propels the controls once secured in the key positions and relations: the 'new' relations are preshaped and predetermined. (It might be necessary to point out that these comments do not imply or suggest that totalitarian control, once established, is unbreakable, but that breaking it depends on changing the very basis of totalitarian society.)

If the critique of totalitarianism, instead of 'constructing' its target, would look at the actual theories and at the reality of totalitarianism, it could hardly assert that totalitarianism is a logical impossibility. Popper cites Mannheim's proposition that 'the power of the State is bound to increase until the State becomes nearly identical with society'; he calls this proposition a 'prophecy' and the 'intuition' expressed in it the 'totalitarian intuition'. Now I think it is rather obvious that the cited passage has long since ceased to be a 'prophecy' and has become a statement of fact. Moreover, one may criticize Mannheim on many grounds, but to count him among the 'holists' and to charge him with the 'totalitarian intuition' is to confuse an analysis of observable trends with their advocacy and justification.

This confusion is characteristic of Popper's concept of 'holism', which covers and denounces equally theories with a totalitarian and those with an anti-totalitarian 'intuition'. By the same token, the concept obliterates the fundamental differences between the critical notion of inexorable historical laws, which sees in these laws the feature of an 'immature' and oppressive society, and the conservative notion, which justifies these laws as 'natural' and unchangeable. The idea that the Nation or the State or the Society are totalities over and above the individuals who must be subordinated to the inherent laws governing these totalities has often justified tyranny and the enslavement of men by the powers that be. But the category of 'holism' is also applied by Popper to the opposite theoretical tradition, exemplified by Marxian theory. According to this theory, the appearance of the Nation and the State and the Society as separate totalities reflects only a specific economic structure of class society, and a free society involves the disappearance of this 'holism'. Popper joins the two incompatible theories with what he calls 'Utopianism' and thus establishes the alliance of Plato and Marx – a fantastic syndrome playing an important part in his demonstration of the 'unholy alliance' between historicism and Utopianism. The latter notion soon reveals its concrete political content:

... we find historicism very frequently allied with just those ideas which are typical of holistic or Utopian social engineering, such as the idea of 'blueprints for a new order,' or of 'centralized planning'.

For Popper, Plato was a pessimistic Utopian holist: his blueprint aimed at arresting all change; Marx was an optimist who 'predicted, and tried actively to further' the Utopian ideal of a society without political and economic coercion.

We do not wish to dwell again on the semantics of the term Utopianism: as the word loses more and more of its traditional content, it becomes an instrument of political defamation. Industrial civilization has reached the stage where most of what could formerly be called Utopian now has a *'topos'* among the real possibilities and capabilities of this civilization. Moreover, ideas and efforts which once were 'Utopian' have been playing an increasingly decisive part in the conquest of nature and society, and there is awareness of the tremendous forces which may be released and utilized through the encouragement of 'Utopian' thought. In the Soviet Union, science fiction writers are being taken to task for lagging behind science in their dreams and phantasies and they are told to 'get their imagination off the ground' (*New York Times*, 9 July 1958). Political interest in maintaining the status quo rather than logical or scientific impossibility today makes real possibilities appear as Utopian. Popper lends weight to his attack on Utopianism by again 'constructing' the theory he attacks rather than criticizing the theory as it actually is. It is hardly justifiable to call Marx's brief outline of the initial institutional prerequisites for socialism a blueprint for the 'social engineering' of an ideal society (he did not make centralized planning the distinguishing feature of socialism, and he never designated socialism as an 'ideal society').

But this may be irrelevant exegesis: what really matters to Popper is the argument against the 'holistic' idea of social change, i.e. the idea that 'social experiments, in order to be realistic, must be of the character of Utopian attempts at remodelling the whole of society'. We have already indicated the basis for Popper's rejection of this idea: his contention that 'the whole of society' is a logically and scientifically untenable notion. Against it, Popper advocates the 'piecemeal' approach to social experiments, concentrating on the fight against 'definite wrongs, against concrete forms of injustice or exploitation, and avoidable suffering such as poverty or unemployment'. He supports this position by a pluralistic philosophy of history. According to it, one may interpret history in terms of class struggles, or of religious ideas, or of races, or of the struggle between the 'open' and the 'closed' society, etc.:

All these are more or less interesting points of view, and *as such* perfectly unobjectionable. But historicists do not present them as such: they do not see that there is necessarily a plurality of interpretations which are fundamentally on the same level of both suggestiveness and arbitrariness (even though some of them may be distinguished by their *fertility* – a point of some importance).

The parenthesis contains indeed a point of some importance – so much so that the concept of 'fertility', if elaborated, may well cancel the complete relativism expressed in the preceding passage. And as to the historicists not seeing this relativism: the view expressed by Popper has been one of the most representative positions of traditional historicism.

IV

Popper has herewith restated some of the philosophical foundations of classical liberalism; Hayek looms large in the supporting footnotes, and the critique of historicism is largely a justification of liberalism against totalitarianism. Liberalism and totalitarianism appear as two diametrically opposed systems: opposed in their economics and politics as well as in their philosophy. The question is: does this picture correspond to the actual relation between liberalism and totalitarianism? It is a vital question, and especially vital for a genuine and effective critique of anti-liberal philosophies. One does not have to accept the Marxian thesis that free, competitive, private capitalism leads, precisely by virtue of its inherent normal development, to totalitarianism (i.e. increasing centralization of economic and political power, ultimately exercised by the state) in order to suspect that a liberalistic society is not immune to totalitarian trends and forces. The tendency towards the increasing power of the State is sufficiently noticeable in societies which are not exactly characterized by a predominance of 'holist' doctrines and in which the 'piecemeal' rather than the totalitarian approach prevailed. Were liberal gradualism and pluralism perhaps derived from the belief in a 'law' no less 'inexorable' than that assumed by the 'holists', namely the law of the market, expressing the harmony between the freely competing private interests and the general welfare? Has the market equalized or aggravated the initial inequality and the conflicts of interests generated by it? Has free competition, economic and intellectual, prevented or promoted the concentration of power and the corrosion of individual liberties? Have not these trends, in the democracies too, reached the point where the State is increasingly called upon to regulate and protect the whole? The existence of countervailing powers seems to be of little avail if they themselves impel centralization, and if the opposition is in the same boat as the power which it opposes. Moreover, industrial civilization has, at the national and international level, so closely interrelated economic and political, local and large scale, particular and general processes that effective 'piecemeal social engineering' appears as affecting the whole structure of society and threatening a fundamental change. Whether or not these trends lead to terroristic totalitarianism depends, not on a philosophy of history and society, but on the existence of social groups willing and strong enough to attack the economic and political roots of totalitarianism. These roots are in the *pre*-totalitarian era.

If these are really the observable trends, then the abstract opposition between liberalism and totalitarianism implied in Popper's presentation does not adequately express the state of affairs. Instead, the latter rather seems to suggest a 'dialectical' relationship between two historical periods of one and the same form of society. Popper's rejection of dialectics is not incidental: an anti-dialectical logic is essential to his argument. It is so because dialectical logic is throughout permeated with what he designates as 'historicism': its methods and its notions are shaped in accordance with the historical structure of reality. Far from 'denying the validity of logic', dialectical logic intends to rescue logic by bridging the gap between the laws of thought and those governing reality – a gap which is itself the result of the historical development. Dialectical logic attempts to accomplish this task by bringing the two manifestations of reality to their actual common denominator, namely, *history*. In its metaphysical form, this is also the core of Hegel's dialectic: Subject and Object, Mind and Nature – the two traditional 'substances' – are from the beginning conceived as an antagonistic unity, and the universe as the concrete development of their interrelation. This undertaking involved a redefinition of the forms and categories of traditional logic: they lost their mode of 'yes' or 'no', 'either–or' and assumed that 'ambiguous', dynamic, even contradictory character which makes them so ridiculous to the protagonists of purity but which corresponds so closely to reality. The realistic character of dialectical thought comes to fruition in the interpretation of history. The latter may best be illustrated by contrasting it with Popper's view that historians are interested in 'actual, singular, or specific events, rather than in laws or generalizations'. In contrast to the opposition between 'singular' and 'law', 'specific' and 'general' expressed in Popper's statement, the dialectical conception holds that the actual, specific, singular event becomes comprehensible only if it is understood as constituted by the 'general', as the particular manifestation of a 'law'. And this 'general' is something very concrete and demonstrable, namely the society in which the specific events occur at a specific stage of its development. The dialectical notion of historical laws implies no other 'destiny' than that which men create for themselves under the conditions of unmastered nature and society. The less a society is rationally organized and directed by the collective efforts of free men, the more will it appear as an independent whole governed by 'inexorable' laws. The manner in which men explain and exploit nature, and the societal institutions and relationships which they give themselves are actual and specific historical events, but events which occur on a ground already prepared, on a base already built. Once institutionalized, each society has its framework of potentialities defining the scope and direction of change. Historical determinism has freedom as a constitutive element: the latter is defined and confined by the 'whole' – but the whole can be (and constantly is) redefined, so much so that the historical process cannot even be regarded as irreversible. There are 'laws', there is historical *logic* in the sequence of ancient slave society, feudalism, 'free' industrial capitalism, state capitalism and contemporary socialism: one emerges *within* the other and develops, under the prevalent conditions, its own laws of functioning as a whole system of material and intellectual culture – a demonstrable 'unity'. However, these very laws do not allow predictability of progress. The present situation indicates clearly enough that a return to original barbarism appears as a historical possibility. Again: certainly not as an inexorable 'destiny' in a cycle of growth and decay, progress and regression, etc. but as a man-made destiny, for which responsibility can be assigned and which can be explained (as failure, impotence, even impossibility to act otherwise) – explained in terms of the structure of the established society and the forms of control, manipulation, and indoctrination required for the preservation of this structure. It then appears that the alternative to progressive barbarism (and there have always been alternatives!) may well involve a change in the *structure* of society, in other words, a 'holist' change which is Popper's real *bête noire*.

Here, I suggest, is the driving force behind Popper's attack on historicism. It is, I believe, in the last analysis a struggle against history – *not* spelled with a capital H, but the empirical course of history. Any attempt to rescue the values of liberalism and democracy must account for the emergence of a society that plays havoc with these values. At the attained stage, this development threatens to obliterate the difference between war and peace, between military and civilian drill, between technical and intellectual manipulation, between the rationality of business and that of society, between free and dependent enterprise, privacy and publicity, truth and propaganda. These tendencies are afflictions of the whole: originating from the centre (i.e. the basic societal institutions), they penetrate and shape all spheres of existence. Moreover, they are not confined to totalitarian countries; they are not attributable to a 'holist' or 'Utopian' philosophy; and they have asserted themselves within the framework of pluralistic institutions and gradualist policies. Contemporary society is increasingly functioning as a rational whole which overrides the life of its parts, progresses through planned waste and destruction, and advances with the irresistible force of nature – *as if* governed by inexorable laws. Insistence on these irrational aspects is not betrayal of the liberalistic tradition, but the attempt to recapture it. The 'holism' which has become reality must be met by a 'holist' critique of this reality.

Freedom and the
Historical Imperative

[1969]

Publisher's note: This essay was delivered in English as a lecture at the Rencontre Internationale de Genève in 1969 and first published in French as 'La Liberté et les impératifs de l'histoire' in *La Liberté et l'Ordre Social*, Éditions de la Baconnière, Neuchâtel, 1970. The text used here is the author's English original.

'Historical Imperatives': the phrase suggests the existence of historical laws governing the development of civilization, and, if linked with the concept of freedom, it suggests the idea of progress in history. I shall try to discuss the topic without accepting the highly questionable assumptions implied in the formulation of the theme.

Imperatives occur in history first as individual, personal necessities of action, derived from the acceptance of specific goals, ends. They are never categorical because they depend, for their validity, on the acceptance of such goals. To use again the familiar example: if Caesar wanted to defeat Pompei, it was imperative for him to cross the Rubicon. This course of action was prescribed, in Caesar's evaluation, by the end to be achieved and by the prevailing circumstances. These were 'given', thus the 'ought' followed from the 'is' – a conditional 'ought'. But the same example may serve to illustrate a very different imperative, which contains the individual goal and the conditional 'ought' while transcending them towards a supra-individual 'goal' to be achieved by supra-individual action: *praxis*. The institutions of the Roman state were no longer adequate to cope with the conflicts which had developed with Roman society, and no longer adequate to translate into reality the possibilities of growth opened by this society. Self-preservation and growth made imperative sweeping changes in the existing institutions: the transformation of the city state into the empire, of the republic into the monarchy. Hegel's 'cunning of reason': in and through the personal ambitions and actions of Caesar, the transition to a 'higher' stage of the historical development, i.e. of freedom, is taking place: the Subject, without losing whatever freedom it may have had, becomes the Object of historical necessity. I shall come back to the concept of the 'higher' stage of 'progress' explicit in Hegel's notion: there are good reasons to reject it – reasons which become more evident every day. Now I want to discuss the question whether Hegel's theory must be rejected because it is based on a mere 'value judgement', namely, that progress in freedom (quantitatively and qualitatively) is a historical necessity. The answer does not depend on acceptance or denial of his concept of Reason as the driving force in history. We can well assume some sort of impulse, instinctive striving for freedom inherent in man, with Reason superimposed on it by the requirements of the Reality Principle. To justify the concept of objective historical imperatives, we have to recognize only one fact (or 'value') as historical datum, namely, that the dynamic of human existence is self-preservation *and* growth, i.e. not only satisfaction of biological needs but also development of the needs themselves in accordance with the possibilities which emerge in the constant struggle with nature (and with man). And it is also a fact that this struggle with nature has led to ever more and larger possibilities of satisfaction of needs. If this is the case, we can meaningfully speak of growth (in the sense indicated) as a force in history (without any teleological and moral connotations, regardless whether this kind of progress is good or bad, and whether it implies progress in freedom). And then we can meaningfully speak of historical imperatives in as much as the operation of this force depends on changing given social and natural conditions which define specific alternatives of praxis: the 'is' *contains* the 'ought'; the latter must be freed *from* this containment by obsolescent, and surmountable, forms of reality. Now we can raise the question whether freedom is implied or postulated by these imperatives. In one sense it certainly is: the individual must be free to acquire the means to attain his end: self-preservation and growth. However, this kind of freedom is variable to the highest degree: in history, it ranges from the mere physical ability to accept and use the means of subsistence, to the power of domination and exploitation. And it includes a rich freedom of choice within a strong framework of repression, of unfreedom. There is one brute fact which must guide any unideological discussion of freedom: since the beginnings of recorded history and to this very day, the liberty of some has always been based on the servitude of others, and the only concept of freedom that corresponded to the facts was the concept of 'inner' freedom, inalienable and practicable even in prison and at the stake. Whether called Christian freedom, or freedom of conscience and worship – this has been to this very day the *only* freedom available to man as man: 'essential' human freedom. Essential indeed if the body is inessential, and if this is the only freedom which can be claimed as pertaining and as granted to all men, regardless of class, race, religion. Freedom of thought is already of a different order and far less 'real': it is freedom only if translatable into expression, and the latter has been politically restricted throughout history – if not by direct censorship then by withholding, from the larger part of the population, the intellectual and material means which would enable them to develop and express free thought. If freedom is man's ability to determine his own life without depriving others of this ability, then freedom has never been a historical reality – to this very day. Does this mean that the imperatives of history preclude the realization of freedom in any other than a partial, repressive, ideological form? In other words: have the historical conditions not yet matured to the point where the self-preservation and growth of human existence would be real self-determination, not only of certain groups or individuals but of the species man – humanity? The affirmative answer is familiar: such integral freedom is precluded by the persistence of scarcity, the requirements of the struggle with nature, and the asocial character of human nature. Marxian theory integrates these three factors into the general concept of history as the history of class struggles. The objective imperatives of history were defined by the necessity of assuring the preservation and growth of a specific form of class society which militated against the realization of freedom. However, the productive forces (the term designating the sum-total of the resources for liberation available to a given society) developed within the class societies have reached the stage where they tend to explode the class organization itself: at this stage, freedom becomes an objective possibility; at this stage too, the historical Subject appears capable of building a society in which the imperatives of self-preservation and growth can become the imperatives of freedom: reconciliation of necessity and liberty. Again, the 'is' implies the 'ought', the status quo calls for its abrogation: the prevailing material and intellectual conditions demand a radically different form of society in order to sustain human progress.

I have briefly re-stated the Marxian conception in order to show how its very limitations, nay its obsolescence, testify to its validity. If there is any conceivable sense in which it can be said: 'if the facts contradict the theory, the worse for the facts' – here it is. One could imagine Marx looking at the world today and saying: 'I told you so, not in my predictions but in my analysis of your society.' This analysis showed that all development of the productive forces by the established society would perpetuate and increase the productivity of destruction and repression, and that this fatal link could be broken only by the praxis of a class whose vital need was, not the perpetuation and amelioration but the abolition of the established society. And this abolition would be liberation: freedom appears first as negation; the 'positive' definition of freedom remains an X, an open variable – just: self-determination.

It must be noted that, in this conception, freedom does not appear as a historical imperative, in the sense that the prevailing conditions 'prescribe' it as the necessary next (or higher) stage of the development. The prevailing conditions are objectively *ambivalent*: they offer the possibility of liberation, and that of streamlined servitude, i.e. the vast administrative '*Gehäuse der Hörigkeit*' (house of bondage) which Max Weber envisaged. This is the ambivalence of progress: quantitative and/or qualitative; technical progress and/or the emergence of self-determination as the way of life, intellectual and material, of a new rationality and sensibility. Qualitative progress may well entail not only a re-direction but also a reduction of the development of the productive forces where the latter promotes waste and aggression, and demands the subjection of man to the machine. The transition from servitude to freedom requires a total transvaluation of values but it does not require that self-propelling quantitative progress on which capitalism depends for its survival.

Quantitative progress, as historical imperative, is part of the ideology and praxis of domination. To the degree to which the latter depends on the technological increase in the productivity of labour and on the private appropriation of surplus value, it must of necessity foster and expand the production of commodities. And the higher the level of the productivity of labour, the larger the mass of luxury goods which become necessities of life and which have to be purchased by intensive, alienated labour. Under the technological imperative, society creates all the needs for the satisfaction of needs with a minimum of toil while subjecting the satisfaction of needs to the constantly expanding apparatus of labour. In other words, within the capitalist framework, technical progress creates the preconditions for freedom while at the same time undermining them. Liberation does not depend on the prevalence of abundance (a self-propelling notion which allows the constant 'postponement' of freedom), and the formula 'to each according to his needs' does not imply the insatiability of human nature. The latter concept too belongs to the arsenal of domination: it justifies the perpetuation of alienated labour and the submission to it. Freedom presupposes a stage in the conquest of nature where the vital necessities of life can be procured with a minimum of work and time so that production beyond the necessities can become a matter of self-determination. Marx believed that this stage was in sight, in the advanced industrial countries, already in the 1860s. Lacking were, not the material conditions but the political consciousness of the working classes and their organizations. *'The root* of things is man': the analysis of the prospects of liberation must break through the reification which mystifies the established society as well as the alternatives. It takes the historical Subject of change as something that exists like an object, while in fact this Subject (Marx's revolutionary class) comes into being only in the process of change itself. It is a *collective* Subject, and in this sense an abstraction, but the abstraction comes to life in the individuals acting in solidarity in a common interest.

The Subject emerges as the decisive factor: the historical imperatives are in the last analysis given by *men*. For the objective conditions which define these imperatives are never 'unilateral', unambiguous: they always offer, not one, but several alternatives. The historical *choice* : socialism or barbarism, each of the two in different forms. The Subject is free to choose: in this choice of a possible historical praxis which transcends the established praxis is the essence of human freedom. And this freedom is not a 'fact', neither a transcendental nor a historical fact – it is the faculty (and activity) of men 'synthesizing' (organizing) the data of experience so that they reveal their own (objective) negativity, namely, the degree to which they are the data of domination. And this radically critical synthesis of experience occurs in the light of the real possibility of a 'better world to live in', in the light of the possible reduction of pain, cruelty, injustice, stupidity. To the extent to which this dual experience has seized the consciousness and sensibility of man, to that extent has he placed himself under the historical imperative κατ' ἔξοχεν: the revolutionary imperative. It is indeed not only a political but also (and perhaps even primarily) an intellectual and moral imperative, for intelligence and morality themselves become revolutionary factors if freed from their service as handmaidens of repression. Apparently one can live quite happily in stupidity, and in a world where genocide, torture, and starvation are easily acceptable as just 'the way of life' – but it is getting increasingly difficult and requires the increasingly global management of human needs and faculties.

'To comprehend the world in order to change it': this formulation of the revolutionary imperative is an empirical postulate, derived from the very banal (and quite 'unscientific') experience of unnecessary suffering – unnecessary in as much as it is not required by the struggle for existence but imposed by the manner in which this struggle is organized and directed. Since there is no scientific logic according to which this imperative can be validated, it is indeed a *moral* imperative. There has always been a dual morality in history: that of the status quo, and that of its subversion: affirmation and negation – not for the sake of negation, but of 'saving' human values invalidated by the affirmation. This revolutionary morality is repressed in all those who have learned (or were forced) to live with this suffering – easily when it is the lot of others out of sight who bear it nicely, less easily when it is the introjection of all the frustrations required by status and business. With the achievements of technical progress under advanced capitalism, this immorality of the beneficiaries of the high and blind standard of living has spread over a large part, probably the majority of the population; thus it has become a vital element in the cohesion and perpetuation of the status quo and its streamlined extension. Under these circumstances, the validity of the imperative seems anything but universal: applicable only to the technically backward peoples of the earth, and even there the imperative seems to be no more than the truism that people will try to subvert intolerable existential conditions. In order to clarify this problem, we have to raise the question: which is the structure and content of freedom as envisaged in the revolutionary imperative?

I suggested that the essence of human freedom is in the theoretical and practical syntheses which constitute and reconstitute the universe of experience. These syntheses are never merely individual activities (acts) but the work of a supra-individual historical Subjectivity *in* the individual – just as the Kantian categories are the syntheses of a transcendental Ego *in* the *empirical* Ego. I have intentionally used the Kantian construction of experience, that is to say his epistemology rather than his moral philosophy, in order to elucidate the concept of freedom as historical imperative: freedom originates indeed in the mind of man, in his ability (or rather in his need and desire) to comprehend his world, and this comprehension is *praxis* in as much as it establishes a specific order of facts, a specific organization of the data of experience. The human mind is constituted in such a way that it subjects the data received by the senses to certain concepts of rigidly universal order in time and space, and this act is the precondition of all activity, practical as well as theoretical. For Kant, the organization of experience is universal because it happens to be the very structure of the human mind: the transcendental a priori rests on the acceptance of a fact. The universality of this structure is a formal one: time and space and the categories constitute the general framework for all experience. Now I suggest that Kant's transcendental construction of experience may well furnish the model for the historical construction of experience. The latter would be distinguished from the former in as much as the forms of intuition in which the sense data appear are *political* space and *political* time, and their synthesis takes place under political categories.

In the universe of this experience, all things appear as data of a hierarchy: an order composed of relationships of domination and subordination. To be sure, things are immediately experienced as specific use values, as aesthetic, sexual objects, etc. However, reflection reveals that their *Stellenwert* is determined by the power structure prevailing in society. If Marx defines the social wealth of a capitalist society as a mass of commodities, he makes this reflection the methodological principle. As commodities, things express and perpetuate exploitation, unfreedom – they are available according to purchasing power, which is in turn determined by the class character of the productive process. The synthesis of the data under political categories is an empirical synthesis, its universality is a relative, historical one, but valid for the entire society in all its branches, in its material and intellectual culture. It transforms everyday consciousness and common sense into political consciousness and political sense. And in this transformation originates the historical imperative of freedom: not only liberation in order to obtain a larger slice of the cake, or in order to participate actively in the administration and management of the established system but replacement of the system itself by one of self-determination on the basis of collective control of the means of production. This socialist formula is not restricted in its applicability to the advanced industrial societies: self-determination and collective control have always been possible alternatives of the organization of the struggle for existence; *mutatis mutandis*, the imperative of freedom has always been the repressed imperative of history.

Today, this repression (material, intellectual, psychological) has attained an intensity and effectiveness which makes it questionable whether the imperative of freedom will ever be translated into reality. Today, it is more than ever before an imperative in the sense that it expresses an 'ought' which imposes itself on the individual *against* inclination (*Neigung*), personal need, interest. These needs, satisfactions, interests seem to invalidate the imperative, or at least to make it appear as an abstract idea, relic of a previous political tradition, surpassed and contradicted by the reality of the advanced industrial societies. There, liberation easily appears as the disruption, even destruction of a material (and cultural) well-being in which even the prevailing inhuman working conditions may seem the lesser (and reducible) evil compared with the terrifying uncertainties and horrors of revolution. The material and intellectual culture which is the mark of oppression in these societies may well continue to integrate the population into the capitalist system, and the latter may well be able to reproduce itself on an enlarged scale through neo-colonial exploitation abroad and militarization at home, plus the profitable conquest of outer space, and the collaboration of the Soviet Union. To be sure, this kind of progress is the manifestation of the aggravating internal contradictions of the system, but it can go on for a very long time, ravaging the people, the land, the sea, and the air, polluting the bodies and the minds – with the latter adapting themselves to the situation. So that the final explosion of these contradictions will not be the transition to a higher historical stage but rather to a perfect barbarism where freedom and automatism coincide.

Conflict between liberty and liberation: the latter, i.e. self-determination, would indeed reduce, and perhaps even abrogate, those liberties of choice and expression which reproduce, in the individuals who enjoy them, the established system. For self-determination presupposes liberation from this very system. Seen in the light of this system and its very material benefits, liberation appears not only as a subversive but also as a highly abstract, 'intellectual', utopian idea. Triumph of the morality of affirmation, of positivism. Not the 'materialism' of the people is to blame, not the high level of well-being, but that it is precisely the kind of well-being which is required in order to reproduce and protect the existing power structure: the satisfactions are aggressive and yet submissive, administered and yet spontaneous, standardized and yet individual. This unity of opposites permeates the entire structure: it finds its supreme expression in the fact that the people freely elect the rulers who perpetuate unfreedom. The liberty of the masters goes hand in hand with the liberty of the slaves – once the latter have accepted the proposition that real self-determination of the one is irreconcilable with that of the other – provided that self-determination means more and other than the free choice of commodities, varieties of alienated labour, and of political bosses.

Still, the argument against liberation is a very strong one. In whose name and authority can the revolutionary imperative be imposed upon millions and generations of men who lead a reasonable, good and comfortable life? I believe there is one answer (and not an adequate one), namely, the right is with the victims of this system of well-being, the victims who pay such a large part of the costs and who are excluded from its blessings, the objects of internal as well as external colonization. For them, freedom means first of all liberation from brutal and corrupt regimes of exploitation, foreign and indigenous. This process will inevitably shatter the cohesion of the societies of well-being. Confronted with this threat, they mobilize and militarize themselves to protect the right order with brutal force, thereby proving their self-validating hypothesis that freedom demands repression. In fact, they are proving that *their own* freedom is incompatible with that of the others. But the answer is inadequate because the liberation of the backward people can never be effective and lasting without a corresponding change in the advanced societies, who are capable of meeting and containing the threat for a long time to come.

In these societies, the process of change assumes new forms, called for by the prevailing conditions of cohesion and integration. In the most advanced sectors of the capitalist orbit, the imperative of liberation appears as that of *contestation*. It is first of all a sign of weakness: absence of a revolutionary situation. A revolutionary class does not contest, it fights for the seizure of power. But the contestation shows a feature rarely manifest in the historical revolutions, namely, the total character of its claim. The contesting groups and individuals refuse to recognize the established culture in its entirety – they reject participation in its politics, intellectual activities, etc., they refuse recognition of the prevalent forms and standards of behaviour, morality, etc. This makes for the essential isolation of these groups and their essential minoritarian character, and for their desperate efforts to link their cause with that of the 'masses', without which no radical change is imaginable. It also makes for the 'abstract' and often bizarre character of the contestation: the difficulty to focus action on specific, concrete issues which could involve larger strata of the population.

The total and abstract character of the protest reflects the actual condition of an integration the concreteness of which extends to all classes of the population. The Great Refusal aims at cutting the fatal link which ties the self-propelling satisfaction of needs to the reproduction of the capitalist system. This link is fastened in the individuals themselves; the needs of a repressive society have become their own; social compulsion appears as the liberty of the individual. Consequently, the revolutionary imperative assumes the form of a negation: to reject the needs and values which increase the social wealth while strengthening 'voluntary servitude' among the privileged population of the metropoles, and streamlining enforced servitude in their colonies, in the Third World. The idea that the latter can liberate the First World is utterly unrealistic: it misjudges the sheer force of the material and technical base of advanced capitalism. This force can be reduced only from within. The signs are there that the process has begun. Its manifestations are strangely unorthodox: the revolt of the intellect, of the senses, of the imagination; the weakening of the social fibre; the discrediting of the values on the operation of which the system depends; and the vast release of aggression spreading mental disturbances.

Après la mort de Dieu, la mort de l'Homme : the conquest of outer space, planetary competition and aggression are being executed by robots in machines – still programmed and directed by men, but by men whose goals are circumscribed by the actual and potential power of their machines. And this power is in turn projected and used in accordance with the requirements of profitable competition on a global scale. Competition is becoming the work of machines: technical, political machines, and the minds which direct the machines are dealing with men as objects, and this reification transforms their mind into a machine. Thus, liberation includes liberation *of* the machine, *of* technique and science from their ghastly use – liberation from the men who today determine their use. For a free society is unimaginable without the progressive automation of socially necessary but dehumanizing labour.

On the basis of the capitalist mode of production, dehumanization is irreversible. Quantitative progress in aggressive competition is the historical imperative dictated by and dictating the self-preservation and growth of the system. Quantitative progress would turn into qualitative progress to the degree to which the destructive potential itself would be destroyed: use of science and technology for the total reconstruction of reality, with priority on the abolition of poverty and exploitation, and with the goal of creating an environment *à la mesure de l'homme*. The goal implies self-determination in the mode of production. The objective conditions (material and technical resources) are there, their liberating utilization depends on the emergence of a new Subject: a consciousness and a sensibility unwilling to reproduce the status quo – refusal to cooperate. Such a consciousness would have to emerge among those social classes which assume an increasingly vital role in the process of production, namely, the cadres of the technical and scientific intelligentsia, who in turn would activate the consciousness of the traditional working classes. Schools and universities, the non-integrated youth appear as the catalysts in this development.

Its unorthodox character (priority of the subjective factor, dislocation of the revolutionary potential from the old working classes to minoritarian groups of the intelligentsia and white collar workers) corresponds to the new and unique historical situation: possibility, imperative of a revolution in a highly advanced and effectively functioning industrial society, with a well-organized and constantly improved military and police apparatus, and a largely satisfied population. In this situation, the idea of freedom appears in a new light.

For the beneficiaries of corporate-capitalist prosperity, freedom is what they have anyway (especially compared with the co-existing socialist countries): a rather rich freedom of choice, political, cultural, in market terms. This freedom is real and practicable within a rigidly structured social system, and it depends (or seems to depend) on the continued functioning of corporate management and administration. This administration itself is, behind the technological veil, dependent on the continuation of the struggle for existence, i.e. alienated labour and exploitation. Thus, the 'given' liberties militate against freedom, that is self-determination. The latter seems less and less imperative, less and less 'valuable' and essential to the human existence: the supreme choice, which is the origin and precondition of all other, namely, the choice of one's way of life, is not a vital need. Unless and until it becomes a vital need, restructuring the thought and action, the rationality and sensibility of the individuals, the chain of exploitation will not have been broken – no matter how 'satisfying' life may be. There is no historical 'law of progress' which could enforce such a break: it remains the ultimate imperative of theoretical and practical reason, of man as his own law-giver. At the attained stage of the development, this autonomy has become a real possibility on an unprecedented scale. Its realization demands the emergence of a radical political consciousness, capable of shattering the equally unprecedented repressive mystification of facts – it demands the political synthesis of experience as a constitutive act: to recognize the politics of exploitation in the blessings of domination. I believe that, in the militant youth of today, the radical political synthesis of experience is taking place – perhaps the first step toward liberation.

Index

226